T0330052

*Regions and Regionalism in History*

14

# THE RISE OF AN EARLY MODERN SHIPPING INDUSTRY

## WHITBY'S GOLDEN FLEET, 1600–1750

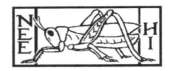

*Regions and Regionalism in History*

ISSN 1742–8254

This series, published in association with the AHRB Centre for North-East England History (NEEHI), aims to reflect and encourage the increasing academic and popular interest in regions and regionalism in historical perspective. It also seeks to explore the complex historical antecedents of regionalism as it appears in a wide range of international contexts.

*Series Editor*
Prof. Peter Rushton, Faculty of Education and Society, University of Sunderland

*Editorial Board*
Dr Joan Allen, School of Historical Studies, Newcastle University
Prof. Don MacRaild, School of Arts and Social Sciences, Northumbria University
Dr Christian Liddy, Department of History, University of Durham
Dr Diana Newton, School of Arts and Media, Teesside University

Proposals for future volumes may be sent to the following address:

Prof. Peter Rushton,
Department of Social Sciences,
Faculty of Education and Society,
University of Sunderland,
Priestman Building,
New Durham Road,
Sunderland,
SR1 3PZ
UK
Tel: 0191–515–2208
Fax: 0191–515–3415

Peter.rushton@sunderland.ac.uk

# THE RISE OF AN EARLY MODERN SHIPPING INDUSTRY

## WHITBY'S GOLDEN FLEET, 1600–1750

ROSALIN BARKER

THE BOYDELL PRESS

First published 2011
The Boydell Press, Woodbridge

ISBN 978-1-84383-631-5

The Boydell Press is an imprint of Boydell & Brewer Ltd
PO Box 9, Woodbridge, Suffolk IP12 3DF, UK
and of Boydell & Brewer Inc.
668 Mt Hope Avenue, Rochester, NY 14620, USA
website: www.boydellandbrewer.com

The publisher has no responsibility for the continued existence or accuracy of URLs
for external or third-party internet websites referred to in this book, and does not guarantee that any content on such websites is, or will remain, accurate or appropriate.

A CIP record for this book is available
from the British Library

Papers used by Boydell & Brewer Ltd are natural, recyclable products
made from wood grown in sustainable forests

Typeset by
Frances Hackeson Freelance Publishing Services, Brinscall, Lancs
Printed in Great Britain by
CPI Antony Rowe, Chippenham and Eastbourne

# Contents

List of Illustrations                                      vi

Foreword                                                  ix

Preface and Acknowledgements                              xi

List of Abbreviations                                    xiv

Part 1: 1600–1689

    Introduction: A Small Port in Yorkshire         3

1   Foundations                                       18

2   The Early Seventeenth Century                     34

3   Upheaval                                          50

4   Stabilisation and Confidence                      58

5   Overview of the Seventeenth Century               82

Part 2: 1690–1750

6   The Established Port                              101

7   'They That Go Down to the Sea in Ships'           128

Conclusion                                                152

Appendix 1:    The Size of the Fleet                 159

Appendix 2:    Pressgang Instructions                165

Appendix 3:    The Naming of Ships                   168

Appendix 4:    The Burnett Papers                    171

Glossary and Definitions                                  172

Selected Bibliography and Further Reading                 177

Index                                                     185

# List of Illustrations

**Figures**

| | | |
|---|---|---|
| 1.1 | Datum line showing excess of baptisms over burials in Whitby during the seventeenth century | 30 |
| 1.2 | Datum line showing excess of burials over baptisms in Harwich during the seventeenth century | 31 |
| 2.1 | National and local vital events, 1621–1635 | 42 |
| 2.2 | Account from the voyage book of *John*, Browne Bushell, master | 48 |
| 4.1 | Occupations recorded in Whitby Parish Register, 1651–1680 | 62 |
| 4.2 | Occupations relevant to seafaring, listed in Whitby parish registers during the seventeenth century | 64 |
| 4.3 | Whitby vital events, 1658–1690 | 67 |
| 4.4 | Hearth Tax data: Hearths per household, Whitby east and west, 1673 | 69 |
| 4.5 | Rates of exemption from Hearth Tax in the seventeenth century | 71 |
| 4.6 | Population estimates for Clark and Hosking's 'small towns' shown by the Compton Census and the Hearth Tax | 75 |
| 4.7 | Estimated size of the Whitby fleet, 1600–1675 | 80 |
| 4.8 | Estimated population of Whitby, 1600–1689 | 80 |
| 5.1 | Alum voyages in Whitby vessels, 1612–1678, from Whitby Port Books | 84 |
| 6.1 | Engineering drawing of Whitby Piers | 107 |
| 6.2 | Ratio of Newcastle to London chaldrons | 120 |
| 6.3 | Profitability, 1716–1728 | 122 |
| 6.4 | Profitability, 1756–1786 | 125 |
| 7.1 | Birthplace, other than Whitby, of servants recorded in Muster Rolls, 1747–1748 | 138 |
| 7.2 | Annual wages paid aboard *Three Sisters*, 1761–1787 | 140 |
| 7.3 | Mean annual wage costs, ten vessels, 1632–1765 | 142 |
| 7.4 | The age range of masters, Muster Rolls, 1747–1749 | 150 |

**Maps**

| | | |
|---|---|---|
| 0.1 | The coastline of England showing Whitby and major ports in the early modern period | 6 |

0.2    Lionel Charlton's map of 1778                                          10
3.1    Map of the Sledway and the approaches to Whitby              57

**Plates**

Between pages xiv and 1

i                     Argument's Yard
ii                    Ghaut, or alley, leading to harbour
iii                   Bakehouse Square
iv                    Whitby's modern piers
v                     The brig *Crisis*
vi                    Driven on to a lee shore
vii                   Ropewalks, Spital
viii                  Spital bridge
ix (a) and (b)  'Taking the ground'
x                     Masts in a townscape
xi (a)–(c)       Anti-scorbutic herbs growing near Whitby
0.1                  The topsail schooner *Alert*, in 1888                      17
2.1 (a)            Luke Foxe and the Claim to Hudson's Bay               38
and (b)                                                                                   39
5.1                  An eighteenth-century drawing of a ketch              87
6.1                  Whitby piers from the air in rough weather           106
6.2                  Engraving of one of Whitby's eighteenth-century   118
                       drawbridges

**Tables**

1.1          Whitby vessels leaving and entering Whitby                 25
2.1          The alienation of Cholmley real estate in the late
               1630s                                                                       43
3.1          National and local vital events, 1654–1680                   53
4.1          Home ports of colliers clearing from NE, 1614 and
               1687–1688                                                               60
4.2          Durham and Yorkshire Ports: Hearth Taxes for
               1672–1674                                                               73
5.1          The daily rate of pay at sea on the ketch *Judith*, 1679   89
5.2          The ports visited by *Judith* between September and
               December 1681                                                         93
5.3          Houses with three or more hearths in West Whitby     95
5.4          Houses with three or more hearths in East Whitby      97
6.1          Tonnage owned in leading outports in 1702              109
6.2          Shareholding in *Hannah*, 1716–1718                      113
6.3          Profits in *Hannah*, 1715–1718                              113
6.4          Share-holders in *Hannah*, 1716–1718                    114

6.5          Share-holders in *William and Jane*, 1718–1726            116
6.6          Charges for Winter-work                                    121
7.1          Stability of *Judith*'s Crew, 1677–82                      134
7.2          Apprenticeship of Alexander Sibbald                        136
7.3          William Barker's career on board *Three Sisters*           137
7.4          The voyages of *Archer* in the Transport Service,
             1775–1788                                                  144
7.5          Seamen's Hospital petitions, by type of injury or
             cause of death                                             149
Appendix 1.1 Tonnage in principal English ports                        160
Appendix 1.2 Tonnage burthen for selected ports, excluding that
             involved in coal, salt, lime and fishing                  161

# Foreword

Whitby is famous for St Hilda, Dracula and Captain Cook. Cook learnt his craft at Whitby. In 1747/8 he was one of no fewer than 1,256 apprentices, or as we might say today cadets, indentured with masters in the town. It was here he learnt navigation and it was here he learnt the importance of the Whitby diet of fresh vegetables, especially the wild plants growing on the cliffs to north and south containing vitamin C to ward off scurvy. Whitby in the eighteenth century was the nursery of English seamanship.

What has not been fully understood until the publication of this eye-opening work is that in the middle of the eighteenth century Whitby was the base of one of the largest merchant fleets in England. This is all the more remarkable when one considers that Whitby was a cramped harbour at the mouth of a small river with an isolated hinterland on a largely inhospitable coast. Rosalin Barker uses for the first time a remarkable collection of documents held in the town to demonstrate the importance of the fleet in England's maritime history. Starting with just two vessels in the early seventeenth century it rose to 318, with a total carrying capacity of 78,000 tons in the late eighteenth. It all began with alum, produced from the deposits of alum shale in the cliffs of northern Yorkshire. Whitby ships brought coal from Newcastle and urine from London, both vital in the production process. But the business soon expanded into a large slice of the carrying trade of the North Sea based on the transport of coals from Newcastle to London and timber from the Baltic to English ports. It extended into the Atlantic and in the eighteenth century into commissions from the navy to carry stores and troops world wide as well as into Greenland whaling. The vessels themselves were unadorned working boats, the eighteenth-century equivalent of Masefield's dirty British coasters, complete with cargoes of Tyne coal. But it was black gold to Whitby's ship owners.

Whitby was never a great port in itself. It was the home of a fleet owned by Whitby men. And until the vessels got too many and too big it was where they were built, where they wintered and were refitted. Barker's sources enable her to reveal the business side of this industry, financed through stocks and shares; the stock to provide working capital for the master to use on each trip, and to enable the burden of repairs to be carried equally by the holder of each share, the shares the division of holdings in individual vessels which were rarely owned by just one man. Their business was shipping, and they enriched the town by their business. Barker is also able to explore the seaman's life and career, dangerous but relatively well-paid and, in the Whitby fleet, relatively well cared for. All this is set in a meticulously researched account of the town's growth in the seventeenth and eighteenth centuries. Clinging to the cliff sides east and west of the river, it was, she suggests, an unusually healthy place to live if only because the tide regularly cleared the sewage out to sea.

Eventually Whitby was sidelined by the sheer growth in British world-wide trade, the concentration of ship owning in London, the increase in the size of ships and the isolation of its harbour. It struggled on during the nineteenth and twentieth centuries, its remaining shipping captured in the haunting photographs of Frank Meadow Sutcliffe reproduced below. The railway brought a surge in fishing and tourism. Now the fishing has largely gone: tourism remains. Whitby mariners make as much money from trips around the bay in replicas of its eighteenth-century vessels as they do from the harvest of the sea.

Rosalin Barker has spent many years immersing herself in the little known shipping archives of Whitby, held by the Literary and Philosophical Society, especially the voyage books and the Seamen's Hospital papers. These hidden treasures underpin the vivid account she gives of the many men who went down to the sea in ships and brought unprecedented prosperity back to the town. They have enabled her to bring this golden age back to life, when Whitby was the home of a great international carrying fleet and a thriving maritime industrial centre. As such the work is an important contribution to British maritime history. But it is also a study of the early modern town that will become an indispensable point of reference for all its future historians.

*Professor Anthony Pollard*

# Preface and Acknowledgements

This work, *The Rise of an Early Modern Shipping Industry: Whitby's Golden Fleet, 1600–1750*, is the distillation of some twenty years of research, much of it undertaken while working in university adult education, an environment which introduces the historian to unexpected elements of history, as he or she responds to the questions raised by students with a wide experience of the communities, both geographical and professional, in which they spend their daily lives.

One may, in the end, decide to specialise in one aspect of history, in this case the history of the merchant sailing fleet of a small but important seaport on the North Sea coast of England. Inevitably, however, all the other aspects of history one has investigated over many years come into play. The study of demography and epidemiology, of urban development and agricultural practice, of religious and sectarian influences, and of fiscal, legal and probate documents, as well as the wider history of British and European history in which the merchant fleet plied its trade, reveal their importance as the links between these aspects become less tenuous, and strengthen with each new examination of apparently insignificant events.

The development of information technology has made possible the systematic collection of historical data, and even more importantly, has enabled the historian to discern connections between apparently trivial, and tiny, scraps of evidence, and produce an informed whole in which all these scraps which have been electronically squirreled away can suddenly play a significant rôle, and help the historian to make sense of long-gone events. It is the small print of local and regional history which in the end illuminates the great narrative of national and international history.

Inter-disciplinary studies are increasingly important in the modern age, when access to the work of scholars in other fields is so readily accessible, both through the traditional library and through the electronic media. Perhaps, as far as this book is concerned, the most germane is the excavation of the wreck of the *General Carleton* of Whitby, lost near Gdansk in 1785, over the last fifteen years by the marine archaeologists of the Polish National Museum of Gdansk. The artefacts and clothes which have emerged from the wreck are astonishingly well-preserved, and redolent of the lives of the thousands of Whitby and other seamen who sailed through the Sound and into the difficult Baltic Sea over many centuries.

Whitby is a community bound to the sea, but by the sea it is bound to the wider world in ways which would have bemused the people who lived in inland towns, villages and remote hamlets in the early modern period in which this book is set. Its world-wide links are most cogently expressed by two unrelated events at the beginning and the end of the period. In 1631 Luke Foxe, mariner, of Hull, where he was born, and Whitby, where he married and lived for much of his life, sailed a 40-ton pinnace, the *Charles*, to the Arctic, in yet another search for the fabled North-west Passage. He found instead Hudson's Bay, in which he reinforced the British claim to that area of what became Canada, and called it 'New North Wales'. He made the return voyage within one year and with all his crew alive, despite the dreadful toll normally exacted by scurvy. Some 140 years later another Whitby-trained navigator, who also made his name in Canada, as a hydrographer during and after the Seven Years' War, James Cook, made landfall on the east coast of Australia, in the area now called 'New South Wales'. He too brought his crews home from their voyages of discovery, in Whitby-built ships, without losing anyone to scurvy.

The source for much of the research for this study of the town's merchant fleet is Whitby Museum, whose collection mirrors so much of Whitby's seafaring past. The ship-models, the equipment, the navigational instruments and the ship-building tools are deeply embedded in Whitby's history. So too are the exotic treasures brought from around the world by past generations of seamen. The library is full of books for the instruction of the ambitious young mariner, and has a bound copy of the mathematical notebooks of a small boy sent to sea at the start of the eighteenth century. With six-figure logarithms and elegant drawings of 'pyrit' ships and naval vessels, it is a delight. Mathematics were a good deal more important than spelling when it came to survival. From the Seamen's Hospital, sad letters survive telling of loss at sea, or incapacitating injuries, while vessels' account books and logs describe, often laconically, long voyages, at times with unlikely cargoes, such as a donkey named Sulphur, bound for Carolina, along with several horses, on board a brig called *Flora*.

The book is divided into two parts, the first of which covers the first ninety years of the seventeenth century, and charts the growth of the port and its fleet, and it increasing importance in the industry as a whole. The Introduction describes Whitby, and the sources, both primary and secondary, for the book, as well as the time frame. The first four chapters account for the early years and the difficult period of the Civil War, and the confidence which came with Whitby's dominance of the coal trade in the years leading up to the Glorious Revolution. The final chapter in this section gives an overview of the century.

Part 2 deals with the first half of the 'long' eighteenth century, until around 1750, although any exact stopping-point for what was a very dynamic industry is difficult to pinpoint. It is divided into two much longer chapters than those of Part 1. Chapter 6 is subdivided into sections describing all aspects of Whitby's fleet and, importantly, the town which it supported and which in turn supported the industry. Chapter 7 covers in detail the all-important workforce, with an examination of the sources, and the work, rewards and risks inherent in seafaring. The Conclusion is followed by four Appendices, a Glossary and Selected Bibliography.

It has been a work which has consumed many months and years, and given me great affection for this remote and often inaccessible town. It is a work which has also been a great source of pleasure, and introduced me to events and people who have, over many centuries, made this place, and above all, who enabled its 'golden fleet' to come into being.

My chief debt is to the countless master mariners, clerks, officials, writers of private letters, and public servants who kept the records on which this study is based. They are recorded in the footnotes, and in the bibliography, but without this unique record the work would have been impossible. To them must be added the members, officers and volunteers of the Whitby Literary and Philosophical Society, founded in 1823, who have assiduously gathered and recorded this archive, and the diligent officials of Whitby Seamen's Hospital Charity, founded in 1675, who kept such detailed records of the seamen who depended on them for their assistance. Thanks are also due to Michael Shaw of the Sutcliffe Gallery for his patient help with photographs by Frank Meadow Sutcliffe.

I have been willingly assisted by the professional staff of other archives from the Northern Isles to East Anglia and the home counties, as well as The National Archives and the British Library. The research was set in motion many years ago with a post-graduate grant from the Open University, and has been encouraged since by other grant-aiding bodies, notably the Marc Fitch Fund. I am also indebted to the University of Hull for its generous award of an Honorary Fellowship which has given me access to all the facilities of a major academic institution, as well as the fellowship of other academics.

To friends, colleagues and students from several universities, whose lively minds have brought great insights to my work, I give thanks, as I do to the patient master mariners and seafarers who have answered my queries about technicalities. The Cambridge Group for the Study of Population and Social Structure (CAMPOP) enabled my forays into historical demography, many years ago, and I am very grateful to them for their guidance, as I am to Professor Glyndwr Williams and Professor Anthony Pollard, who urged me to write this book. I am further indebted to Professor Peter Rushton, the commissioning editor of NEEHI for his patience and encouragement, to NEEHI itself for their financial support towards publication, and to Boydell and Brewer, the publishers.

Above all, I must thank Sophie Forgan and Victor Gray for their encouraging, and perceptive, comments on the completed manuscript, and for their suggested emendations. Surviving blots or misinterpretations are my own.

This book could not have been written without the support, patience and tolerance shown by my family to the piles of books and papers, and my general air of abstraction while I was working.

# List of Abbreviations

| | |
|---|---|
| BL | British Library |
| Clark and Hosking | C. Clark and J. Hosking (eds), *Population Estimates of English Small Towns, 1550–1851*, revised edition, University of Leicester Press, 1993 |
| Corfield | P. J. Corfield, *The Impact of English Towns 1700–1800*, Oxford University Press, 1982 |
| Davis | R. Davis, *The Rise of the English Shipping Industry in the Seventeenth and Eighteenth Centuries*, Macmillan, 1962 |
| ERO | Essex Record Office |
| FMS | Frank Meadow Sutcliffe |
| Gaskin | R. T. Gaskin, *The Old Seaport of Whitby*, first published Forth, Whitby, 1909, Caedmon reprints, 1986 |
| HBCA | Hudson's Bay Company Archives, Winnipeg |
| IAB | Ian Barker |
| Lewis | D. B. Lewis (ed.), *The Yorkshire Coast*, Normandy Press, 1991 |
| NAS | National Archives of Scotland |
| NRO | Norfolk Record Office |
| NS | Nan Sykes, botanist |
| NYCRO | North Yorkshire County Record Office |
| OA | Orkney Archives |
| RRB | the author |
| SBC | Scarborough Borough Council |
| SRO | Ipswich and Suffolk Record Office |
| TNA | The National Archives |
| TWRO | Tyne and Wear Record Office |
| WLP | Whitby Literary and Philosophical Society |
| Woodward | D. Woodward (ed.), *Descriptions of East Yorkshire: Leland to Defoe*, East Yorkshire Local History Series no. 39, 1985 |

Plate i: Argument's Yard. A photograph by Frank Meadow Sutcliffe of one of the most photogenic yards leading down to the harbour.

Plate ii (above): A narrow ghaut, or alley, leading down to the harbour, photographed by Frank Meadow Sutcliffe. These were gradually filled in with housing as the population grew. Plate iii (below): Bakehouse Square, showing evidence of infill on the west side, photographed by Frank Meadow Sutcliffe.

Plate iv (above): Whitby's present day piers in a northerly gale, showing their effectiveness at calming the harbour, and also their piecemeal construction over the centuries. (photograph: Scarborough Borough Council). Plate v (below): *Crisis*, a brig launched in the slump after the Napoleonic Wars, and named accordingly. This pierhead painting is one of Whitby Museum's fine collection of the genre.

Plate vi (opposite, above): Driven on to a lee shore; this was one of the most dangerous fates for a sailing vessel. It occurred when an on-shore gale proved stronger than the anchor and cable holding her to ride out the storm, which either failed or dragged, or when a rudder broke in similar circumstances. Photographed by Frank Meadow Sutcliffe.

Plate vii (opposite, below): Ropewalks, Spital. At Spital bridge, near the site of the mediaeval leper hospital, there was a timber pond where baulks of timber could be stored; by the time Frank Meadow Sutcliffe took this photograph it was used as a haven for cobles. Alongside can be seen the covered shed of a lengthy ropewalk.

Plate viii (above): Spital bridge as it is now, with signs in the walls of the sluice-gate system which kept the pond's level at the right height. (Photograph: the author)

Plate ix (a) (above) and (b) (opposite, above): 'Taking the ground'. Not every small importer had access to a quay, and vessels often came aground and unloaded coal into wagons on the beach. The vessel sitting almost upright next to the pier (a) shows just why these vessels were so popular with the government as transports. They could be grounded safely for unloading (b) where no harbours existed or for repairs to the hull, and they did not topple over while they were aground. Photographs by Frank Meadow Sutcliffe.

Plate x (below): It is difficult now to imagine what a seaport like Whitby looked like in the days of sail. Masts were often tall enough for their tops to be level with the parish churchyard on the east cliff. A large number of them in port at once would have a dramatic effect on the townscape. Photograph by Frank Meadow

Plate xi (a) (above, left), (b) (below) and (c) (above, right): Anti-scorbutic herbs which grow on the cliffs near Whitby, and would have been known by most of the men who sailed in Whitby ships: (a) scurvy grass (Cochlearia officinalis); (b) wild cabbage (Brassica oleracea); and (c) wild celery (Apium graveolens) (NS).

# Part 1

1600–1689

# Introduction

## A Small Port in Yorkshire

There has been no case study hitherto of the merchant fleet of a single port over a long period of growth and stability in the early modern age. This book considers the constituent parts of such a fleet between 1600 and 1750, and the capitalisation, profitability and risk inherent in such an enterprise. It also examines the changes in the infrastructure of the port, and the effects of this industry on the community that financed, built, repaired, owned, manned and supported it.

Since Ralph Davis's *The Rise of the English Shipping Industry in the Seventeenth and Eighteenth Centuries* was published in 1962, there has been an increasing interest in maritime history, though much of this has concentrated on the economic effects of overseas trade, or on the development of ports within studies of urban history.[1]

Associated industries, such as the coal trade, the Yorkshire fishing industry and whaling in the north-east of England, have been well studied, and even some individual ports have been examined.[2] Indeed, Stephanie Jones's PhD thesis of 1982 studied the trade and harbour development of Whitby itself between 1700 and 1914. Simon Ville looked at a single family of shipowners.[3] Sarah Palmer examined the effect of particular legislation.[4] Marcus Rediker looked at shipping on the Atlantic, and described its work-force.[5]

In many ports such an exercise would be difficult to the point of impossibility, because of serious gaps in the source material on which such a case study would depend. There are certainly, particularly from the eighteenth century onwards, national sources for most ports, such as Port Books, Port Registers, Customs and Excise archives, and the records of Admiralty and other statutory bodies. However, such sources give an external view of the town, based on information imparted, often reluctantly, to the government of the day, and therefore suspect. In any case, many of these documents deal with the late

---

1  P. J. Corfield, *The Impact of English Towns 1700–1800*, Oxford University Press, 1982; G. Jackson, *Hull in the Eighteenth Century: A Study in Economic and Social History*, Oxford University Press for the University of Hull, 1972.

2  J. Hatcher, *The History of the British Coal Industry*, vol. 1, *Before 1700: Towards the Age of Coal*, Clarendon Press, 1993; M. W. Flinn (with D. Stoker), *The History of the British Coal Industry*, vol. 2, *1700–1830: The Industrial Revolution*, Clarendon Press, 1984; T. Barrow, *The Whaling Trade of North-East England, 1750–1850*, University of Sunderland Press, 2001; A. Credland, *The Hull Whaling Trade*, Hutton Press, 1995; P. Frank, *Yorkshire Fisherfolk*, Phillimore, 2002.

3  S. P. Ville, *English Shipowning during the Industrial Revolution: Michael Henley and Son, London Shipowners 1770–1830*, Manchester University Press, 1987.

4  S. Palmer, *Politics, Shipping and the Repeal of the Navigation Laws*, Manchester University Press, 1990.

5  M. Rediker, *Between the Devil and the Deep Blue Sea*, Cambridge University Press, 1987.

eighteenth and nineteenth centuries, and provide only limited information about earlier periods.

The town of Whitby had been bereft by the dissolution in 1539 of its abbey, of which it had been a dependent borough. In the years after the dissolution it had passed to the Cholmley family, still as a dependent town with a low economic status. However, the discovery at the start of the seventeenth century of alum deposits stirred its small fishing and ship-owning community into action. The heavy debts inherited by Sir Hugh Cholmley I from his spendthrift father, Sir Richard Cholmley, and the fines later imposed on him by Parliament for his support of Charles I during the Civil War, led to considerable sales of property in the town. These sales greatly loosened the manorial tie, while leaving the town without the constraints on enterprise that the charter of an incorporated borough might have imposed. This led to extraordinary growth, from being a remote and under-used port with a merchant fleet of two vessels in 1600 to the granting of a Harbour Act in 1702 for a port that was probably the sixth most important ship-owning outport in England.[6]

It is the function of a local history to highlight the *minutiae* of the larger regional, national or international picture.[7] It is the task of the local historian to set his or her story into the contexts that surround it. Scholars have come to accept that all historical study is part of a larger whole. British history is part of European history, which is in itself part of world history; moreover, regional history is part of national history, while local history must be considered as an insight into each wider field.[8] The study of individual communities leads to comparisons, and thus to the establishment of a norm, and consequently to the ability to pick out the exception to that norm. Furthermore, the study of that exception can enhance our understanding of the mechanisms by which all communities grow and prosper, or shrink and decline.

It is accepted that each community belongs to a series of societies, and that its history must take account of each of these, and of the time-scales of each, if it is to be of value.[9] Too often a study of a community looks at its inhabitants in only one sphere of action, and ignores most of the others. This has been a problem with much early study of Whitby, as of other communities, in that it has failed to take into account either the relationship with the greater picture, or the variables of time and place in which the community is set.

However, recent work on academic local history goes a long way to redressing the balance, in particular through the occasional papers of the Department of Local History at the University of Leicester.[10] These have been supported

6   1 Anne cap. 19 (8).
7   R. R. Barker, 'The Small Print of History', *Local Historian*, vol. 15, No. 8, pp. 486–489.
8   H. P. R. Finberg, *The Local Historian and his Theme*, Leicester University Press, 1952, pp. 4–5.
9   C. Phythian-Adams, *Rethinking English Local History*, Leicester University Press, 1987, Chapter 3.
10  P. Clark (ed.), *Country Towns in Pre-Industrial England*, Leicester University Press, 1981; D. Marcombe, *English Small Town Life: Retford 1520–1642*, Department of Adult Education, University of Nottingham, 1993.

by the research encouraged and published by *Local Population Studies* and *Midland, Southern* and *Northern History*, among other journals.[11]

This case study draws on the methods of several specialised branches of history, and uses them to bring together the threads both of a small urban society in a remote corner of England, and of its quite unexpectedly successful and sophisticated shipping industry. It shows how each affected the other, and how they were completely interdependent. Among its intentions is to prove that it is impossible to make a complete study of an industry without a close examination of the society that developed it, and that to study a society as complex as that of Whitby without detailed knowledge of its principal industry and the effects that industry had on all aspects of Whitby's life is a futile exercise.

### The choice of Whitby

The most important factor influencing the choice of Whitby for study is that the town lends itself to the kind of examination suggested by both Phythian-Adams and Finberg in their work on English local history. It fits into more 'societies' than do most comparable communities, and has a national and international importance and involvement totally disproportionate to its size. Its recorded history is lengthy and diverse, and despite the town's apparent isolation, there have been few periods since the Norman Conquest when it was not playing some important rôle *vis-à-vis* national events. At the same time it is quite clearly different from the 'norm', as a town, and as a port. Because of these factors, it can well act as a model for studies of other ports and their fleets, or even for other towns with single industries, or groups of industries, which are closely related.

At the same time, while Whitby is well known to maritime historians for its success as a port in the late eighteenth and early nineteenth centuries, there persists an erroneous view that its fortunes were built upon ship-building, which Young records as starting largely around 1730. However, it can be seen from the seventeenth-century evidence, patchy as it may be, that Whitby's eighteenth-century fortune was built on much earlier enterprise, on alum, on the connections that industry gave it to other ports, on opportunism, on self-confidence and possibly even on keeping careful records. It may be that the Society of Friends, whose record-keeping was meticulous, contributed to this; it certainly contributed to the survival of the record, as Quaker shipowners and their friends deposited their papers in the Whitby Literary and Philosophical Society's archives after 1823.

England is heavily dependent on the sea as a means of transport and travel and as a source of its temperate climate. The south and east coasts face Europe, and the west coast faces Ireland and the Atlantic. For the inland areas, natural access to the sea is by major rivers and estuaries, on which have developed

---

11 C. Phythian-Adams, 'Local History and Societal History', *Local Population Studies*, vol. 51, 1993, pp. 30–45, emphasises in particular the most recent approach.

large river- and sea-ports which were and are significant urban centres – ports
such as Gloucester, York and Nottingham. These major river systems have
large market hinterlands, and in many cases significant primary products such
as mineral deposits, or the produce of rich agricultural land. Such ports are
thoroughly examined in the secondary literature by Corfield, Davis, Ville and
Jackson.

Map 0.1: The coastline of England showing Whitby and major ports in the early
modern period

Whitby on the other hand has a minimal estuary on a dangerous stretch
of coast, little hinterland and very little primary production, except the fish
which were common to all coastal communities. It has neither river system nor
agricultural hinterland of any note, and its market area was occupied with the
produce of pastoral farming, such as butter, cheese, hides and wool.

As an urban society Whitby meets most of the criteria devised by Clark
and Slack to define a town. The characteristics of towns which they emphasise
are:

1. an unusual concentration of population
2. a specialist economic function
3. a complex social structure
4. a sophisticated political order
5. a distinctive influence beyond the town's immediate borders.[12]

Whitby's main apparent aberration, the lack of 'chartered' status and there-fore of political sophistication, is shown to be vital to its subsequent growth. For a town that became so important during the eighteenth century, Whitby was deviant from the norm. The town was governed by a manor court; there was also a Select Vestry, and a residual 'burgess court'.[13] It appears likely that the membership of each of them was much the same, and that the group, some-times referred to as the 'chief citizens', functioned as a self-selecting oligarchy. Since there was no effective charter of incorporation, changing rules to suit cir-cumstances was probably much easier than in a rigidly-incorporated borough, especially when the power of the manor began to decline after the Civil War, though it retained much of its influence.

This oligarchy was sufficiently independent-minded to bring into being the Harbour Act of 1702, despite being initially discouraged by the actions of other ports whose corporations objected to Whitby's ambitions. The Harbour Act enabled the town to build highly effective piers, paid for out of a tax on coal carried from the north-east to London.[14] A photograph taken for Scarborough Borough Council during a gale in 1999 (Plate 6.1) shows the efficacy of the piers in protecting the harbour. The piers were extended by a further Harbour Act in 1740, and finally in 1910. That a (supposedly) politically unsophisti-cated town should manage to persuade Parliament to allow it a tax on coal to provide such a superb facility must have been very galling for its rivals.

As a port Whitby rose during the eighteenth century to become one of the six chief ship-owning ports of England, in three principal trades; the north-eastern coal trade, the timber trade and, in time of war, the hired naval transport trade. An outport was a port other than the Port of London, and a document in the British Library shows Whitby as the sixth ranking outport in 1788, with 257 vessels, and almost 48,000 measured tons.[15] That represented between 6 and 8 tons for every man, woman and child in the town. It is probably the first time that national statistics came anywhere near an approximation of the accurate

---

12 P. Clark and P. Slack, *English Towns in Transition 1500–1700*, Oxford University Press, 1976, pp. 4–5.

13 This was the only consolation left to the town after it lost its charter c. 1210. The burgess court was permitted to meet three times a year.

14 The Bill presented to Parliament in 1696 failed because of pressure from ports such as Ipswich and Scarborough, whose pre-eminence in the coal trade was already being challenged by Whitby. The dues for the Winterton Lights (NRO/HMN7/186, 771X7; Winterton Lights, 1687/8) showed that Whitby had already displaced Newcastle, Yarmouth, Lynn, Ipswich and London as a coal-carrying port.

15 BL/Additional Ms 69087, an abstract of the total number of ships, with their tonnage, registered in the British Dominions on 30 September 1788. For an explanation of tonnage and further analysis of this, see Appendix 1.

measurement of national tonnage, two years after the passing of the Act that made the registration of shipping compulsory.

At various times Whitby produced public figures whose stature placed them on an international stage, either for their influence or for their particular technical skills. Among such figures are Luke Foxe, the seventeenth-century explorer of Hudson's Bay; Captain James Cook, navigator and hydrographer; William Scoresby, senior, and his son, also William Scoresby, who were whaling masters, navigators and inventors. John Beecroft, a Whitby-trained master mariner, was despatched in the nineteenth century to help fight the slave trade at its African end. Abel Chapman and his sons became leading figures in the national ship-owning societies and in Lloyds at the turn of the eighteenth and nineteenth centuries; George Chambers, initially apprenticed to the sea, became a renowned nineteenth-century marine artist.

The sources for the community in which this industry was based reveal that the experience of Whitby, so far from the norm as a port and urban centre, shows that it was possible for a community with few facilities to become a ship-owning and -managing port whose success far outweighed its natural advantages. This success had a profound effect both on the industry itself and on the community it served and in which it had its base, as well as on the wider world. More importantly, this success, by generating diverse documentary sources, enables light to be thrown upon the national shipping industry. It is also clear that Whitby's economic success was due to the ability to seize a chance offered once, and to use it to stimulate a culture of opportunism and entrepreneurial skill of a high order, and with these two assets to force disadvantage, such as the lack of incorporated status, to become advantage.

## Geography

Whitby is set at the mouth of the River Esk in North Yorkshire, with a hinterland of high moorland, and no major river system. It serves only a coastal plateau, unlike other ports of the north-east which have either major river systems, such as the Humber complex, or else major and fertile agricultural hinterlands, such as those in the area served by Scarborough, and even both, as in the hinterland of the Tees. The navigable part of the harbour itself is only 120 yards wide, and viable for only one mile upstream. At its maximum depth the harbour has probably never drawn more than 16 feet, and even with modern dredging can take only vessels of up to 2,000 tons.[16]

However, the harbour defines the townscape. Unlike many ports, such as Yarmouth, Ipswich or Liverpool, Whitby is bisected by its estuary, so that the streets of the original planted town abut both banks of the river, thus giving the original occupants much greater access to the port.[17] The harbour-side

---

16  Personal communication from Captain Peter Roberts, former harbour-master at Whitby.
17  TNA/E179/261/32, Hearth Tax Returns, Wapentake of Whitby Strand, show clearly that by 1673 the number of households on each side of the River Esk, and their status, was roughly equal.

has, however, only a narrow strip of land at river level, and much of the town clings to the steep sides of a ravine. This geography has implications for urban congestion, since there is little building land close to the hub of commercial activity, but at the same time offers advantages for urban health, since the cliffs are well-supplied by fresh-water springs, and the fast-flowing river has always enabled detritus to be carried out to sea quickly, thus reducing the effects of disease.

## The sources and their use

The available sources are both extensive and extremely diverse, but are also unique, and require great care in manipulation. The early record is also defective, in that there were periods of dearth of evidence, and that several of the sources had to be used 'against the grain'. For instance, the Pierage Accounts for Scarborough, 1613–36, are simply lists of dues received from each vessel trading from the Tyne, towards the rebuilding of Scarborough's storm-destroyed pier.[18] They record the painfully slow gathering of a sum sufficient to restore a desperately needed 'harbour of refuge'. However, they can be, and in the course of this study have been, used to give a crude estimate of the number, identity and capacity of vessels from individual English ports engaged in the Tyne coal-trade at that period.

The primary sources fall into two groups. On the one hand there are those sources that provide much of the material routinely used in shipping history, and which are to be found in the national archives, since they cover mercantile and naval shipping in a national perspective. These include such systematic sources as Port Books, 'causes', or lawsuits, in the High Court of Admiralty, and national returns to the Admiralty proper, to Customs and Excise, or to institutions such as Trinity House.

Such sources have formed the basis of much of published shipping history, and there are recognised ways of analysing their content. There are also the archives of individual trading and merchant companies, such as Mariscoe-David and Henley, and they too have been thoroughly examined by other historians.[19] Whitby, along with most other outports with any pretensions to importance, is recorded in all of these categories.

Whitby, however, has a unique range of sources which have not hitherto been analysed in detail. These are mainly found among the various collections of the Whitby Literary and Philosophical Society and Whitby Seamen's Hospital Charity, with additional collections in the Orkney Archives in Kirkwall, in Tyne and Wear Record Office and among the archives of other east coast outports. Principal among them are the papers associated with the Seamen's Sixpence, a levy of 6d per man per month at sea for the upkeep, initially, of Greenwich

18 NYCRO/DC/SBC/Pierage Accounts.
19 H. Roseveare, *The Financial Revolution 1660–1760*, Longman, 1991; S. P. Ville, *English Shipowning during the Industrial Revolution: Michael Henley and Son, London Shipowners 1770–1830*, Manchester University Press, 1987.

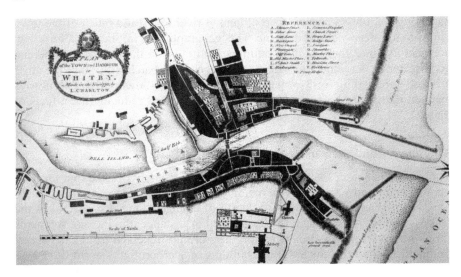

Map 0.2: Lionel Charlton's map of Whitby, 1778

Hospital, and then extended, from 1747, to several provincial seamen's charities, among them Whitby Seamen's Hospital, founded in 1675. This collection,
in the care of the Whitby Literary and Philosophical Society, contains minutes,
appeals and disbursement books, mainly unfoliated. There are also listings of
vessels, dating back to a time when the building seems to have been used as
an office by various organisations connected with the sea, such as the Customs
and the Shipowners' Society. Foremost, however, are the annual muster rolls
for Whitby vessels from 1747 to 1818, listing names, ages, places of residence
and posts on board of most Whitby seamen for over seventy years. Some are
fragile, others incomplete, but they are a rare record, matched by a similar
collection for Hull shipping, which is held in the archives of the University
of Hull. Even more unusually, Whitby also has enrolled volumes, in much
better condition, into which the schedules were copied. The port registers of
shipping, from 1786, are kept in the North Yorkshire County Record Office
in Northallerton. These are of immense importance for the later history of
Whitby's merchant fleet.

Amongst the shipping papers in Whitby is a series of voyage books, from
1677 to 1840, books of accounts listing every expenditure made, and reconciled,
usually annually, to show either profit or loss. These are an invaluable source
of information about wages, chandlery, repairs, victualling, fitting-out, and factoring and freighting of cargo. They list names of crew and also of tradesmen,
and give evidence of the diet, cleanliness, risks, and problems of merchant
seafaring. To these can be added logs, navigation exercise books and a rare
notebook listing the costs incurred in the training of Crispin Bean's apprentices
at the end of the eighteenth century. Among the papers of Balfour, Scarth and
Watt in Orkney and Edinburgh are letters from two Whitby/Orcadian families

for the period 1764–1810, as well as shipping accounts and a voyage book of *Flora* which matches the log preserved in Whitby of the same brig. In Ipswich are the receipt books of an official called the Coal-meter, covering more than a century, recording the arrival of every cargo of coal or salt into the port of Ipswich with the name and home port of the vessel and the master.

Part of the uniqueness of these records lies in their routine nature, routine, that is, to the men and women who compiled them. Some voyage accounts from other ports have been analysed by Davis, but only those held, because of financial 'causes', in the High Court of Admiralty. In any case those are narratives of the lives of four different vessels, all engaged in foreign trades, and all but one belonging to London.[20] Analysis of them without the benefits of modern information technology must have been difficult. They seem to have given no idea of the complexity of share-ownership, of disbursement, of individual masters and members of the crew. There is no clear indication of the existence of that vital part of a vessel's assets, the stock, although, being London-based, the owners would have had access to marine insurance and to London investment. Others, among private estate papers associated with colliery owners, have been examined by Flinn, but only in so far as they show the profitability of the coal trade.[21]

The Whitby 'voyage books', together with three from Scarborough which are in the same collection, are detailed accounts of the day-to-day running of a vessel, of its purchases, large and small, of its building costs, of its shareholders and its annual disbursements. They show the cost of freight and of factoring, the number of 'posts on board' and the fluctuating wages paid to their holders, and in some cases the loss of the vessel. They are the 'day-books' of moderately-sized business enterprises, joint-stock companies in effect, some well run, some not quite so successful.

Other financial papers are held in the Court of Chancery. By their very questionability in court, these are suspect, as Davis infers.[22] Those held in Whitby have, on the other hand, been agreed by masters, ships' husbands and shareholders as presenting an acceptable record of local practice at the time they were presented. This very acceptability probably makes them as near to a true picture of the reality of a fleet as we are ever likely to find. The compiler of one of the longest voyage books, that of *Three Sisters*, 1761–88, George Galilee, was described in old age by his wife as one man in a million, for his good nature, but more importantly for this study, for his integrity.[23]

20  R. Davis, *The Rise of the English Shipping Industry in the Seventeenth and Eighteenth Centuries*, first published, Macmillan, 1962, National Maritime Museum, Modern Maritime Classics Reprint No. 3, 1972, pp. 338–62.

21  M. W. Flinn (with D. Stoker), *The History of the British Coal Industry*, vol. 2, *1700–1830: The Industrial Revolution*, Clarendon Press, 1984, p. 172.

22  Davis, p. 364.

23  When charged by her Quaker granddaughter with hypocrisy for opposing her marriage to a non-Quaker, Mary Galilee explained her excellent reasons for choosing the non-Quaker George. (Personal information from a descendant, quoting papers in private hands.)

Not only are the sources unique, but so is the number and time-scale of them. There are voyage books relating to more than one vessel with the same owners; there are vessels of all sizes and trades; there are voyage books for the entire life of a vessel, from building to loss. The same vessels have, after 1747, their complete muster schedules and enrolments for the Seamen's Sixpence. Earlier voyage books include the musters and the rates of pay in their accounts. In addition, routinely described events can be related to the national archive, and the *personae* described in these documents appear from time to time on the national scene. Luke Foxe, James Cook, William Scoresby, father and son, John Beecroft and Abel Chapman are well-known, but other, more obscure, masters and men figure in lists of transports, lists of prisoners, letters from captivity and official returns which bear out the accuracy of the local record.

That the locally preserved records of Whitby's fleet have survived when those of many other ports have vanished is probably due to two factors. First, from 1654, when George Fox himself visited the town and established there a Meeting of the Religious Society of Friends, or Quakers, the Society dominated commercial and financial life in the town. Noted for their integrity and for their careful record-keeping, they preserved much that in a town with more disparate influences might have been lost.

The other factor is the decline in Whitby's importance as a port in the nineteenth century, mainly due to its remoteness and the impossibility of enlarging the harbour. As firms declined, so their records were placed in the archives of the Whitby Literary and Philosophical Society, founded in 1823 by a community strongly convinced of the need for education and for scientific discovery. In other, larger, continuing ports, such records remained in shipping offices among the docks which were a principal focus for the bombing raids of the Second World War, and were thus lost.

Whitby's unique shipping archives have a long time-span, sufficient to reflect the progression of events, both in peace and in the difficult conditions of wartime, and of changes in shipownership practices, and in ship-handling and provisioning. But it is their breadth that enables us to see beyond the period in which they were compiled to a more distant past, to find within them the continuum that characterises the occupation of seafaring, even when immediate primary evidence is lacking. The evidence in the early modern period, when the archive begins to broaden exponentially, is redolent of the medieval practices, particularly the codification and refinement of the laws and customs of the sea, beginning with the late twelfth-century Laws of Oléron, and recorded in the large volumes of *The Black Book of the Admiralty*.[24] Therefore within the broadening evidence from Whitby is to be seen not a new beginning of the industry, but the continuation of developments of the previous five hundred years.

The laws stipulated the number of daily meals at sea, and care for the sick or injured seaman far from his home port. They set down the over-arching

---

24  T. Twiss (ed.), *The Black Book of the Admiralty*, vols 1–5, 1871–76, Rolls Series, 55.

rights of the master, even to his right to sell or jettison cargo for the sake of the safety of the ship, but included the prohibition on ill-treatment of his men by that same master. Limitations were placed on punishment, and the laws set out the harsh reality of the essential rôle of the pilot, the spreading of risk, and the diligent keeping of accounts. All these provisions and limitations are overt in the Whitby archive, and sufficient evidence survives of the 'watch ashore', the wives and families of the seafarers, over time to make clear that with modern demographic and social history techniques, this case study of Whitby from 1600 to 1750 can serve as an exemplar of those involved in merchant shipping for a much longer period in the past.

However, in any 'regulated' industry, the ideal can often diverge from the actual, and there is evidence of it falling short at times. Not all voyages were profitable, and not all vessels were well, or even honestly, run. However, there was clearly a high level of social control in the closely knit town of Whitby.

The voyage books of a range of the early vessels show the perceived costs and profit and loss of each individual vessel, showing the return on running expenses, the accepted method of calculating profit.[25] They can be more exactly analysed, however, to show the return on capital invested, depreciation, and the effect of war and peacetime slumps on a whole industry, and to reveal something of the quality of life for their crews. Both the analysis of running costs for individual vessels and the aggregation of all the accounts gives a surprising insight into the value of ship repair and maintenance to the national economy. The contribution to the 'retail' trade of the north-east of England by the fleets of the three north-eastern headports and their subsidiaries can be estimated with reasonable confidence, and can be shown to amount to some £270,000 per annum in the eighteenth century, spent on chandlery and victualling in the north-eastern ports.[26]

## Secondary sources

A wide range of secondary sources has been used to provide a background to this study. The works most closely used have fallen into two groups. The first of these contains books written in Whitby, dating from the eighteenth to the twentieth centuries, and often using sources now no longer available. Principal among these are the works of Charlton, Young, Gaskin, Browne, Jones and Weatherill.[27] The two early histories by Charlton and Young (1816) contain

---

25 The notion of profit as a return on capital invested does not appear in the Whitby record until the nineteenth century. See also S. P. Ville, *English Shipowning during the Industrial Revolution: Michael Henley and Son, London Shipowners 1770–1830*, Manchester University Press, 1987, pp. 120–1.

26 R. R. Barker, 'Tea for the Cabin'; paper presented at the conference of the Centre for the History of Retailing and Distribution (CHORD), September 2003. A revised and expanded version of this has been accepted for publication.

27 L. Charlton, *The History of Whitby*, York, 1779; G. Young, *History of Whitby*, 2 vols, Whitby, 1817; R. T. Gaskin, *The Old Seaport of Whitby*, first published Forth, Whitby, 1909, Caedmon reprints, 1986; H. B. Browne, *Chapters of Whitby History 1823–1946*, Brown, 1946; R. Weatherill, *The*

useful comments on their own times and Charlton attempts some anecdotal evidence as to the remarkable development of the fleet.

Gaskin, scion of a whaling family of some note, used national sources for his book, which was posthumously published, and his view of the seventeenth century is probably more accurate, though since his book is arranged topically rather than chronologically, and without an index, it is more difficult to use as a resource. Perhaps the best known of these Whitby volumes is that of Richard Weatherill, *The Ancient Port of Whitby and its Shipping*, a compilation unique in its detail of all the vessels he was able to trace through local private archives, many of which are now lost. That Weatherill missed many vessels of which details have since come to light, is immaterial; as a 'census' of the fleet of any port it is without equal. He compiled three lists; vessels recorded in Whitby before 1786, when registration became compulsory, those built in Whitby post-1786, and those built elsewhere post-1786. Where possible, he gave the fate of each, and any stories of their voyages for which he could find evidence. However, he was largely silent on any vessels belonging to the early modern period, recording only the later history of a few built in the second decade of the eighteenth century. Sadly he does not even give the name of the builder. Their very mention, however, is a tribute to the strength of the vessels built in Whitby. Some of these early ones were still at sea in the 1790s.

Bridging the gap between early works on Whitby and later works on the national shipping industry is a PhD thesis by Stephanie Jones, 'A Maritime History of the Port of Whitby 1700–1914' (1982), which examines the trade of Whitby and the development of the harbour up to the First World War, including the age of steam.

Among the most consulted and most valuable secondary works on the larger picture have been the seminal studies of Clark and Slack, Davis, Corfield, Ville, Starkey, Palmer, Rediker and Jackson. Without these, which offer many opportunities for comparison and contrast, as well as vital information about the national shipping industry, the broader claims of this study would be invalid. Of these, the works of Clark and Slack on the development of towns have been invaluable. Davis's *Rise of the English Shipping Industry in the Seventeenth Century* is, of course, the standard work on the growth and organisation of the national merchant fleet, and Ville's *English Shipowning during the Industrial Revolution* has been important as a comparison for Whitby ship-owning practices, albeit at a later date. Rediker's *Between the Devil and the Deep Blue Sea* is useful as a study of seamen's lives, for the purposes of comparison. As a general history of seafaring it prompts some misgivings, however, as it contains a picture barely recognisable in the light of the primary sources available in Whitby. Sarah Palmer's recent book on the repeal of the Navigation Acts has

*Ancient Port of Whitby and its Shipping*, Horne, Whitby, 1908; S. K. Jones, 'A Maritime History of the Port of Whitby 1700–1914', unpubd PhD thesis, University College, London, 1982; S. P. Ville, *English Shipowning during the Industrial Revolution; Michael Henley and Son, London Shipowners 1770–1830*, Manchester University Press, 1987; M. Rediker, *Between the Devil and the Deep Blue Sea*, Cambridge University Press, 1987.

been most timely for its analysis of the concept of 'the shipping interest' and as a reminder of sailing practices long after the end of the period under study.

N. A. M. Rodger's two volumes of naval history, *The Safeguard of the Sea* and *The Command of the Ocean*, give a valuable insight into the development and growth of the Royal Navy in both peace and war. Though this book is a study of a merchant fleet, to consider it without regard to the often present enemies of this country would be impossible. Regular naval action both by national ships and by inimical privateers affected Whitby's shipping enterprise, by blockade of the port, by loss to sinking or capture, or by profit made from a long association with the Royal Navy in the transport and victualling services.

A small and only recently reprinted book is *A Seaman's Pocket-Book*, published in 1943 'by authority of the Lords Commissioners of the Admiralty' for 'hostilities only' seamen. It was designed to give them what was termed 'sea-sense' in order to ensure as far as possible their safety, their survival, their efficiency and their care for their fellow-seamen. Although it refers specifically to modern warships, and there is much that is technologically far removed from the problems of the early modern merchant fleet, it contains a surprising amount of valuable information about terminology which can aid interpretation of earlier shipping records. Above all it serves to enhance the sense of continuity that runs through seafaring from the earliest times.

Inevitably, any study of a single industry must owe a great deal to standard works of general history, and particular tribute must be paid to the volumes of the *New Oxford History of England*, and to the work of the Cambridge Group for the History of Population and Social Structure.

## The time frame

Several factors contributed to the choice of time frame for this study of Whitby's merchant fleet. The great expansion of the Whitby merchant fleet occurred in the seventeenth century, up to the beginning of the reign of William and Mary. Thereafter the period of exponential growth was over and the remaining sixty or so years were times of consolidation and change. The survival of the voyage accounts of three vessels, two that had sailed from Scarborough and one from Whitby, in the first three decades of the eighteenth century; the development of the harbour following the Harbour Act of 1702; the discovery of an important document on the coal trade of the late seventeenth century; and the realisation of the growing influence of the Society of Friends, made it clear that for the purposes of this volume the early modern period should be defined as running from 1600 to 1750.

This is a time frame during which remarkable national events took place, which had dramatic effects on the national life and on the shipping which was of such great importance to an island nation. In 1603 England and Scotland were united by the accession of James VI and I, and the century began with some twenty years of peace. Charles I's reign began with European war, and continued into the horror of civil war which convulsed Yorkshire as much as, if not more than, the rest of the country.[28] The Commonwealth period involved more war, especially at sea, and also the continued breakdown of local government already damaged by the civil wars. The restoration brought more stability at home but more war abroad, ending with the Exclusion Crisis and the eventual so-called 'bloodless revolution' and the arrival of William III and Mary; and more European war. Two Jacobite rebellions and the South Sea Bubble formed the background to the period of eighteenth-century consolidation of Whitby's fleet, providing yet more challenges and opportunities.

The Act of 1747, which made selected provincial seamen's charities eligible for some of the proceeds of the levy known as the Seaman's Sixpence, originally imposed to support Greenwich Hospital, led to the inclusion of Whitby Seamen's Hospital in the scheme, and indirectly gave the historian access to the muster rolls of almost all the vessels belonging to the port.

It must be remembered that a fleet is a dynamic entity, and that its state in any particular year is a snapshot of a group of vessels, only a small percentage of which will be exactly contemporary. Some vessels were lost on their maiden voyages, others carried on working for decades. Plate 1 shows *Alert*, built by George and Nathaniel Langborne in 1802, photographed by the eminent photographer Frank Meadow Sutcliffe in 1888, still going strong. *Liberty and Property* was built by Thomas Fishburn in 1752 and spent 102 hard-working years in the coal and Baltic trades before disappearing from the records. The bracket half-model made by Fishburn's yard for the vessel's unknown first owners is still extant – the oldest such model in existence, it is in the care of Merseyside Maritime Museum. Some 96 per cent of the Whitby fleet would have been built before 1747, and, at an attrition rate of 4 or 5 per cent, the oldest vessels would have dated back to the 1720s, or even earlier.[29] The evidence of individual vessels indicates that at least some of the vessels recorded in the first 1747 muster rolls must have been built during the seventeenth century. It is therefore imperative that the time frame should include the early years of these muster rolls, since they reveal so much of the vessels and individuals who manned the fleet. The lines of the topsail schooner *Alert* (Plate 0.1), built in 1802, would not be greatly different from those of ships built fifty years earlier, within the compass of this book.

The first five chapters of the book cover the growth in the seventeenth century as Whitby's shipping industry emerged from the obscurity that followed the dissolution of the abbey and the serious reduction in the status of the town. These are shorter chapters, each of the first four dealing with a twenty-year period in which it has been possible to make an informed judgement about the development of the fleet, and ending with a summary of the status of the fleet at the end of this period of Whitby's enormous growth in size, wealth and stature as a port within the national shipping industry.

28  J. Binns, *Yorkshire in the Civil Wars*, Blackthorn Press, 2004.
29  Davis, p. 87, suggests around 4 or 5 per cent were lost annually.

Plate 0.1: The topsail schooner *Alert* in 1888

In Part 2, Chapters 6 and 7 deal with the dynamic change within the fleet over the following sixty years, and offer a much more detailed analysis of the internal workings of the fleet, its trades and financial structures and its manpower. The concluding chapter looks forward to the later development and eventual decline of the fleet in the next century.

# 1

# Foundations

## The mediaeval background

There was already a *vill*, or settlement, and a port at Whitby in 1078, when William de Percy granted land for the foundation of a Benedictine abbey, dedicated to St Hilda, on the ruined site of an abbey that had flourished from the seventh to the ninth century.[1] The refounded abbey prospered and the abbots became entitled to wear a mitre, a coveted status. (In 1225, Abbot Roger de Scarborough was a witness to the major reissue of *Magna Charta*.) The land held by the abbey was very early elevated to the status of a Liberty. That privilege gave the abbey a great measure of independence from the Crown, such as the right to offer 'sanctuary', but also gave it the responsibilities of a major centre of provincial power so near the Scottish frontier. The records of the medieval period show many incursions and raids by Scots and Scandinavians.

In 1128 'burgage', the right to plant a town, was granted to the settlement at the foot of the abbey cliff. The extent of the medieval burgage area is not recorded, but later documentation makes the confines of the town clear, and by 1801 the township was defined as containing 48 acres, about half of which was inter-tidal mud. Housing in the neighbouring 'constablery', or township, of Ruswarp eventually abutted in part with that of the township of Whitby.[2] This limitation of size, the probable extent of the original burgage, became of great importance to the development of the town in the later eighteenth and early nineteenth centuries.[3] In fact, by the time of the 1831 census, Whitby had the most densely populated central township in the north of England.

Towards the end of the twelfth century the town's status was elevated to that of a 'free' borough, with a 'burgess court'. However, an early thirteenth-century abbot became alarmed by the fiscal consequences of that freedom. Supported by the Earl of Northumberland, who was high steward of the abbey, he persuaded King John to rescind the charter, and the town reverted to its former dependent status, despite a long fight through the courts until the middle of the fourteenth century. By that time the town was prosperous despite the loss of free status. The only survival of that freedom was the burgess court, or

---

1  J. C. Atkinson (ed.), *The Whitby Cartulary*, Surtees Society vols. 69 and 72, 1878–1879; the first volume contains a chronicle of the early days of the abbey.

2  Maps of 1740, 1778 and 1828 show a small amount of expansion into Ruswarp township where it adjoined Whitby township, but only an expansion of middle-class housing. Artisanal housing was still confined to the old township.

3  A proposal to extend the boundaries of the township by including the suburb of Ruswarp, was made, and rejected, in the late eighteenth century. Lionel Charlton's map of the proposed boundary changes (Map 0.2), unwittingly provides excellent corroboration of the exact mediaeval boundaries.

Fifteen, which eventually seems to have elided with the Select Vestry.[4] The Select Vestry in Whitby is of ancient origin, and had already superseded the normal vestry by the time of this study.[5] The Fifteen retained, and made good use of, certain rights in the harbour.

It is likely that in the long run King John's action benefited Whitby, since the town was not curbed by the kind of restrictive practices that characterised other corporate boroughs. Furthermore, the manorial bonds weakened after the dissolution of the abbey. However, during the Middle Ages, the abbey exerted a strong influence over commerce and development, an influence which became much clearer with the fall of the abbey itself.

During the Middle Ages both harbour and town prospered. In 1301 Edward I imposed a Lay Subsidy, or taxation, of one-fifteenth of all goods, movables and chattels, on the whole country to pay for the war against the Scots. The assessments for Yorkshire largely survive, and have been published by the Yorkshire Archaeological Society. Of the Yorkshire towns whose assessment for 'a fifteenth' in 1301 survive, the assessment for the provincial capital, the city of York, was the highest by a factor of eight over its neighbour and nearest rival, the abbey and liberties of St Mary at York. Next in rank to St Mary's, which had originally been founded from Whitby abbey, was Whitby itself, and its Liberty. Whitby was clearly a wealthy town. Merchant houses of substantial quality survive in the town; a goldsmith existed in 1301, and merchants from Lombardy and from northern Europe lived and traded in the town.[6] Wine was imported into Whitby, and Whitby's obligation to provide a ship of war against the Scots at regular intervals equalled that of other apparently more viable ports, such as Hull. The developing surnames of the early fourteenth century give clear indication of the ports with which Whitby traded, and from which migrants came, and also of the trades within the town. Place-name surnames, such as Lombard, or Lincoln, and those of occupations, such as Walker, Baker and Mason, all occur.

Whitby remained, like all ports, a frontier town, with the added risk of attack by pirates, and by land from Scotland, despite the fact that the de Brus family, of which King Robert I, 'the Bruce', was a cadet member, were major benefactors

---

4 Parochial records, particularly a 'brief' book, of charitable appeals sanctioned by the Crown, which also contains the elections of churchwardens and other officials, emphasise the rôle of the Fifteen. It is clear from some of the elections, which appointed known Quakers as parish officials, that the concern was for the good governance of the town rather than for ecclesiastical conformity.

5 English parishes had, over several centuries, developed a form of local government, based on the annually held Vestry meeting of the parish church. This was generally held on the Wednesday in Easter week, and elected churchwardens and later, statutory officers such as Overseers of the Poor and Highway Surveyors. As towns grew in population and economic strength, the number of people anxious to have a say at the annual meeting grew, and the whole became too cumbersome, so a Select Vestry would be elected to conduct the parish affairs. The Select Vestry usually became an oligarchy, electing replacement members without consultation. It was not until the Sturgess-Bourne Act of 1818 (58 Geo. III c. 69) that any national attempt was made to regulate such activity.

6 W. Brown (ed.), *The Lay Subsidy of 1301*, Yorkshire Archaeological Society, vol. xxi, 1896. The record of the Lay Subsidy of 1301 is extant for much of Yorkshire, and shows two goldsmiths; one in York, taxed at just 7d, and one in Whitby, taxed at 4s 6³/₄d. Unfortunately there are no returns for the recently established but thriving port of Kingston upon Hull.

of the abbey. Nonetheless by the end of the fourteenth century Whitby was already trading in coal.[7] Its principal trade, however, was in fish, particularly in white herring, caught off Whitby and processed in the town. This added value must have led to the importation of salt, and evidence of that becomes apparent at the end of the sixteenth century, though by then the processing had turned from white herring to red.[8] There is clear evidence in the mediaeval record of trade with the Baltic, foreshadowing Whitby's pre-eminence in the Baltic trade at the end of the eighteenth century.

Appointments at regular intervals of customs officials to deal with *specie*, wine, coal, wool and contraband bear witness to Whitby's continued activity as a port, defining the town as such, and with the burgesses sharing revenue.[9] The harbour was deep enough and secure enough to contain a captured French war fleet, and its captors, in the mid fifteenth century.[10] The quays seem to have been largely assigned to the abbey, and the bridge, an essential part of a town divided by its harbour, to the burgesses. So too were the liabilities divided, and the national record shows grants of quayage and pontage for lengthy periods to each.[11] Storms did recurring damage to Whitby, especially as it is likely that the present Tate Hill Pier, once the Burgess Pier, was the only pier protecting the harbour until the mid seventeenth century, when Sir Hugh Cholmley built a pier on the west side to protect his coal staithes. The Harbour Act of 1702 saw the west pier lengthened and re-aligned and a new east pier built.[12]

National political control, such as it was, over both English and Scottish ports, had been exercised by the Exchequers of the two kingdoms since the Middle Ages. A system of headports covered the coast, in England from Berwick southwards to the Channel, then along the south coast and up the west coast to Lancaster.[13] Each port covered a designated area of coast, and that area was subdivided into lesser, or *creco* (creek) ports. It was a system designed to facilitate the collection of customs dues, administer such limited lightage

---

7  References in both Close and Patent Rolls throughout the Scottish Wars of Edward I and Edward II emphasise this precarious position. J. C. Atkinson (ed.), *The Whitby Cartulary*, Surtees Society vols. 69 and 72, 1878–1879, contains a transcript of the *compoti* for 1394–96, which give account of several coal deliveries in vessels from Whitby and other English ports.

8  Port Books: TNA/E190/185/11*, Surveyor, 1600/01, Coastal; E190/185/3, Surveyor, Easter to Michaelmas 1592, Coastal; E190/185/4, Searcher, Michaelmas 1593/4, Overseas; E190/185/9, Surveyor, Michaelmas 1598/9, Coastal. White herring was unsmoked, while red herring was both cured and smoked.

9  *Specie* is coin of precious metal, and may be of any denomination, or currency of any country. It was often in mixed currency, which could be changed in most large ports (see Calendars of Close and Patent Rolls at various times).

10  R. T. Gaskin, *The Old Seaport of Whitby*, first published Forth, Whitby, 1909, Caedmon reprints, 1986, p. 74.

11  See: Definitions and Glossary.

12  J. Binns, 'Sir Hugh Cholmley of Whitby, 1600–1657: His Life and Works', unpubd PhD thesis, Leeds University, 1990. The existence of the pier is confirmed in a map of c. 1740, which shows a later addition to that pier.

13  D. Woodward, 'The Port Books of England and Wales', *Maritime History*, vol. 1, pp. 147–165, explains the Exchequer port system in detail.

and buoyage as existed, and deal with national communication.[14] It was also a system with built-in tensions, as creek ports grew in size and economic importance, and headports silted up over the centuries. Liverpool, for centuries a dependent port of Chester, serves well to highlight these anomalies. At the end of the sixteenth century, of the ten most important ship-owning outports listed by Davis, only two were creek ports, Aldeburgh and Leigh.[15] By 1709, a listing of far higher tonnages owned in the outports was actually headed by Scarborough, which was a creek port of Hull, and the same listing of ten ports contained three other creek ports; Whitby, Sunderland and Liverpool.

Whitby was a creek port of Newcastle upon Tyne, and the area of coast dominated by Whitby, although expanded over time, included the lesser, mainly fishing, ports of Staithes, Runswick and Robin Hood's Bay. The limit of the port was at first Spital Bridge, the probable upper limit of the mediaeval burgage, but was extended in the eighteenth century to the high water limit at Ruswarp, giving control over a tidal reach approximately one mile long.

North-westwards Whitby's neighbour was Stockton-on-Tees, another creek port of Newcastle, and south-eastwards was Scarborough, the most northerly creek port of Hull. It is an anomaly of the coast that Whitby's estuary enters the sea in a northerly direction, so that the coast faces north, and this was important to both the town and the fleet. It was not until after the Harbour Act of 1702 that Whitby was an official 'harbour of refuge', a coveted status, which could lead to national financial assistance with repair of piers and other harbour installations.

The dissolution of the abbey at the end of 1539 seems to have caused an implosion. There had been evidence of increasing dearth in the hinterland before this date, though Leland recorded that the quay was being rebuilt, just before the fall.

> ...4 miles to Whitby, where is a havenet holp with a peere and a great fischar toun ... Whitby wher a new key and port is yn making of stone fallen down yn the rokkes thereby.[16]

The burgesses remained, but the collapse of the abbey seems to have outweighed the strength of any burgess activity. The town's revenues, from abbey expenditure, from corrodians ('pensioners' who had given the abbey either land or money in return for their care for the rest of their lives, often sent to the abbey as a reward for faithful royal service) and from pilgrims, went immediately to London, to be retained initially by Henry VIII. In due course the abbey and its lands were leased to various landowners for several years. During Henry's lifetime, part of the abbey land was sold to the Cholmley family, who were able to purchase most of the remaining land during the reign of Edward

---

14  J. Naish, *Seamarks; Their History and Development*, Stanford Maritime, 1985; the early chapters describe in detail the gradual provision of seamarks and warning buoys for the growing international merchant fleets.

15  Davis, p. 35.

16  John Leland, c. 1540, quoted in Woodward, p. 16.

VI. The benefice of the parish church went to the archbishop of York, who leased it to lay rectors, at times wealthy Whitby shipowners, until the reforms of the middle of the nineteenth century.

The sums calculated by the *Valor Ecclesiasticus* of 1536 indicate that the net economic loss to the town of Whitby, the probable chief recipient of abbey expenditure, was well in excess of £400. The two religious hospitals closed, presumably leaving the inmates as a burden on the community. The identity of the town was destroyed, part of its defining rôle gone; it had been to a large extent a 'company town'. It vanished from the national record, its quay became ruinous, its fleet diminished, its harbour trade was minimal, until alum was discovered c. 1608.[17] It is from this nadir in Whitby's fortunes that this study of the rise and consolidation of both fleet and town commences.

### The beginning of growth

Most histories of Whitby, or references to Whitby in more general works, have assumed that Whitby's eighteenth-century prosperity had its origin in the profits of ship-building and coal-trading in that same century.[18] However, these first chapters show the infinitely more complex mechanisms behind a much earlier growth. What changed in the eighteenth century was not that Whitby suddenly emerged as a port of considerable importance, but that it was already at the end of a long period of growth and consolidation. The turn of the seventeenth and eighteenth centuries saw changes of a different kind, as Whitby made the most of its skill, enterprise and growing prosperity to maximise its potential. By then the embryonic stage was long past. The child had been born and was growing very rapidly to adulthood.

Just two merchant vessels apparently regarded as 'belonging' to the town can be identified from the scanty resources available at the very start of the seventeenth century.[19] It is known, however, that there was at least one Whitby vessel trading with the Baltic in 1590, when it was recorded as paying a Sound Toll at Elsinore.[20] There was also something of a fishing fleet. The importation of several cargoes of salt suggests some kind of food processing, at least in part of fish. In 1609 there were exports, mainly in Scots vessels, of both butter and 'white' herring, both requiring salt for their the preservation.[21] 'Red' herring

---

17  BL/Additional Ms 32656, fo. 54, a certificate of 1544, describes great decay in the harbour, and a much reduced fleet, just before the dissolution of the abbey.

18  G. Young, *History of Whitby*, 2 vols, Whitby, 1817, vol. 2; S. K. Jones, 'A Maritime History of the Port of Whitby 1700–1914', unpubd PhD thesis, University College, London, 1982. Neither Davis nor Corfield comments on the suddenness of the appearance of Whitby as a major ship-owning port in 1702 and 1709 respectively.

19  TNA/E190/185/11*, Surveyor, 1600–01, Coastal, names among the 28 vessels calling at Whitby two belonging to the port.

20  N. E. Bang, and K. Korst, *Tabeller over Skibsfart og Varetransport gennem Oresund, 1497–1783*, Copenhagen and Leipzig, 1906–1953, 7 vols, record the Danish tolls exacted at Elsinore from vessels passing through the narrow Sound between Denmark and Sweden. The Sound was the shortest route into the Baltic Sea.

21  This trade appeared in the mediaeval records.

were also exported in 1611.[22] The herrings must have been caught locally, probably by Whitby vessels, and processed ashore. In 1576 Whitby had been one of the fishing ports which signed a certificate recording the increase in the number of fishing boats of between 10 and 30 tons following the passing of the Act of Parliament which added Wednesdays to the days of abstinence from meat.[23]

There was a small harbour trade, much of it carried in vessels from other English ports, and some from Scotland and the Netherlands.[24] There were no primary products amongst the exports, except for a little specialised timber, and the only value-added products were the white and red herrings, together with butter from the largely pastoral hinterland, and 'refuse', or re-cycled, bark from the tannery, sold for tanning fishing nets.[25] The timber consisted of 'crooked timber for boats' knees', suggesting that if there was any local boat-building, it was not on a sufficiently large scale to absorb the available supply, or else was so impoverished that more money was to be made from exporting the raw material than by using it, analogous to eating the seed-corn of the community. Yet, despite the apparent inability to utilise such materials at this early stage in the century, by 1625 Whitby had shipyards and at least one ship-builder, Andrew Dickson. Dickson was sufficiently well-financed, or at least creditworthy, to build *Great Neptune*, 500 tons, for the New England Company. At the time it was the largest merchant ship afloat, and when the Company failed to pay its debt to the builder, it was bought into the Navy.[26]

The trade of Whitby harbour in the years before 1612 was very sparse. In the busiest year, 1606/7, there are twenty-eight entries for Whitby in the Port Books, just over one every two weeks.[27] Of these twenty-eight voyages, just two, to Kampveer in the Netherlands and to Elsinore, were in a Whitby vessel, *Jacob*. In the earliest year for which the Port Books survive, 1600, just two Whitby vessels, *Isabel* and *Mary*, are named. By 1604 *Mary* had vanished from the record, but

22  White herring were gutted and salted and packed in barrels. Red herring were gutted and heavily dry-salted and then smoked. Kippers are smoked after being lightly brined and are split open. See www.historyshelf.org/secf/silver (visited 27 September 2007).

23  R. H. Tawney and E. Power (eds), *Tudor Economic Documents*, vols 1-3, Longmans, 1951, vol. 2 p. 122, quoting SPD Eliz., vol. 107, No. 67; 5 Eliz cap. 5.

24  Including a cargo in *Durtie Megge* from Burntisland. Vessel names, as will be seen in Appendix 3, often reflected their owners' aspirations. The owner of this vessel must have been a stern realist; TNA/E190/186/10, Searcher, Christmas 1609–10, Overseas; E190/186/11, Controller, Christmas 1610–11, Overseas; E190/186/6, Customer, Christmas 1606–07, Overseas; E190/186/8, Controller, Christmas 1607–08, Overseas; E190/186/9a, Searcher, Christmas 1608–09, Overseas.

25  In fact the Port Books describe the substance as '*refuge*' bark. Again the importance of the pastoral landscape is emphasised, since, like butter, tanning was an industry based on cattle-farming.

26  *Calendar of the Acts of the Privy Council, 1623-5*, pp. 439-40. Presumably either Andrew Dickson had exhausted the local assizes, or else there was some doubt as to which branch of the law applied; if the issue of debt was intractable, then the Privy Council would have been acting as a court of last resort.

27  TNA/E190/185/6, Customer, Christmas 1606/7, Overseas. There may well have been other books, now lost, for coastal shipping. W. Childs (ed.), *The Customs Accounts of Hull, 1453–90*, Yorkshire Archaeological Society Record Series, vol. 144; the surviving Whitby Port Books show that 28 vessels entered and left the port in the year, on average one every two weeks. By comparison, in the late fifteenth century the port of Hull might receive cargo from between 65 and 80 vessels per annum.

another vessel, *George*, had appeared. It is not safe, however, to assume that these represented the entire fleet for, as has been seen, the early Port Books do not survive in a continuous sequence.[28] Three more vessels were named before 1612, but in 1612 at least twelve vessels were recorded as belonging to Whitby. The concept of 'belonging' is all that is available, in practical terms, to the historian before the first form of registration in 1786 – it represented the home port declared to the Customs at any given time.

However, during the first decade of the century the discovery that was to end Whitby's stagnation had already been made, even though the town's early struggles belied any possibility that the changes could become so dramatic. Around 1608 (the exact year is variously ascribed) alum shale was discovered in several places near to and north-west of Whitby, and processing began.[29] Hitherto alum had been a papal monopoly, based in continental Europe, and after Henry VIII's breach with Rome the need for home-produced alum became urgent. The product was essential for the woollen industry, in which it was used to fix dyes, and for brewing and other industries, and it had been desperately sought in England. There had been abortive attempts to refine it during the sixteenth century on the Isle of Wight and other places, but in the North Riding of Yorkshire there was an ample supply of the shale which could be processed to produce alum, and indeed the industry endured for around 250 years. Alum required considerable capital investment, some of which probably came initially from London to back that of the original patentees, who were local landowners.[30] The industry also needed men to work the alum banks, and shipping to carry imported raw materials and to carry away the output. The additional raw materials required were coal for fuel, and ammonia, usually derived from urine, as part of the chemical process. The latter was augmented by kelp, initially processed locally and later imported from mainland Scotland and eventually from Orkney.[31]

There is some coal on the North York Moors, but not of a sufficient quality to be used industrially, so coal had to come from the coalfields of Tyneside and Wearside. Urine could be, and was, obtained locally, and the Alum Accounts in the Audit Office make clear that there was a considerable infrastructure carrying urine from 'producer' to the alum banks.[32] The shortfall in local urine was made good by urine from London, which had to be shipped to Whitby. The Audit Office accounts show the initial use of Dutch and Scots vessels for the transport of coal to Coatham, at the mouth of the Tees. The industry also made heavy demands on timber, partly for construction work, but partly also

28  TNA/E190/185/3,4,9 and E190/186/11.
29  D. B. Lewis (ed.), *The Yorkshire Coast*, Normandy Press, 1991, pp. 46-9, describes the difficult early stages.
30  Lewis, p. 47, recounts the early financial development.
31  By the third decade of the eighteenth century Whitby's long networking links with Orkney were well-established.
32  TNA/AO3/1243/3A, Accounts of Alum Monopoly; there were many payments to carters for the transportation of urine over land. According to the first edition of the *Encyclopaedia Britannica*, 1768–71, urine was still used as well as lees of kelp at that time.

for tool handles and for making wheelbarrows, thus generating local income to woodworkers and owners of woodland, and to carriers of wood, and also fairly quickly changing the landscape as woodland disappeared. The export of 'crooked timber for boats' knees' ceased completely.

Jack Binns' thesis identified six Whitby-owned ketches in 1612, but the detailed analysis of the extant Port Books of most of the east coast ports shows that in 1612 there were at least twelve vessels belonging to Whitby, which made forty-six voyages in that year.[33] Table 1.1 shows a much more systematic trade carried in Whitby vessels, apparently dedicated to the new alum trade, carrying either coal in or alum out. Given that even in the heyday of eighteenth-century coal-carrying, few colliers managed as many as ten trips to London per year from sophisticated and well organised ports like Newcastle, the four London voyages of *Allome An* with alum from the economically backward port of Whitby is evidence of attempts at good management. That the *Fortune* managed seventeen trips with coal from Sunderland is even more remarkable. It may not be very far, but the vessel still had to be loaded at the difficult barred harbour of Sunderland, sail to Whitby, be delivered, load ballast, and sail back, without guarantee of favourable wind and tide.

**Table 1.1** Whitby vessels leaving and entering Whitby

| Vessel | Master | Cargo | Trips | Total carried |
|--------|--------|-------|-------|---------------|
| *Allome An* | *Foxe* | *alum* | *4* | *217 tons* |
| Amity | Williamson | coal | 4 | 80 chaldrons |
| B.....ser | Henson | *(illegible)* | 1 | *(illegible)* |
| Benjamin | Gregg | coal | 2 | 39 chaldrons |
| Fortune | Harrison | coal | 17 | 286 chaldrons |
| Fox | Farley | coal | 1 | 14 chaldrons |
| Heaven | Brown | coal | 3 | 58 chaldrons |
| Henry | Brown | coal | 9 | 190 chaldrons |
| John | Ratcliffe | malt | 1 | 20 quarters |
| Robert | Woodhall | malt | 1 | 20 quarters |
| Rose | Boynton | *(illegible)* | 1 | *(illegible)* |

(Source: TNA/E190/187/6, Customer/Controller, Christmas 1611–Christmas 1612, Coastal. Vessels leaving in italics.)

---

33 J. Binns, 'Sir Hugh Cholmley of Whitby, 1600–1657: His Life and Works', unpubd PhD thesis, Leeds University, 1990, p. 191. The ketch was the most common vessel trading round northern Europe in the seventeenth century; it may be that the six vessels for which Dr Binns does not account were smaller hoys.

Luke Foxe's *Allome An* was initially recorded as belonging to London and then to Whitby, showing, perhaps, that this was the year during which Foxe settled in the town.[34] The year 1612 is the first in which there are more than sporadic entries for Whitby vessels, and the alum industry was clearly beginning to have an impact on the volume of local shipping.[35] For the first time there is clear evidence of the importation of coal into the port in more than domestic quantities. The amounts carried by individual vessels were small by comparison with later cargoes, though an exact estimate is impossible, since it is not known whether the coal was being measured into Whitby in Newcastle chaldrons (about 53cwt) or London chaldrons (about 27cwt). Probate evidence makes it clear that turf (peat) was burnt as domestic fuel even at the end of the seventeenth century, so importation of coal on such an increased scale is further evidence of industrialisation.[36]

There are some extant entries for trade in ships from other ports during the blank period after 1612, and these, particularly in 1619, serve to confirm the importance of Scotland and Scots vessels in early seventeenth-century shipping. This may have led to the ease of changeover to kelp from Scotland when local supplies proved inadequate – the links would already have existed through the harbour trade. The import is of rye, deals, wine, malt and salt. Outwards went the 'refuse' bark, together with some cloth and two hawks.[37]

Deeds in private hands from the first half of the seventeenth century show that there were coal staithes on the west bank of the Esk beside the street called Haggersgate, and they probably date from this period.[38] They may have been used to hold coal for transportation by the recognised 'road' along the sands at low tide from Upgang to the Mulgrave alum works about three miles away. The account books held in The National Archives for the alum works at Sandsend and Mulgrave refer to the Whitby storehouse.[39] The growth (by an estimated 500 per cent) of the Whitby fleet between 1600 and 1612 thus appears to be a response to the growing importance of the alum trade.

The early alum accounts show that there was what appears to be a dedicated rather than a casual workforce.[40] It is likely that the initial workforce was in part recruited locally, but it is probable that there was some inward migration. Regrettably the volume of the parish register which would have contained the

34 Foxe later achieved fame for his unsuccessful search for the North-West Passage in Charles I's 40-ton pinnace, *Charles*, and became Marshall for the Vice-Admiralty of the North Riding.

35 TNA/AO3/1243/3A, Accounts of Alum Monopoly; Lewis, pp. 51-2; kelp imports probably began during the lacuna in the Port Books between 1612 and 1634, when the first record of kelp is extant.

36 Various probate inventories record turves in the garth.

37 TNA/E190/188/10, Searcher, Christmas 1618/19, Overseas; E190/188/9, Customer, Christmas 1618/19, (In) Overseas; E190/189/10, Collector of New Impots, Michaelmas–Easter 1626/7, (In) Overseas; all are books shared with other creek ports of Newcastle.

38 At the present time Yorkshire Water is doing core sampling along the west waterfront in the town; it may be that the eventual report will yield clear evidence to confirm the staithes.

39 TNA/AO3/1243/3A, Accounts of Alum Monopoly.

40 TNA/AO3/1243/3A, Accounts of Alum Monopoly; these show regular payments to named workmen of all levels.

Elizabethan transcript made in 1598, and the early years of the seventeenth century, has been lost, since that would have shown more clearly which were the 'new' surnames. We know that Luke Foxe at least was an immigrant, and there were probably others.[41]

The early Port Books and Audit Office accounts show that in 1612 much of the transportation of urine and of coal was still in Dutch or Scottish vessels, but there is anecdotal evidence, quoted in the following century, and part of the oral tradition of the community, that the more important fishermen of Whitby acquired larger vessels in order to enter this trade.[42] Lionel Charlton places this as happening about 1615, and the presence of Luke Foxe in 1612, in his *Allome An*, reminds us that there would have been a need for masters to migrate from other ports, to sail in and out of Whitby in this trade. Seafaring, particularly coastal pilotage and deep sea navigation, were skills which could not be learned quickly, and this new industry would initially attract enterprising seamen either with capital to invest or with already-owned vessels. Even the larger vessels bought by successful local fishermen for this new trade would need extra, and differently skilled, seamen, especially as their export trade in processed herrings would be too valuable to be allowed to lapse until the new industry was securely established.

What these changes reveal is that both enterprise and opportunism must have played a large part in the decision-making. However, there must also have been a sufficient amount of ready capital to permit the upgrading of the vessels for the much more complex business of cargo-handling, and for the necessarily increased length of voyages, particularly round the dangerous coast of East Anglia to the River Thames. Over the succeeding centuries, the sandbanks of the Norfolk, Suffolk and Essex coasts claimed the vessels and the equipment, but more importantly the lives, of many Whitby crews. John Naish, in his book on seamarks, recounts the long struggle to provide adequate buoyage and lightage on these dangerous shores.[43]

When its growth began in the seventeenth century, Whitby was still dominated by the secular lordship of the Cholmleys, who had first leased and then bought the dissolved abbey lands from the Crown. They were an established gentry family, well connected by marriage, typically trained in the law, and holding high office under the Crown. Apart from the Whitby abbey estate, they held land in various parts of England.[44] Until late 1603 Henry Cholmley, the lord of the manor at the start of the century, was a Roman Catholic. His wife, Margaret Babthorpe, had spent several periods of imprisonment in York, and he himself had been heavily fined, and was spendthrift to boot. The endowments

---

41 M. Christy (ed.), *The Voyages of Captain Luke Foxe and Captain Thomas James in Search of a North-West Passage*, Hakluyt Society Nos. 88 and 89, 1894, in which Foxe, in his own account of his great voyage, describes himself as from Hull. He was, in fact, born in Hull, and describes himself so in his journal of the voyage.
42 L. Charlton, *The History of Whitby*, York, 1779, pp. 307-8.
43 J. Naish, *Seamarks: Their History and Development*, Stanford Maritime, 1985.
44 One had been Justiciar of England, another Verderer of the royal forest of Pickering.

of the parish church of St Mary had been given separately to the archbishop of York at the dissolution, and were farmed out to lay rectors, so that only a perpetual curate ministered to the town, an apparently sad conclusion to a long period of distinguished church history.[45]

Probate records for the first two decades of the seventeenth century reveal no urban occupations save that of a beer-brewer, and only a single mention of a 'burgess'. No minutes of either manor court or burgess court are known to survive from this period, and the only institutional officers whose names are known are the curate and the three churchwardens who signed the parish register from time to time.[46] The town did, however, appear to have a specialised economic function, in that it was still a port; moreover, its probably reduced population was still concentrated within its medieval streets; and its solitary deceased burgess indicates the remnants of its once more complex government. Thus three of Clark and Slack's criteria for defining a town are met.[47] Nonetheless, Whitby was apparently a small, unimportant and isolated community, with only vestigial remnants of its wealthier past.

It is impossible to estimate with certainty the size of the population *c.* 1600. Clark and Hosking show no totals for Whitby from the diocesan surveys of 1563 and 1603.[48] The parish register is missing before 1608, a critical date in Whitby's development. A solitary Bishop's Transcript for 1600/1 shows seven baptisms between October 1600 and March 1602, and seventeen burials. Unfortunately, there are no records for the known severe outbreak of plague in 1603, though its severity is attested by the large number of deaths in the small sub-dependent fishing port of Runswick.[49] The evidence is far too scrappy for an accurate estimate of population, but a crude guess can be attempted. Between May and December of 1608 thirty-one baptisms were recorded, and during the whole of 1609 there were forty-six. For some reason both years recorded only small numbers of burials, five in each year in what appears to be a very deficient burial record. It might, however, indicate that there had been a serious outbreak of plague in Whitby in 1603. Such serious epidemics took the most vulnerable members of the community, and succeeding years might therefore

---

45  The instrument of dissolution is found in TNA/Close Roll No. 421, 31 Henry VIII, part 4, 213.

46  The early modern records of the manor of Whitby were until very recently thought to have been lost. At the time of writing they have been rediscovered, but are as yet unlisted and unarchived.

47  P. Clark and P. Slack, *English Towns in Transition 1500–1700*, Oxford University Press, p. 5, lists these.

48  C. Clark and J. Hosking (eds), *Population Estimates of English Small Towns, 1550–1851*, revised edition, University of Leicester Press, 1993, p. 175. This study appears to have included the acreage of the present parish of Ruswarp with Whitby. Ruswarp is *now* a ward of the town, but in the period of this study was outside the township, which is given in the early population tables in the *Victoria History of the North Riding* as 48 acres, the probable limit of the medieval burgage. It was not until the late eighteenth century that the township began to expand into the constablery of Ruswarp. Even the parish church and abbey were technically in the adjacent constablery of Hawsker-cum-Stainsacre.

49  P. Slack, *The Impact of Plague in Tudor and Stuart England*, Routledge and Kegan Paul, 1985, p. 279, quoting Lady Margaret Hoby's Diary; Parish Registers of Hinderwell, North Yorkshire. Runswick, like the larger fishing port of Staithes, was a township of Hinderwell.

show an uncharacteristically low number of burials.[50] Assuming the baptismal record to be accurate, then the use of the crude birth rates suggested by Wrigley and Schofield for the whole of pre-industrial Europe, that is between twenty-two and forty per thousand, produces a potential population for the town in 1608-9 of between 1,150 (4 per cent ) and 1,750 (2.2 per cent).[51]

Since Clark and Hosking calculate that at the time of the hearth tax of 1670 and the Compton Census of 1676 there were respectively 1,980 and 3,520 inhabitants, and an eleven-year moving average of baptisms shows a clear upward trend from 1609 to the end of the century, it is likely that the lower calculation, 1,150, more nearly represents the population of Whitby at the start of the century than does the higher figure.[52] This is supported by the fact that during the period of fuller registration after 1610 it is quite clear that normally baptisms exceeded burials in Whitby, which would imply a higher fertility level.

The smaller Essex port of Harwich, with which Whitby vessels traded regularly during this century, was much less healthy than Whitby.[53] Harwich also faced due north, but lay at the end of a peninsula at the confluence of the Orwell and the Essex Stour, at the point where both joined the mouth of the Thames estuary. Unlike Whitby, with its superabundance of springs, Harwich had no fresh water at all within the confines of the medieval borough and the estuarial tides washed the effluent of the town from one side of the peninsula to the other. Harwich had the further disadvantage that the town was surrounded by the notoriously malarial Essex marshes.

The datum line for Harwich shows a very different picture, with fearsome outbreaks of plague, typhus and enteric fevers, as well as the constant attritional mortality from malaria. However, as many major towns such as London and York were on flat, low-lying sites, like that of Harwich in topography if not in size, the contrast serves to show the comparative health of Whitby. The town had, therefore, advantages in continuity of population and thus of collective experience over time, an important factor in the days before systematic recording of such catastrophic events as flood, and during which there was no

50 E. A. Wrigley, and R. S. Schofield, *The Population History of England*, Cambridge University Press (paperback), 1989, pp. 545-6, Table A2.4, showing the corrected totals for deaths by year, does not appear to demonstrate this phenomenon in the years following 1603 and 1625, both notorious plague years. However, the national totals include many parishes which were not affected by plague, and the phenomenon is most obvious in individual parishes. Aggregative analysis of the registers of the Tendring Peninsula in Essex, and of a group of parishes around Saxmundham in Suffolk all show clear evidence of years of low mortality following serious mortality crises, but often at different periods.

51 Wrigley and Schofield, p. 174. They suggest that no western European country would have had a birth rate of less than 22 per 1,000 in pre-industrial times.

52 Clark and Hosking, pp. 175-6.

53 R. R. Barker, 'Comparing Demographic Experience: Harwich and Whitby', *Local Population Studies*, vol. 46, 1991; in this article the author showed the differences between a healthy and an unhealthy town.

Figure 1.1 Datum line showing excess of baptisms over burials in Whitby during the seventeenth century

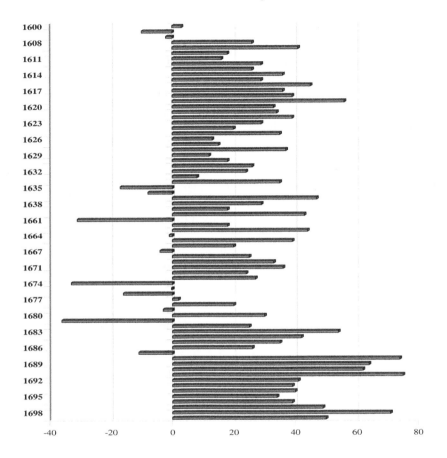

Datum line showing baptismal surplus or deficit in the seventeenth century in Whitby; 0 = parity; -n = deficit, of baptisms relative to burials in same year; +n = surplus of baptisms over burials in same year.

routine forward planning to meet disaster, save perhaps through what is termed 'folk memory'.[54]

Continued aggregative analysis of the Whitby parish register shows that as the shipping industry stabilised and the population presumably reached a more

54  When considering the importance of collective memory to a community, an interesting example is that, during the 1953 storm surge, the older communities of Essex, such as Walton-on-the-Naze and Harwich, suffered far less loss of life, indeed in the former, no deaths at all, than the new settlements like Canvey Island and Jaywick, where there was no collective memory of previous disasters, or awareness of the risk of certain weather conditions, and which suffered catastrophically.

Figure 1.2 Datum line showing excess of burials over baptisms in Harwich during the seventeenth century

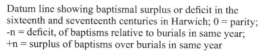

Datum line showing baptismal surplus or deficit in the sixteenth and seventeenth centuries in Harwich; 0 = parity; -n = deficit, of baptisms relative to burials in same year; +n = surplus of baptisms over burials in same year

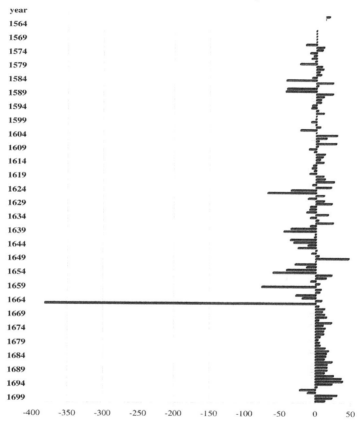

usual age-balance, by the end of the 1650s, so the relationship between baptism and burial grew much closer, although still subject to increasing swings which will be discussed in due course. The pattern of baptism, burial and marriage in Whitby in the first part of the seventeenth century is such as to show that considerable and dramatic changes in vital events were taking place in a community in which it can be seen that there were unusual developments in a new industry. It is likely, therefore, that the two phenomena were closely intertwined.

In 1600 there were probably some eighteen towns in England with more than 5,000 inhabitants, one of them being London, with an estimated population of 200,000, and three others – Norwich, Bristol and York, provincial capitals – containing more than 10,000.[55] Of these eighteen towns, eleven were ports, and all were incorporated boroughs, subject both to the protection and to the constraints of a very structured and oligarchic system. Among the third tier, between 5,000 and 10,000, was the port of Newcastle-upon-Tyne, of which headport Whitby was a member. Thus in 1600 Whitby was very much smaller than any of the eighteen largest English ports or inland towns.

Of those principal ship-owning outports whose tonnage in 1582 and 1629 was listed by Davis, few appear in the 1563 and 1603 population estimates of Clark and Hosking for small towns.[56] Although Scarborough does not appear in the 1629 listing for tonnage, there survives in the Scarborough Borough Archives a copy of the Admiralty order of 23 December 1628, which led to the return.[57] Presumably that port, an incorporated borough with a royal castle, was considered large enough to warrant a copy of the order. Whether Whitby also received it is unknown, and in any event no return from either port is extant. Of the listed ports, Newcastle, Hull, Lynn, Great Yarmouth, Exeter and Bristol were towns too large to qualify for inclusion in the population listings for small towns, and of the others, only Southampton, with an estimated population of 3,210, and Aldeburgh, with 1,200, have population estimates for 1603.[58]

Judging by later shipping and demographic statistics, Aldeburgh was already declining at the start of the seventeenth century, although Southampton's fleet continued to grow, but at a much slower rate than did that of Whitby.[59] The crude estimate given for Whitby earlier in this chapter puts the town far down in any scale of outport population. It is thus clear that Whitby's population ranking at the beginning of the century was low, but there were, as shown above, some unusual mechanisms occurring in its baptismal and burial rates in the two following decades. It thus appears likely that some disturbing, possibly economic, influence was at work.

What *has* become apparent is that the low population ranking at the start of the century, and the probable total population, as well as the economic structure, made Whitby only marginally urban. Whitby had its medieval harbour, which was still working, but its humble status is further emphasised by the state of the harbour trade and probable ship-owning activity.

Such parish register evidence as there is does show a significant rise in the mean number of baptisms centred on the years 1613–1620. That the burial and marriage totals remain constant may be an indicator of an inward migration of steady, married men in the prime of life, perhaps masters and mates of vessels.

---

55  P. Corfield, *English Urban History 1500–1780*; Open University, Course A322, 1977, Unit 10, p. 42.
56  Davis, pp. 35–6; Clark and Hosking, pp. 175–6.
57  M. Y. Ashcroft (ed.), *Scarborough Records 1600–1640*, North Yorkshire County Record Office Publication No. 47, (Draft) 1991, p. 197; Copy of order, Admiralty to Vice-Admiralties, 23 December 1628.
58  Kings Lynn does not appear in Corfield's list of towns of above 5,000 inhabitants in 1600, but does not appear either in Clark and Hosking either.
59  Davis, pp. 35–6; Corfield, pp. 36–7.

Such men would contribute to the baptismal rate, while having little effect on the marriage rate. Their ages would be below those at which death from natural causes would be expected, so that the apparent imbalance would have been due in large measure to such inward migration. Having said that, Luke Foxe, the only identifiable immigrant, from Hull, married a Whitby bride, Ann Barnard, on 13 May 1613, to contribute to the stable marriage rate and the growing baptismal rate. This does, of course, simply emphasise the problems of examining demography with inadequate sources. Of the twenty-one masters recorded in the first two decades, only one other, Andrew Gregg, master of *Marie*, apparently married in Whitby. However, four others fathered children in this period, adding to the imbalance of baptisms and marriages. As far as can be traced, nine children were born to the families of ships' masters between 1608 and 1618. Since the names of crew members are unknown at this stage, it is not possible to establish exactly how many births the seafaring community as a whole added to the population of the town.

Wrigley and his colleagues of the Cambridge Group for the History of Population and Social Structure have shown that average *infant and child* mortality could be as high as 23 per cent and no lower than 15 per cent in the period, and have also shown that the percentage of the population of England and Wales who were aged over forty-five ranged from 21 per cent in 1601 to over 25 per cent a century later. Within these percentages there were fluctuations due to changing economies, climate, food crises and urbanisation, as well as the problems of crisis mortality.[60]

There can be no doubt that it was during the second of these two decades of the seventeenth century that the discovery of, and early attempts to exploit, the alum shale in the area provided the impetus that set Whitby upon its remarkable growth curve, both of the town and of the fleet. That in the eighteenth century the alum became a minor part of Whitby's prosperity is irrelevant; it had completed the important work of 'kick-starting' the economy, and was to provide a thread, at least in the background, of continuity throughout the early modern period.

60 E. A. Wrigley, R. S. Davies, J. E. Oeppen and R. S. Schofield, *English Population History from Family Reconstitution, 1580–1837*, Cambridge University Press, 1997, pp. 207, 216 (Figure 6.1), 294–5.

# 2

# The Early Seventeenth Century

## Economic progress

It is clear that the first two decades of the seventeenth century saw the start of a new economic phase in Whitby, together with the demographic change necessarily accompanying it. It was in the next forty years that, despite all the vicissitudes of a period that was very hard for much of the whole country, Whitby managed to progress, to make political and economic decisions, and to increase the size of both population and fleet, and its consequent prosperity. During those years there was both foreign and civil war, in the second of which the Cholmleys were heavily embroiled, as were their kin.[1]

As with the earlier period, evidence is still spasmodic, but it increases and diversifies, partly because of Whitby's increased economic activity and partly because Whitby had once more ascended the national stage rather than the local one where the town had spent the years since the dissolution of the abbey. For the first time it is possible to find more than one source for a single event or a sequential change and therefore to begin to understand the complex nature of Whitby's development.

Such simple, but in truth misleading, evidence is to be found in the Scarborough Pierage Accounts of 1614–36.[2] There are no more Whitby vessels recorded as leaving the Tyne at the end of the series than at the start, suggesting little growth in Whitby's involvement in the coal trade. The trade from the Tyne was dominated, then, as later in the century, by the ancient East Anglian ports of King's Lynn, Great Yarmouth and Ipswich, as well as by London and by Newcastle itself. However, in the later 1630s, it becomes clear, from Port Books once more extant, from the sources associated with the alum industry and from the first known voyage book for a Whitby vessel, that the Whitby fleet did undertake a considerable trade in coal, but with Sunderland, on the Wear, where the alum investors had by the 1630s already bought a colliery at Harraton. The investors were then shipping their Harraton coal from

---

1   Sir Hugh Cholmley was the Governor of Scarborough Castle throughout the year-long siege of 1644/5. After the castle fell to Parliament he was permitted to go into exile until 1651. His cousin, Browne Bushell, sometime owner and master of the vessel *John* of Whitby, was beheaded as a traitor in 1652, and his Scarborough (sic) cousins, Sir John Hotham and his son, were also executed by Parliament after the fall of Hull. The widowed Lady Hotham retired to a Cholmley manor near Robin Hood's Bay. The Newtons, of Bagdale Hall, remained Parliamentarian in their sympathies. J. Binns, *Yorkshire in the Civil Wars*, Blackthorn, 2004, gives a vivid account of the destruction war brought to Yorkshire in this period.
2   NYCRO/DC/SBC/Scarborough Borough Records, Pierage Accounts.

Sunderland, thus avoiding the payment of dues to the Hostmen of Newcastle.[3] Few records of pierage have survived from Sunderland, unlike those for the Tyne.[4]

It is within this period of gaps in the systematic shipping record that we find two glimpses of an aspect of the shipping industry that was to dominate at the peak of Whitby's pre-eminence in the late eighteenth century. Whitby does not feature in Davis's table of major ship-*owning* outports for 1629, but there is national evidence that Whitby was developing a ship-*building* industry at this time.[5]

## Ship-building

Trinity House certificates for the arming of vessels trading in the Thames are to be found in the State Papers Domestic of the reign of Charles I. The certificates of 1626 list three Whitby-built vessels, all belonging to other outports. The certificates allowed vessels to carry defensive ordinance, and all three vessels were over 100 tons, presumably tons burthen. One, *Pelican* of Newcastle, was of 170 tons. The Whitby ship-builders named were Henry Potter and Christopher Bagwith.[6] Nothing further is known of Potter as a builder, although one Thomas Potter was a purchaser of a Cholmley tenement in 1638. However, in 1635, Phineas Pett, the King's Master Shipwright, set sail for the north of England in search of timber and other materials for a great new ship to be built at Woolwich. The weather drove his vessel back from the approach to Newcastle and it put in to Scarborough, whence Pett rode to Whitby. He lodged with the ailing, and in fact dying, Captain Luke Foxe, and 'found much kindness at the hands of one Mr Bagwell, a shipwright and yardkeeper'; with little doubt, Christopher Bagwith the ship-builder.[7] That the great man felt it important to ride to Whitby over twenty-one miles of rough moorland and back again suggests that Bagwith had a well established yard, worthy of his attention. However, given Pett's subsequent reputation for peculation and for use of poor materials, this may be less of a recommendation than it seems.[8]

Others had thought Whitby a good place to build. In 1624/5 Sir Ferdinando Gorges, Governor of Plymouth, a Dr Gooch, and others of the Council for New

3   D. P. Pybus and J. Rushton, 'Alum and the Yorkshire Coast', in D. B. Lewis (ed.), *The Yorkshire Coast*, Normandy Press, 1991, pp. 51–2; Hatcher, J., *The History of the British Coal Industry*, vol. 1, *Before 1700: Towards the Age of Coal*, Clarendon Press, 1993, pp. 254–5, explains the investment in some detail.

4   NYCRO/DC/SBC/Scarborough Borough Records, Pierage Accounts; only one sheet remains from Sunderland.

5   R. Davis, *The Rise of the English Shipping Industry in the Seventeenth and Eighteenth Centuries*, first published, Macmillan, 1962, National Maritime Museum, Modern Maritime Classics Reprint No. 3, 1972, p. 35.

6   TNA/SP16/88, Trinity House certificates; to these ship-builders must be added Andrew Dickson, builder of the vessel *Great Neptune* in 1625/6.

7   W. G. Perrin, *The Autobiography of Phineas Pett*, Navy Records Society, Vol. 2, 1918, p. 159.

8   N. A. M. Rodger, *The Safeguard of the Sea: A Naval History of Britain, 660–1649*, Harper Collins, 1997, pp. 365–75.

England commissioned Andrew Dickson of Whitby to build a ship to be called *Great Neptune*, of forty guns, and over 500 tons burthen, costing £1,100, for the New England trade which, like that of the Levant, required large and sturdy vessels fit to defend themselves against pirates.[9] Fortunately for this study, Gorges failed to pay his bills, and the vessel comes to light in the Acts of the Privy Council, when Dickson petitioned for his money. The ship, the largest merchant vessel then afloat, was eventually bought for the Navy.

In his analysis of the early Stuart period, Rodger shows that dishonesty and fraud were rife among government suppliers, and amongst naval officials.[10] So too was the failure to pay bills, often over many years, a practice which in turn encouraged fraud by suppliers who had to make money somehow, or else starve. The Council for New England may have used up all their credit in the southern ship-building ports, and may have felt that a builder in Whitby would be a more innocent target. They were wrong.

Apart from this evidence that Whitby had the skills to build substantial vessels, even if caulkers had to be brought from London for *Great Neptune*, there is the unwitting testimony that the harbour itself was capable of accommodating the draught and beam of large vessels.[11] There is sadly no evidence of where these yards were, although common sense suggests they were in the safety of the upper harbour, implying, of course, that the contemporary bridge was capable of being opened to a width which would allow the passage of a 500-ton vessel.[12] The only other possible site, the area behind the original east pier now known as Tate Hill Sands, would at that time, before any west pier had been constructed, have been too exposed to northerly and north-easterly gales for such a valuable construction project.

During this period, Luke Foxe, who had experience of the Spitzbergen whaling industry in which the Dutch were predominant, persuaded Charles I to send him in the 40-ton pinnace *Charles* in search of the elusive north-west passage.[13] He survived and returned after exploring the west coast of Baffin Land and leaving his name on both land and sea.[14] Foxe is particularly admired among historians of Arctic navigation for achieving his feat within a single season. His journal described himself as of Hull, his birth-place, and he may have been living away from Whitby at the time of his voyages. On the other hand, when he petitioned the king for permission to undertake his voyage, he may have felt that Hull carried a greater cachet than the relatively unknown Whitby.

9   C. D. (*sic*), 'Records of the Council for New England', *Proceedings of the American Antiquarian Society*, 1867, from TNA/Colonial Papers, vol. 2, No. 6.

10  Rodger, pp. 364–78, in which the Administration of the Navy from 1603 to 1630 is discussed.

11  C. D. (*sic*), 'Records of the Council for New England', *Proceedings of the American Antiquarian Society*, 1867, vol. 2, No. 6, records the struggle to find enough specialists for this enterprise, from TNA/Colonial Papers.

12  Whitby Bridge has been replaced several times since 1600, the last time being early in the twentieth century. Early versions seem to have been lifting or draw-bridges. It is now a swing bridge.

13  L. Foxe, *North-West Fox, or Fox from the North-West Passage*, London, 1635, reprinted by Johnson Reprint Corporation, Canada, 1965, A1–2.

14  Both Foxe Land and Foxe Channel were named by him.

Hull was after all the King's Town, a place of which Charles was to become only too well aware at the start of the Civil War.[15] However, Foxe also served as Admiralty Marshall for the North Riding, and documents extant in the High Court of Admiralty clearly show that he was sailing in and out of Whitby in the 1620s.[16] The voyage is of further note in that Luke Foxe reasserted the English claim to control of northern Canada against the French.[17] It is serendipitous that just as James Cook navigated his ship to what became 'New South Wales', his predecessor as a Whitby-linked explorer 140 years or so earlier had called the area in a different hemisphere which he claimed for the Crown 'New North Wales'.

The text of the document in Plate 2.1 is :

Translation of the Memoriall to the French commissioners, etc., touching Hudsons Bay:
His Maj[es]ties Right to Hudson's Bay
The Northern part of America wherein Hudsons Bay is comprised was discovered in the year 1497 by Sir Sebastian Cabot by particular Commission from King Henry the 7th.
In the yeare 1610 Mr Henry Hudson his Maj[es]ties subject sailed into the Streights and Bay of Hudson, and took possession thereof, giving names to severall places therein by which they have been since called and known in the Mapps of these parts, as well Foreign as English.
In the year 1612 Sir Thomas Button an Englishman sailed into the said Streights and Bay and took possession of severall places particularly of the River of Port Nelson and territories thereunto belonging in the name of his Master King James the First, and called the said River and Port wherein they then wintered by the name of Port Nelson from the Commander of the Ship wherein he sailed whose name was Nelson.
In the Year 1631 **Capt Luke Foxe** by command of his late Majesty King Charles the First made a voyage to Hudsons Bay and amongst other places within the said Bay he entered the River of Port Nelson and finding there a Cross which had been erected by Sir Thomas Button, with an inscription defaced, he set up the said Cross againe with a new inscription declareing his Maj[es]ties Right and possession and then named the adjacent countries upon the said River, New North Wales as it's called to this day in the Mapps of America...

Between 1612 and 1634 there are no extant Port Books, so that it is not possible to plot clearly the development of the fleet between these two dates, apart from the glimpse of ship-building above and the adventures of Foxe. Significantly, none of the vessels known to have been built in Whitby during this

---

15  Though generally known as 'Hull', its real name is Kingston upon Hull, the 'Hull' part being the River Hull, which enters the Humber estuary at that point.
16  TNA/HCA/49; Examination of Luke Foxe, Admiralty Marshall for the North Riding of Yorkshire. This examination refers to a case held in the manor court at Whitby, when Foxe was unsuccessfully sued by his articulate or apprentice for salvage money.
17  HBCA A.9/1 fols. 8d–9, Transactions between England and France relating to Hudson Bay, 1687–88

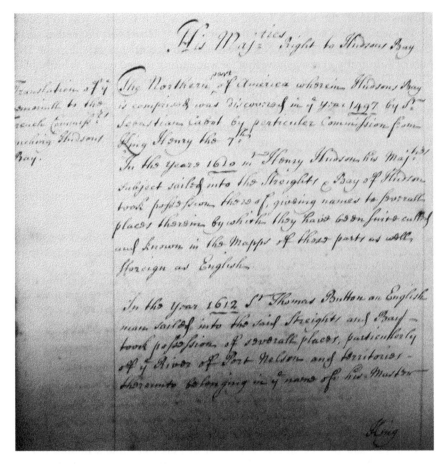

Plate 2.1: Luke Foxe and the Claim to Hudson's Bay
(a) HBCA A.9/1, fo. 8d: Part of the Claim to Hudson's Bay

brief period became part of the town's fleet. Of the vessels known to belong to the town, we have no building records. There survives, however, a part of the voyage accounts of *John*, Browne Bushell master, for 1632, showing clear evidence of trade with northern Europe and, carrying coal and passengers, to London.[18]

18  TNA/HCA30/638, Voyage Book of *John*, of Whitby, Browne Bushell, Master. Bushell was a cousin of both Hugh Cholmley and John Hotham, both Royalist governors who had changed sides, and also of Isaac Newton, Parliamentary governor of Whitby. The value of the voyage book as a resource will be discussed later in this chapter.

Plate 2.1: Luke Foxe and the Claim to Hudson's Bay
(b) HBCA A.9/1, fo. 9.

## Civic status

There is also evidence of civic developments between 1620 and 1632. In 1626 Trinity House, London, had issued a certificate supporting the petition of agents of the burgesses of Whitby for the improvement of the harbour, ostensibly as a refuge for vessels sailing between London and the Tyne.[19] This implies, as

19 G. G. Harris (ed.), *Trinity House of Deptford, Transactions 1609–35*, London Record Society, Vol. 19, 1983, p. 61, Certificate dated 12 April 1626.

does a petition to Charles I for incorporated status in 1630, that the burgesses were already finding the economic impetus and political will which was so important for the growth of the fleet.[20] It also suggests that they had already made a sufficient amount of profit to enable them to commence such an expensive process.

These developments reflect some of the problems of Whitby's status as a seigniorial borough. Sir Henry Cholmley, having conformed to the Church of England in 1603, died, with his own affairs in confusion, in 1615/16. He was succeeded by his son, Sir Richard, who, as Gaskin describes in his accounts derived from family papers, soon ran up more enormous debts, incurred in his political activities as High Sheriff and as a member of the Council of the North.[21] There would be little cash, or care, to spare for his town of Whitby, and there was considerable frustration within the growing industry as fabric declined and harbour installations fell into disrepair, as well as with the constraints implicit in manorial control. It is known that before Sir Richard's death he and his son were already alienating property in Hawsker, an outlying township of Whitby, to raise cash.[22] Sir Richard died in September 1631, and it seems likely that his death, and the succession of his son Hugh, whose activities to redeem the family fortunes had a great impact on the town, were the reasons why, having persuaded Charles I of their case for becoming a chartered borough, the chief citizens failed to proceed to incorporation after Letters Patent had been granted. Jack Binns has argued that many or even all of Sir Hugh's improvements and sales of property benefited only himself, and that he did little for the town. He also suggests that the manor prevented much of the potential for individual economic progress through its control of the port. This would have added to the pressure for incorporation. Jack Binns suggests that Cholmley actually intervened to prevent the incorporation through his then close friendship with Thomas Wentworth, Lord President of the North, and a leading adviser and supporter of Charles I.[23]

However, in the face of a lack of written evidence, it is equally possible that the opportunistic, and now prosperous, burgesses bought the offered tenements, which in many cases they already occupied, at a price which, while high, they could afford, and made the most of the opportunities afforded by the attenuation of the manorial link. One of the principal purchasers was Isaac Newton, later to distinguish himself for Parliament in opposition to Cholmley after Cholmley and his cousin Bushell had gone over to the king. The Bushell family home, Bagdale Hall, was purchased by Isaac Newton, described by

---

20  CSPD 1630, pp. 43, *et seq.*, states that the ancient borough and haven, 'commodious for navigation and fishing…of late is very much decayed'. The petition was a request for incorporation since the trouble was due to want of settled government.

21  R. T. Gaskin, *The Old Seaport of Whitby*, first published Forth, Whitby, 1909, Caedmon reprints, 1986, pp. 118–28.

22  I am grateful to Mrs Janet Green of Robin Hood's Bay for this information from deeds.

23  J. Binns, 'Sir Hugh Cholmley: Whitby's benefactor or beneficiary?', *Northern History*, Vol. 30, pp. 87–104.

Bushell in his voyage accounts as 'my cuzsen Newton'.[24] The politics of the Civil War divided this extended family as it did so many.

## Population

During this same period, the parish registers show a steady upward trend in the size of the population, in that the eleven-year moving averages show a gradual increase in baptisms. The number of marriages seems to have remained stable, but the number of burials increased, although still lagging behind the baptismal rate. By this stage there must have been more normalisation of the population profile. The early immigrants would have been assimilated, and would have settled down to a more routine life cycle, such as those shown by Wrigley and Schofield for this period.[25]

At the start of this period, as shown in Figure 2.1, Whitby's proportional rate of baptisms per hundred marriages was high, much higher than the national rate, while the burial rate was lower. The newly developing industry would have attracted young adults migrating in family units, as did the later changes associated with the industrial revolution. There was clearly a vigorous and fertile population. At the same time, men might have been marrying outside the parish, not unusual in a seaport; this phenomenon might also suggest a disproportionate number of men seeking brides in the rural hinterland. Whichever mechanism is in place, there is no doubt that it is the result of Whitby's sudden prosperity and need for a workforce in a predominantly male industry.

However, in the 1630s there was an upward trend in burials, as the early immigrant population began to age. Luke Foxe himself died in 1635, and there is evidence that the bubonic plague which haunted some of the port towns between 1635 and 1638 reached Whitby.[26] However, the plague of 1625, which caused such devastation in the ports of East Anglia, seems to have missed Whitby entirely, although Whitby men are known to have died and been buried in Harwich during the particularly severe visitation in that port.[27]

## Wealth

Whitby's parish registers are scant during the Civil War, but there is much more evidence of shipping and economic activity, especially as a number of the Port Books are extant from 1632. At the same time there is the evidence of the purchase of land and buildings from the Cholmleys during the 1630s, both in Whitby and in Robin Hood's Bay. Some are purchases by tenants, but others

---

24 *Ibid*. There are also many deeds of private property in Whitby, now in private hands.
25 E. A. Wrigley and R. S. Schofield, *The Population History of England*, Cambridge University Press (paperback), 1989; J. Charlesworth, *Parish Register of Whitby, 1600–1676*, Yorkshire Parish Register Society, 1928.
26 J. Charlesworth, (ed.) *Parish Register of Whitby, 1600–1676*; Yorkshire Parish Register Society, 1928.
27 ERO/D/P 170, Vol. 1, Burial Register for St Nicholas's church, Harwich, Essex.

Figure 2.1: National and local vital events, 1621–1635. The figures have been adjusted to the same scale

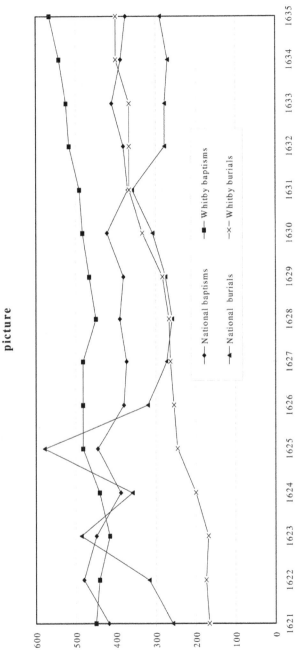

**Relationship between the baptisms and burials of Whitby and the national picture**

are possibly for new use or for investment at a period when growing prosperity in Whitby meant that there was money with which to exploit the Cholmley family's need for ready money.

Table 2.1: The alienation of Cholmley real estate in the late 1630s

| Date | No. of Lease | Price | Purchaser | Occupation or status (bracketed if known from other source) |
|------|------|------|------|------|
| 22/2/1639 | 37 | £16.00 | Aire, Robert | |
| 18/10/1638 | 39 | £80.00 | Bagwith, Christopher | tenant (ship-builder) |
| 21/3/1639 | 63 | | Bower, Thomas | |
| 10/10/1639 | 49 | £80.00 | Cass, Thomas | |
| 2/2/1639 | 36 | £26.67 | Cosin, Miles | gentleman |
| 2/2/1639 | 31 | £40.00 | Craven Charles | |
| 16/10/1638 | 26 | £24.00 | Dodds, William | boatwright |
| 2/2/1639 | 33 | £30.00 | Dunnington, John | (master mariner) |
| 20/5/1640 | 50 | £35.00 | Huntrodes, Richard | |
| 5/9/1640 | 29 | £15.00 | Huntrodes, Roger | |
| 13/10/1638 | 46 | £95.00 | Jackson, William | tenant |
| 18/2/1639 | | £12.00 | Linskill, Henry | tanner |
| 18/2/1639 | 38 | £60.00 | Linskill, Richard | smith |
| 5/1/1639 | 35 | £40.00 | Lockwood, Charles and William | |
| 18/2/1639 | 10 | £40.00 | Martin, John | |
| 30/10/1638 | 45 | £86.67 | Mason, Robert | gentleman |
| 16/2/1639 | 28 | £25.00 | Monkman, William | |
| 2/2/1639 | 53 | £30.00 | Moon, Thomas | |
| 20/3/1639 | 48 | £22.50 | Morrell, Robert | |
| 13/10/1638 | 27 | not known | Newton, Isaac | gentleman |
| 30/10/1638 | 47 | £43.00 | Newton, Lawrence | |
| 18/2/1639 | 7 | £86.67 | Noble, Gawen | |
| 11/2/1639 | 25 | £36.00 | Norrison, Robert | |

| Date (cont.) | No. of Lease | Price | Purchaser | Occupation or status (bracketed if known from other source) |
|---|---|---|---|---|
| 16/10/1639 | 44 | £20.00 | Pearson, William | |
| 30/10/1638 | 42 | £25.00 | Potter, Thomas | (ship-builder) |
| 1/4/1638 | 52 | £58.00 | Rickinson, Ralph | |
| 29/10/1639 | 24 | £16.00 | Sneaton, Henry | tailor |
| 18/2/1639 | 15 | £19.00 | Sneaton, Matthew | |
| 28/2/1639 | 32 | £45.00 | Sneaton, William | tailor |
| 29/3/1639 | 30 | £61.00 | Woodhouse, John | |
| 19/2/1639 | 65 | £16.00 | Wilkinson, Frances and Repentance, with Smales, Isabel | |
| Total raised | | £1,183.51 | | |

The list of buyers of Cholmley land includes a number of families who were involved in the new shipping industry, either actively or as investors. Potter, Newton, Linskill, Sneaton, Huntrodes, Dunnington, Smales, Bagwith, Rickinson, Norrison and Noble were among the new entrepreneurs. It is possible that Thomas Potter was a ship-builder, Bagwith certainly was, and Dodds was a boat-builder. By this stage there was no more exporting of 'crooked timber for boats' knees'. Other deeds in private hands record much changing of property ownership at this time, with the new owners, some of whom are husband and wife partnerships, having surnames belonging to families that became very involved in the new shipping industry

That the sale raised almost £1,200 is an indicator of the growing wealth in Whitby at that time. It is further remarkable when to that sum can be added the value of Whitby's growing merchant fleet, together with the ready money required as operating capital for that fleet. Some thirty-three names occur in Binns' listing of the sales, and many others are recorded in other deeds in private hands as buying property.[28]

The purchases are clear evidence of growing prosperity, since they required a laying-out of cash. It was cash with which to pay creditors that Cholmley

---

28 Several collections of deeds deposited in the archives at Whitby Museum confirm purchases by men and women who can be linked to the shipping industry.

needed, rather than promissory notes. These same purchasers whose families are known to have been involved in the new shipping industry must also have had sufficient funds to buy shares in vessels and in the stock of those vessels, and have been sufficiently solvent on a daily basis to support the often long wait for returns on shipping investments. These were men and women of substance.

During the gap in the Port Books, from 1612 to 1632, there is thus clear evidence of the development of industry, particularly in ship-building and, from the alum accounts, in the production of alum, which involved the importation of coal. There is also evidence of considerable change in the aspirations of those citizens who were becoming involved in these economic changes, and the parish registers show a gradually increasing population. One would therefore expect that when the Port Books are once more available, they would show that there had been similar advances in both the number of ships in Whitby's fleet and in the activity of the port, and indeed this is what emerges.

Some thirty vessels from Whitby alone are to be found trading into and out of the port.[29] A large number of these were importing coal from Sunderland, and in greater amounts than in 1612, when the largest cargo was of 24 chaldrons. The largest cargo in 1634–36 was carried by *John*, and was of 36 chaldrons, an increase in capacity of 50 per cent.[30] This in itself is an indicator of growing confidence, showing that investors were prepared to acquire larger vessels.

Meanwhile, the alum industry was expanding, after a long period in which five-figure sums in capital had been consumed until at last the process was perfected, and the system of production stabilised. These developments led to a much larger export trade in finished alum, and again the cargoes were some 40 per cent larger. Furthermore, the alum was being sent abroad; not simply to the entrepôt of London, but directly to northern European markets. Not only had the papal monopoly been breached to provide alum for the home market but the trade had been carried into Europe.

Where coal was being imported, it was from Sunderland, so that the arrangements with Harraton were clearly successful, and this explains the paucity of Whitby vessels in the Scarborough Pierage records for 1633–36.[31] There was some trade with Newcastle, but the product shipped was salt, although one vessel appears actually to have carried a cargo of coals *to* Newcastle.

Other things emerge from the Port Books of the 1632–38 period, particularly the growing list of names appearing as merchants. Apart from 'HM Alum Works', at least twelve separate merchants were importing and exporting goods

29 The exact number is difficult to ascertain, since some vessel names were particularly popular, and can only be differentiated by the different names of masters. Other entries give only masters' names and no name for the vessel.

30 TNA/E190/190/3 (Controller, Christmas 1632/3, Overseas); TNA/E190/190/8, (Customer/ Controller, Christmas 1633/4, Coastal); TNA/E190/191/2 (with Stockton), (Controller, Christmas 1635/6, Overseas); TNA/E190/191/8 (Customer, Christmas 1636/7, Overseas).

31 NYCRO/DC/SBC/Scarborough Borough Records, Pierage Accounts, 1613–36.

in Whitby. Seven of them were dealing in alum, while others dealt in butter, a growing trade, in rye, and in preserved fish. Butter was to become an important export from Whitby, in response to the desperate need of London for what was in effect a universal grease, used fresh for eating and rancid for industrial use.[32]

A Port Book for 1641 shows ten voyages in which masters were factoring their own cargoes. This meant that the vessel's owners had entrusted to the master a sum, either in cash or bills of exchange, with which to buy a cargo at his port of outset and sell it on his arrival. 'Factoring' masters were often recorded as merchants in the appropriate column. Although the cargoes these men were importing were of tow, flax, hemp, timber, wine, cider vinegar and prunes, factoring became a normal practice throughout the eighteenth century, almost universally so in Whitby's coal trade.[33]

One extremely important document for the history of Whitby's shipping has survived in the cause papers of the High Court of Admiralty, for a year in which the Port Books are no longer extant. It is an excerpt from the voyage accounts of *John*, Browne Bushell, master, for most of the year 1632.[34] Although it had been entered as evidence in the High Court of Admiralty for some now long-forgotten cause and therefore was, as Davis suggested, not entirely above suspicion as an account of what happened, it is a bench-mark document for the history of the port.[35]

The excerpt consists of eleven pages of accounts, running through most of a single year, 1632. It comes to an end in September, and the accounts of the last two voyages are more confused than the rest, with guilders and pounds appearing in the same list apparently indiscriminately. This apparent confusion may be a factor in both a change of employment for Bushell, and for the appearance among cause papers in the High Court of Admiralty, since 1632 is the last year Bushell spent in England before entering the service of the king of Spain. As his final voyage was to Dunkirk, then part of the Spanish Netherlands, it is likely that he, a (possibly impoverished) younger son, was recruited there. It has usually been assumed that he became a mercenary soldier for the next ten years, but his subsequent prowess during the civil war as master of a King's ship, suggests that his Spanish service may have been in part naval. Unfortunately he is not to be found in the lists of sea-captains of the Spanish Netherlands in the *Scheepvaartsmuseum* in Amsterdam. However, the voyage accounts show that he had traded with both Amsterdam and Dunkirk, and the reputed portraits of Bushell and his young wife which hang in Whitby Museum are possibly of Dutch origin. Like his cousins Sir John Hotham and Captain

32  F. J. Fisher, 'The Development of the London Food Market, 1540–1640', *Economic History Review*, 1st series, vol. 5, 1935, pp. 46–64; voyage accounts record the purchase of butter for the men and rancid butter for the ship.

33  In fact, freighting of coal rather than factoring was generally a response to a fall in the price of coal in London.

34  TNA/HCA30/638, Voyage Book of *John*, of Whitby, Browne Bushell, Master.

35  Davis, p. 364.

John Hotham junior, Bushell died on a Parliamentary scaffold, executed for his rôle as deputy governor of Scarborough Castle, which he had handed over to Sir Hugh Cholmley after he, as governor of the castle, and concerned with the direction Parliament was taking, returned his allegiance to the Crown.

Apart from the fact that the voyage book was compiled by a known Civil War figure, it throws some light on the involvement of Whitby's gentry families in shipping. Throughout the early modern period, the active involvement of gentry families in the Whitby fleet, both as investors and as sea officers and ultimately masters, is evident.

One of the most significant aspects of the voyage accounts of the vessel *John* lies in the way they are set out, and in their detail, for they are the earliest known survivors of the long series of such accounts which cover a range of Whitby vessels, of all sizes and trades. The keeping of such accounts was laid down in the medieval period under the various refinements of the Laws of Oléron. Some accounts are the only survivors of a particular owner's records, while others are part of the archive of a fleet. Although the accounts of *John* cover only one year, what is even more important is the continuity of the records through the following period of over 200 years. Each is neatly set out, probably composed from vouchers, such as the eighteenth-century bundle in the care of Whitby Museum, and each records every purchase, from major refits to candles, together with wages and all port dues, set out voyage by voyage, and often including the cost of factored cargo.[36] At the end of each voyage the return, either in terms of freight or of the sale of cargo, is recorded, and an operating profit (or loss) is declared. At no time is any attempt made to calculate a return on investment.[37] The account from *John* is incomplete, and lacks an annual reconciliation, which would have included winter lay-up costs, and repairs, and the restoration of the stock, before disbursement was made to the owners.[38] All the later voyage books relating to Whitby shipping follow the same format as that of *John*, and are transparent to the most unsophisticated share-holder.

Another value of the voyage accounts of *John* is that it is also a benchmark in the progress of the infrastructure of the port. It was already apparent from the problems of recruiting caulkers to work on *Great Neptune* in 1625/6 that specialist facilities in the town were not yet adequate for the booming shipping industry. The voyage book provides a further insight into this, in its account of

---

36 OA/D3, Papers of Watt of Breckness; the letters of Elizabeth Watt show that masters' wives kept the accounts at times of pressure.

37 No attempt is made to show profit or loss on investment till the nineteenth century.

38 R. R. Barker, 'The Stock in Her: A Maritime Enigma', *Business Archives*, No. 86, 2003, pp. 18–26. Each vessel had an allocated sum of money, part of the capital cost, known as the *stock*. The initial amount was established as part of the purchase price of the vessel, and was used for disbursements in cash during each year. At the end of each year the sum was made up again to the set total before any disbursement to share-holders was made, and if inflation occurred, such as during wartime, or if age made the vessel more expensive to run, then the total of the stock was increased. It was a means of ensuring that the multiple owners of pre-insurance days paid their portion of any costs. It died out slowly, as marine insurance became universal, and the number of owners needed to share the risk of owning a vessel diminished.

the supplying of salt beef, and of ship's bread or biscuit. The ox was bought alive; someone was paid to kill it; the men were given beer for salting it down, after the salt had been bought for the purpose. Then the hide was sold to recoup some of the cost. The corn was bought, carried to the mill, ground and baked. Yet there were already signs that some provisions could be bought ready pre-pared at Whitby. At the greater port of Newcastle, on the other hand, bread was always bought ready-baked.

It is clear from the Port Books that by 1641 masters were factoring their own cargoes, but the voyage book of the *John* brings that practice into the previous decade. Although much of Bushell's cargo was carried as freight (that is, his ves-sel was being hired for the purpose of carrying a specific cargo) his first voyage in the year was with a cargo of 47 chaldrons of coal from Newcastle to London. The coals cost him £26 to buy and he sold them for £71. The remaining voyages were for the carriage of various goods to Dunkirk and Amsterdam as freight.

Amongst these important facets of the industry and its development in Whitby are the minutiae of daily life on an early seventeenth-century vessel of unknown rig and size; the struggle with exchange rates; pay for a soldier to guard them at Dunkirk; carrots, cabbages and turnips at Amsterdam; killing the rats; stockfish borrowed from two other masters, to be repaid at Newcastle, 'as God bless me well thether'.

Figure 2.2: Account from the voyage book of *John*, 1632

|  | £ | s | d |
|---|---|---|---|
| pade for thrums and ocum and whenkide[39] | 00 | 03 | 06 |
| pade to John Bereparke[40] for the bridge | 00 | 01 | 04 |
| pade to Mr Heron | 00 | 01 | 06 |
| pade to John Mason for salte | 00 | 00 | 09 |
| pade to my cuzsen Nuton[41] for a 100 of fish[42] | 03 | 00 | 00 |
| pade for butter to Dame Grange | 01 | 09 | 00 |
| paid for corne | 00 | 14 | 00 |
| pade for salte to John Glover | 00 | 04 | 00 |
| pade for bere when our men did salte the meate | 00 | 00 | 06 |
| pade for karring the korne to and making and baking of itt | 00 | 01 | 06 |
| pade for fresh fish at sea | 00 | 04 | 00 |
| pade for killing the oxe | 00 | 02 | 06 |
| item pade for the oxe | 03 | 00 | 00 |
| pade for one barrell of bere to John Grene | 00 | 06 | 08 |
| for candills at Whitbye | 00 | 01 | 06 |

(Source: TNA/HCA30/638, Voyage Book of John, of Whitby, Browne Bushell, Master, fo. 1).

39  A 'whenkide' was a bundle of gorse or furze, which was used to clean the bottom of the hull. The vessel was beached at high tide, and then, as the tide fell, it was pulled over, and gorse was piled alongside, then ignited. It burned very hot and quickly, softening the pitch with which the hull was 'payed', enabling it to be scraped clean of weed and sea-creatures, and re-payed with new pitch. The process was then repeated for the other side. It also enabled the checking of the hull timbers for rot.
40  John Berepark is known from other documents to have been bridge-keeper at this time.
41  The Newtons were cousins to the Bushells, and occupied Bagdale Hall after the fortunes of the Bushells declined.
42  Stockfish, or dried cod.

The purchases listed show the kinds of routine expenditure which, on top of the value of the vessel and the costs of cargo when they were factoring, represents a considerable outlay of either capital or credit for Bushell and his 'partners', who, unfortunately are never named or enumerated. The stock for the vessel *John* was £30; how that related to the capacity of the vessel is not clear, save that we know that *John* was capable of carrying 47 Newcastle chaldrons, or 124 tons, of coal. The only other early Whitby vessel whose stock is recorded is *Welcome*, described in the will of John Haggas as a small ship or hoy.[43] Its stock was £12, and its largest cargo into Whitby, in 1634, was of 15 chaldrons of coal. As well as his investment in *Welcome*, John Haggas, a stonemason who died (possibly of plague) in 1637, owned his house in Baxtergate, an unknown amount of goods and chattels, and was able to bequeath £182 in cash to his grandchildren, as well as his share of *Welcome*. This, together with the evidence from the sales of Cholmley property, and from Bushell's voyage accounts, as well as the capital invested in the alum installations, begins to give a clearer picture of the amount of capital and credit belonging to Whitby at this early period in the seventeenth century. It is perhaps not surprising that the burgesses considered incorporation and demanded from the Crown a new pier to protect their harbour.

Perhaps the most significant evidence for this period is of the easing out of the Scots and Dutch vessels which had dominated the early years of the alum and port trades. Whitby's shipping was on its way to becoming, as the Scots and Dutch fleets had been and would continue to be until the passing of the various Navigation Acts, one of the great carrying fleets of northern Europe, trading between other ports rather than into Whitby itself.

---

43 (In private hands) St. Ninian Papers: NW/U/4; copy of will relevant to title of St Ninian's Church in Baxtergate, Whitby.

# 3

# Upheaval

## Civil War and change

At the start of the Civil War, in 1642, Whitby was a Royalist port which served the Royalist general, the Earl of Newcastle, until his departure from Scarborough, and Whitby's capture by Lord Fairfax and Sir William Constable. Of the period between 1641 and 1650, with its brief glimpse of the development of factoring by the masters of colliers, there is little information from the systematic record of community or port. As in so many parishes, the parish register is deficient until the election of a Civil 'Register', William Jones, in 1653. The Port Books are once again scrappy, as in most ports at this difficult time.

## Town and people

Although there is little local information for the 1640s, Whitby was caught up quite seriously in the events of the Civil War. Sir Hugh Cholmley, the lord of the manor, was governor of Scarborough castle, first for Parliament, then after a meeting with the Queen, for Charles I. His deputy was his younger cousin, Browne Bushell, erstwhile master of *John*. Cholmley enabled the Earl of Newcastle to escape from Scarborough in 1644, and in 1645 finally yielded up the castle and went into exile, having previously made Bushell master of a King's ship.

Gaskin gives an account, culled largely from John Vicars's *Parliamentary Chronicle*, of the fall of Whitby.[1] Vicars described Whitby as a haven-port in the farthest part of Yorkshire, with a very strong garrison of the earl of Newcastle, but he also told of the willing surrender of the town. Most important to this study is the presence of forty vessels in the harbour, greater and lesser. Some may have been of the Royalist navy, and others from other outports, but they are still indicative of a busy harbour, despite the war.

Lady Cholmley was permitted to live in Abbey House during her husband's exile, although the Cholmleys were not re-united as a family until 1652, when Sir Hugh returned from exile on payment of punitive Royalist compositions or fines.[2]

It is from accounts of these events that some scant evidence of the town's fate during this period may be gleaned, and augmented by similarly scant probate

---

1   R. T. Gaskin, *The Old Seaport of Whitby*, first published Forth, Whitby, 1909, Caedmon reprints, 1986, pp. 162–5.
2   The raising of the money to pay these accounts for a second tranche of Cholmley's land sales in Whitby and the dependent port of Robin Hood's Bay.

evidence. The plague of the mid-1640s arrived in Whitby. Nicholas Haggas, the surviving son of the late John Haggas, whose will was discussed in the previous chapter, had survived the plague of the 1630s which took his brother and his father, but died with his wife in this new outbreak. The tuition bonds for their orphaned children bear witness to this. The departure of the three orphans to live in Helmsley, some 34 miles inland, shows how capital could move into and out of a community as a result of epidemic.[3] This is an economic effect of plague which has aroused little comment from historians.

The size of the garrison on which Vicars commented, mentioning in passing the ordnance guarding the 'works', which could be stone quays, fortifications or possibly the alum works, must have had a considerable effect on the town. Some people would have profited, while others would have been victims of plague or of shortage of food, or of the abuses that a garrison whose morale was diminishing could inflict on a civilian population. Yet the port was clearly prospering and would continue to do so.

It was, after all, now free of Sir Hugh's constraints, and may well have been so earlier while the lord of the manor was preoccupied by the war, in which he had been a most active and at times efficacious commander. He never again held office as a Justice of the Peace. He was in exile for several years, and when he did return, he had to sell yet more of his lands and property to pay his Royalist compositions.[4] His beloved and extremely resourceful wife Elizabeth died in 1655, and he devoted the last grieving years of his life to his memoirs, dying in 1657.[5]

In 1653 the chief citizens of Whitby elected William Jones to be their Civil 'Register'. This official was effectively a 'Registrar', a title which is more familiar to the modern ear. He was responsible for registering births, civil marriages and deaths, rather than the baptisms, marriages and burials of the church. In Whitby the events were entered into the normal parish register book, and have therefore survived, while in other parishes a separate book was (presumably) purchased, and lost or destroyed after the Restoration. A loose leaf list of 67 signatories to the election was tucked into a pocket of the parish register.[6] Whether this was the only sheet or one of several is not known. Two church-wardens signed, as well as two constables and the overseer; 'Hugh Cholmley' signed, though it is not clear whether this was Sir Hugh, or his son, also Hugh.

---

3  Borthwick/Archdeaconry of Cleveland, Wills 1648; there is a sad little document in which, after the death of their first guardian, three childish signatures consign themselves to a guardian some 30 miles from home. Noteworthy, however, is that these children, of both sexes, of a stonemason, were all literate.

4  J. Binns, 'Sir Hugh Cholmley of Whitby, 1600–1657: his Life and Works', unpubd PhD thesis, Leeds University, 1990, Appendix, has extracted from both the Calendar of the Committee for Compounding and from the Cholmley Lease Book the transactions which were made; in all Sir Hugh raised over £700 from the sale of local leases in the 1650s, to local entrepreneurs who were consolidating their own positions.

5  J. Binns (ed.), *The Memoirs and Memorials of Sir Hugh Cholmley of Whitby 1600–1657*, Yorkshire Archaeological Society, vol. 153, 2000.

6  J. Charlesworth (ed.), *Register of Whitby, 1600–1676*, Yorkshire Parish Register Society, 1928, pp. 80–1.

The other signatories have names which appear regularly as ship-builders, merchants, master mariners and share-holders in shipping in the documents of the period up to and beyond the Restoration. Many became Quakers when the Society of Friends was established in Whitby soon after by George Fox. The list seems, from the strength of the signatures on the original, to be a confident document, in which Cholmley is not dominant, but simply one among many. His name appears in the middle of the list, without any indication of status or rank.

It is the register itself, kept by the newly appointed officer, William Jones, which restores some of the missing information about the town. Marriages, often conducted by justices living over 20 miles from Whitby, were recorded in detail, with information about occupations appearing routinely. So too births were recorded with somewhat similar care, but of burials none appear to have been recorded, so that the relative health of the community is unknown.

Although it is not possible to construct meaningful moving averages centred upon any years earlier than 1658 for baptisms, 1666 for burials and 1659 for marriages, there is some raw annual data which can be used to show how patterns were changing relative to those of the rest of the country. Table 3.1 shows that by this stage of the seventeenth century the ratio of births to deaths is much nearer the national norm, although the ratio of Whitby births to deaths is on the whole higher. There are some years when the record is clearly deficient and therefore produces apparently aberrant patterns, which have been italicised, but this table gives a picture of a thriving population, one which might well still have been seeking brides outside the town, but with, on the whole, a more normally balanced age pyramid.

When registration ceased during the upheavals of the Civil War, the moving average of births centred on 1635 was 48; when the average can be resumed, centring on 1666, it was 53, rising in ten years to 79. The town was therefore continuing to grow during the Civil War and Commonwealth period, and this should indeed show in shipping figures during that period.

During the years 1650 to 1654 extant shipping records show that shipping activity in Whitby was increasing rapidly. There were still no 'official' figures for tonnage owned in the port, but the number of vessels whose names appeared at this time had increased considerably over those recorded twenty years before. There were in these four years at least sixty-two vessels whose names are recorded in a range of documents. Many of them occur a number of times.[7] Between them they made 402 recorded voyages into and out of Whitby, increasing the number of voyages by a factor of fourteen over the beginning of the century. At the same time there were still many voyages by vessels from overseas and from other outports sailing in and out of Whitby, and many voyages by Whitby vessels into other ports without touching the home port.

---

7  E190/192/8, Collector of Customs, Christmas 1649–52, Coastal; TWRO/659/243 Primage accounts.

Table 3.1: National and local vital events, 1654–1680; Civil years, per 100
marriages

| Year | Whitby births | Whitby deaths | National births | National deaths |
|---|---|---|---|---|
| 1654 | 340 | *blank* | 314 | 283 |
| 1655 | 245 | *blank* | 265 | 193 |
| 1656 | 383 | *blank* | 291 | 220 |
| 1657 | 474 | *blank* | 308 | 363 |
| 1658 | 340 | *blank* | 296 | 456 |
| 1659 | 479 | *blank* | 256 | 309 |
| 1662 | 558 | 408 | 348 | 362 |
| 1663 | 461 | 270 | 347 | 301 |
| 1665 | *675* | 350 | 400 | 570 |
| 1666 | 586 | 443 | 424 | 392 |
| 1669 | *294* | *156* | 433 | 473 |
| 1670 | 452 | 295 | 415 | 460 |
| 1671 | 720 | 473 | 345 | 378 |
| 1672 | 679 | 500 | 412 | 358 |
| 1673 | 581 | 413 | 432 | 367 |
| 1674 | 363 | 485 | 448 | 402 |
| 1675 | 292 | 292 | 430 | 453 |
| 1676 | 529 | 643 | 451 | 399 |
| 1677 | 538 | 523 | 412 | 331 |
| 1678 | 536 | 393 | 426 | 385 |
| 1679 | 464 | 486 | 396 | 533 |
| 1680 | 430 | 280 | 350 | 405 |

(Source: NYCRO/Whitby parish register; Wrigley and Schofield)

## Trade

Unfortunately the Port Books are generally deficient in most ports during the
period of the Civil War and in the years immediately after. As a result, it is
not possible to discover where the Whitby fleet found its coal cargoes during
the period when Harraton colliery was out of action partly because of the dis-
ruption caused by Civil War, between 1642 and a disastrous fire and flood of
1647.[8] At the same time, the Tyne and Wear coal trade had been badly affected
by Royalist blockades, so it is likely that other north-eastern pits acted as

8   Lewis, pp. 88, 236.

suppliers.[9] Certainly later in the century Whitby vessels were obtaining coal from Blyth Nook, Cullercoats and Seaton Sluice.[10] Even the survival in the archives of Trinity House, Newcastle, of clearances from Newcastle Quay for 1650–1654, is of no assistance. Of 6,977 clearances from Newcastle Quay shown in the period, just eighty-five (1.55 per cent) were for a small range of Whitby vessels.[11] Only one of the clearances from the Tyne was for a large cargo, 20 chaldrons carried in *Unity*. Few of the other eighty-four voyages carried cargo in double figures. This may reflect more on the amount available than on demand. It may also reflect somewhat dangerous practices designed to avoid duties. The Whitby Primage accounts for 1647, with only nine entries, nevertheless show that *Hopeful Katherine* of Whitby paid no duty for 'they came but into the roads, loaden, and then went away'. Swaying coal in vats from one vessel to another in Whitby Roads, perilously near to Whitby Rock, required great skill, good anchors and cables and fair weather, not to speak of a frustrated tide-waiter looking on.[12] The coal was destined for Rotterdam. The same record shows other coal heading for the same country, so there may have been a small entrepôt trade in coal from Wearside before the fire. That suggests that the coal trade was by then a major part of the work of Whitby's growing fleet, and that the fleet was possibly already beginning to rival that of East Anglia.

It is tempting to speculate that the growth of Whitby's fleet was a direct product of the Navigation Acts and Ordinances, the first of which was passed in 1650, but a close analysis of the growth in the decade of the 1650s shows that the bulk of the increase had already happened before the first Ordinance and the First Dutch War (1652–54).[13]

Fifty-one cargoes between 1650 and 1654 were sufficiently mixed and varied as to be worthy of study as a reflection of the demands of the growing and prospering town. Being exported were coal, salt, meal, oats, foodstuffs (particularly butter), feather beds, peas, cheese, barley, barrel hoops, tobacco and a range of alcohol and its by-products.[14] That wine and spirits were not likely to have been Whitby-produced adds weight to the concept of a small but

---

9   Lewis, pp. 85–7.
10  Voyage Book of *Judith*, 1677–1682; Whitby Literary and Philosophical Society; NRO/HMN7/186, 771X7; Winterton Lights, 1687/8; recording clearances from the north-east.
11  TWRO/659/231 gives a very good overview of coal shipments for the period, but the acquisition of Harraton Colliery in the alum interest, and the probable growth in importance of other creek ports of Newcastle, suggests that coal shipments from Northumberland and Durham may have been greatly underestimated.
12  Tide-waiters sat, in small rowing cobles, in the 'roads' or seaward approaches to ports, to collect passing dues, and to note activities such as that of *Hopeful Katherine*.
13  Davis, pp. 12–13, explains the effect of the Navigation Acts on English shipping, in that they forbade foreign shipping from participating in a substantial sector of English trade. The Scots, still politically independent despite the Union of the Crowns in 1603 were counted as foreign. The resulting war with the Dutch, the major trading fleet in northern Europe, ended after the capture of over 1,000 Dutch ships which joined the English merchant fleet as prizes.
14  J. Binns, 'Sir Hugh Cholmley: Whitby's benefactor or beneficiary?', *Northern History*, Vol. 30, pp. 87–104, quotes various sources to establish that by 1638 Whitby was the largest exporter of butter to London, with a peak total of 6,566 firkins.

important entrepôt trade. Indeed some of the exported goods appear in other manifests as imports. The imports themselves show a town becoming accustomed to a few luxuries. A great deal of wine was imported, mainly Spanish, all of it through London, the greatest of all English entrepôts. Soap, grocery wares, silver plate, candy, hops for brewing, starch, glasses, figs, apples, tobacco and tobacco-pipes, vinegar and cider also came in. However, most of the voyages were with coal from Sunderland, whether or not from Harraton, and butter and alum to London. A significant new import was of barrel hoops, suggesting more cooperage than could be supplied with hoops by the town's blacksmiths, to contain butter, barrelled fish and alum.

Since there are no extant Port Books for Whitby between 1652 and 1665, the immediate impact of the First Dutch War cannot be seen. There is no evidence that any of the 1,000 prizes that were sold into the merchant fleet came to Whitby.[15] Also lost, as far as Whitby is concerned, is evidence of the disastrous consequences of Cromwell's Spanish War, 1655–60.[16]

Scarcity of evidence makes it difficult to tease out the exact point during the Commonwealth and Restoration periods when Whitby's fleet changed from a fleet serving the port and its small hinterland with a single industrial product to becoming a service fleet. The voyage accounts of *John* show that the process had started to some extent as early as 1632. All vessels carried freight, by definition a service, at some time in their careers. There is a possibility that some of the more thrusting masters may have served in Cromwell's Navy. Capp makes the point that there were a great many mercantile officers in that force, because of the problems of finding politically reliable naval officers among former Royalist officers.[17] Rodger confirms this.[18] Such men probably made contacts, both political and mercantile, which would have stood them in good stead in civilian life. They may also have made money from prizes captured in the First Dutch War. That there were masters in good standing with the Commonwealth authorities can be seen from the list who signed as electors for the Register in 1653, among them Jonas Haggas, then aged twenty-three, who was to become, thirty years later, a major investor in shipping.[19]

That such a small and remote port should have developed entrepôt trade indicates once more the opportunistic and experimental nature of its new entrepreneurs. Entrepôt trade carries a higher risk, in that it is dependent on the availability of vessels to carry the goods onward, and involves the risking of venture capital on goods for which the market may well have slumped by the time they arrive, given the vagaries of wind and tide. There are also

---

15 Only one 'flyboat' or *fluyt* has been identified in Whitby, in the 1704 inventory of the wealthy yard-owner Francis Knaggs.
16 Davis, pp. 12–14.
17 B. Capp, *Cromwell's Navy*, Oxford University Press, 1989, pp. 160 *et seq*; at p. 167 Capp quotes BM Add Ms 11602, that colliers provided some of the senior captains.
18 N. A. M. Rodger, *The Command of the Ocean: A Naval History of Britain, 1649–1815*, Allen Lane, 2004, pp. 50–1.
19 J. Charlesworth (ed.), *Register of Whitby, 1600–1676*, Yorkshire Parish Register Society, 1928, pp. 80–1; Archdeaconry of Cleveland, will and inventory of Jonas Haggas, 1689.

implications for the townscape of the port, in that storage would have to be built. This would have led to conflict of interest with developing ship-yards, with repair and timber-yards, and with staithes for loading and discharge of cargoes. The effective harbour, 800 yards by a maximum of 120 yards, must have been at times a chaotic place. The area known as Bell Island, shown in Charlton's map (Map 0.2), was a large mud bank, dry at half-tide, and thus of no use for construction of anything permanent.

At some stage during this period, Sir Hugh Cholmley had begun to develop the alum banks at Saltwick Bay.[20] Ongoing archaeological investigation of the shore at Saltwick reveals continuous industrial use stretching back to the medieval period, and including a medieval harbour. Much of the shore is of alum shale, into which could be cut channels, rut-ways and post-holes for various installations.

Map 3.1, dating from 1734, shows a channel, known as the Sled, Sledway or Swatchway, across Whitby Rock, an extensive and dangerous triangular shale reef which extends a mile out to sea between Whitby harbour and Saltwick. The Sledway was probably cut in the seventeenth century to enable coal to be taken from the Cholmley coal staithes on the west side of the harbour to the works at Saltwick without vessels having to beat out and in again round the Rock every time.[21] The channel is still occasionally used by fishing craft running for shelter, if the tide is right, although rubble which at times fills the bottom of the channel makes it of little use for boats with fibreglass hulls.[22] To protect his coal staithes Cholmley built a new pier on the west side, using methods that were copied by his son Hugh as Surveyor General when he went, accompanied by Whitby stonemasons, to build the mole at Tangier in 1664.[23]

It is easy to assume that on this period of enterprise and boom and development of the town the sun shone constantly. The reality was rather more mixed. As with many forms of administration in which the financial element was predominant, the actual never lived up to the ideal, and resentment flared quite frequently against neighbouring ports, and against the domination by the headport, Newcastle on Tyne. As economic patterns changed, feelings between Newcastle and Whitby were at times very poor, with dues being withheld, and with a long history of disagreements, especially over the collection of dues for lightage and buoyage, some of which were referred to the assizes.[24] The

20  The enterprise appears to have begun during his exile, when his brother Henry acted as agent. The royal monopoly on the alum industry, as with all other monopolies, had been suspended.
21  Personal communication from archaeologist John Buglass, who suggests that the Sledway was cut at this time. Shale could be cut into with stone-cutting tools, but black powder blasting was possibly also used.
22  The late Captain Noel Jameson, formerly harbour-master of Whitby, explained that to use the Sledway towards Whitby from the east, the rose window in the north transept of the ruins of the abbey church had to be 'rolled' along the top of the land on the port side.
23  J. Binns, 'Sir Hugh Cholmley: Whitby's benefactor or beneficiary?', *Northern History*, Vol. 30, pp. 87–104.
24  TWRO/659/243; Primage, buoyage and beaconage accounts on foreign shipments from Whitby, 1647, with a letter to Mr Gibson from William [indecipherable] complaining that the masters pretended to have paid the duties at other ports; TWRO/659/182; Court case against Whitby merchants

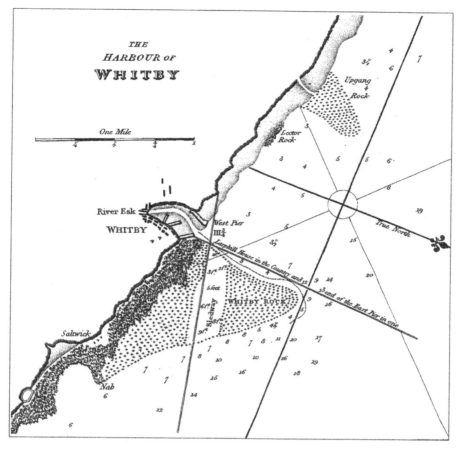

Map 3.1: Map of the Sledway and the approaches to Whitby
Cartographer unknown. From a copy of the Harbour Act of 1734 (8 Geo II, cap. 10) which added to the west pier.

*Hopeful Katherine's* trans-shipment of coal at sea was a symptom of this conflict of interest. It was a common problem; as Ipswich declined in the eighteenth century, its creek port of Harwich pushed very hard against the restrictions imposed by the larger, but failing, headport.[25] Whitby may have been spared arguments with the manor during Cholmley's exile, but other troubles would have taken their place.

---

at York, 1672; Verdict in the case of the Whitby Merchants and Trinity House, 1673; F. W. Dendy, *Records of the Newcastle-upon-Tyne Hostmen's Company*, Surtees Society 105, 1901, pp. 152–3, recounts the attempts to persuade the collector of customs at Whitby, Allan Wharton, to accept a moiety of the takings as collector of dues, in 1672. He declined after consulting Whitby merchants.

25  L. T. Weaver, *The Harwich Story*, 2nd edn (privately published) Harwich, 1976.

# 4

## Stabilisation and Confidence

### Restoration to Glorious Revolution

The thirty years following the end of the Commonwealth and the restoration of the monarchy are the years in which Whitby at last became established as a major port on the east coast. Sufficient evidence survives from different sources to make this apparent.

After the restoration of Charles II in 1660 a much clearer picture emerges of the consolidation of Whitby's fleet, and the effect of that development on the community. Parish registers from this time have survived almost without a break, and it is much easier to observe the demographic patterns and to see how the growth of the shipping industry affected them. Some of the travel writers whose commentaries on English communities give us insight into late seventeenth-century life visited Whitby and were considerably impressed. Probate evidence and transfers of property give a picture of a thriving community. Fiscal evidence provides some unexpected contrasts with the wealth of other, better known, port towns.

Whitby expanded its long tradition of what the French call '*la vie associative*', which has characterised the town's society to the present day, with the provision of a charity for 'decayed and distressed mariners'.[1] Any community which had been run by a combination of manorial homage, Easter vestry and the remnants of a burgess court must have been well conditioned to the idea of committees and trusteeship. Periodicals such as the early nineteenth-century *Whitby Panorama* have reports from many charitable and other societies. The various private Acts of Parliament which controlled the harbour and street lighting and paving, as well as other *minutiae* of urban life, all had their boards of Trustees.

### The coal trade

The growing domination by Whitby of the vital coal trade during this period is revealed in a recently discovered ledger recording the dues paid for the privately owned Winterton Lights, the 'leading lights' for the major port of Great Yarmouth. This small volume demonstrates the swings in the importance of coal-carrying ports during the seventeenth century.[2] There were two sets of lights on Winterton Ness, acting as leading lights for Yarmouth Roads,

---

1    This charity remains in existence, though much altered in its provisions.
2    J. Naish, *Seamarks: Their History and Development*, Stanford Maritime, 1985, pp. 74–5 and 93–4; C. R. B. Barrett, *The Trinity House of Deptford Strond*, London, pp. 40–8.

Yarmouth being a long-designated 'harbour of refuge'. The doubling up was due to some sharp practice by James I, who granted permission to Trinity House to place two lights on Winterton Ness, after many appeals from seafarers, and then also granted a patent to Sir William Erskine and others to set up private lights, and charge for their upkeep by a duty on the amount of cargo carried.

Various unsuccessful attempts were made by Trinity House to have the private lights removed. These attempts included a petition pointing out that the charges were extortionate. However, this petition was unavailing, and subsequently additional protection was given to the private lights by a ruling that vessels could not leave the Tyne without a certificate of payment for Winterton Lights.

Naish, in his excellent account of the development of seamarks, gives a clear account of how the lights worked, and a more detailed study of the protracted squabbles between private owners and Trinity House, who were, in any case, somewhat neglectful of their east coast lights.[3] This neglect, and problems of updating lights and buoys as sandbanks and shorelines shifted over many years, led to a lengthy and despairing correspondence between Whitby shipowners and Trinity House over the need to move the Dudgeon Light, for which the Whitby owners had raised the money in the first place, because it had become a 'false light' and was causing many wrecks. Modern navigation almanacs still show disused lighthouses around the coast of East Anglia and Essex, and Whitby itself has two 'disused' lighthouses on the ends of the eighteenth-century piers, rendered obsolete by the pier extensions, with their own lights, which were built in the early years of the twentieth century.

The Winterton Lights returns confirm the rising importance of the Whitby fleet at this time and its dominance of the coal trade. The returns, recording clearances from the Tyne with cargoes of coal, cover a period of fifteen months between June 1687 and September 1688, from Newcastle, and for a shorter period from the lesser ports of Blyth Nook, Seaton Sluice and Cullercoats. When the figures for the small ports are adjusted to provide an estimate for an equivalent period of time to those of Newcastle, a dramatic picture of change emerges, shown in Table 4.1. The chief interest in the list from the smaller ports lies in the predominance of Whitby among all the vessels recorded. It is possible that the smaller cargoes from Blyth Nook and the other ports were intended to supplement the quantities brought to the Whitby alum works from the alum investors' own colliery at Harraton near Sunderland. Cargoes from the lesser ports were small, presumably because such ports had a much less developed infrastructure, despite the fact that several of the vessels were clearly capable of carrying substantially more, and did so from the Tyne. From both greater and smaller ports Whitby was by far the dominant port recorded.

---

3 NYCRO/ZWvi 11/10/1–9, Correspondence of Whitby Shipowners' Society.

Table 4.1: Home ports of colliers clearing from NE, 1614 and 1687–1688
(ports with ten or more voyages recorded)

| Ports | Newcastle clearances for Scarborough Pierage, 1614 NYCRO/SBC | Newcastle clearances for Winterton Lights, June 1687–Sept. 1688, NRO/HMN7/186 | Whether entering, leaving or continuing coal trade | Movement up or down the rankings | |
|---|---|---|---|---|---|
| **Whitby** | | 308 | entering | ↑ | |
| Yarmouth | 156 | 288 | continuing | | ↓ |
| Ipswich | 218 | 119 | continuing | | ↓ |
| **Hastings** | | 75 | entering | ↑ | |
| **Shields** | | 71 | entering | ↑ | |
| London | 91 | 46 | continuing | | ↓ |
| Newcastle | 123 | 41 | continuing | | ↓ |
| Scarborough | 41 | 40 | continuing | par | |
| **Brightlingsea** | | 39 | entering | ↑ | |
| **Rochester** | 18 | 35 | continuing | ↑ | |
| **Ramsgate** | | 28 | entering | ↑ | |
| Colchester | 31 | 26 | continuing | par | |
| **Seaton Sluice** | | 23 | entering | ↑ | |
| **Stockton** | | 21 | entering | ↑ | |
| Aldeburgh | 55 | 19 | continuing | | ↓ |
| Woodbridge | 50 | 19 | continuing | | ↓ |
| **Cullercoats** | | 14 | entering | ↑ | |
| Margate | 10 | 12 | continuing | | |
| **Lowestoft** | | 11 | entering | ↑ | |
| Bridlington | 13 | 10 | continuing | | |
| Kings Lynn | 173 | | leaving | | ↓ |
| Hull | 80 | | leaving | | ↓ |
| Harwich | 67 | | leaving | | ↓ |
| Sandwich | 58 | | leaving | | ↓ |
| Wells | 37 | | leaving | | ↓ |
| Blakeney | 28 | | leaving | | ↓ |
| york | 24 | | leaving | | ↓ |
| Burnahm | 17 | | leaving | | ↓ |
| Selby | 16 | | leaving | | ↓ |
| Manningtree | 13 | | leaving | | ↓ |
| Dover | 10 | | leaving | | ↓ |

Many more small ports sent vessels for coal perhaps once or twice a year, probably for the domestic market, but these have been omitted from the table, leaving only those ports that shipped ten or more cargoes during the year. The totals from the lesser ports have been aggregated with those from the Tyne. A notable disappearance from the later listings is King's Lynn, but by this date, 1687, Cornelius Vermuyden's great enterprise of draining the fens was finished, and Kings Lynn's shipping was largely involved in the export of agricultural produce. Any coal that the town needed would probably have come in vessels from 'service' fleets such as that of Whitby.

Just before 1687, the year of the Winterton Lights document, the second, and perhaps most illuminating, of the series of voyage accounts of Whitby vessels, those of *Judith*, 1677–82, gives a clear picture of the duration and destinations of forty-five of its forty-seven known voyages, and of the economics, the problems of bureaucracy and government interference, the problems of exchange rates, and the diet and labours of its crew.[4] It also shows that the lack of infrastructure, which had once made the acquisition of provisions for voyages difficult, as for Browne Bushell's *John* in 1632, was a thing of the past.

### The developing town

In 1603 it was apparent that Whitby could barely claim its continued status as a town. The population was small, and its influence slight; the occupational structure is unknown and the single industry, as a port, was sadly reduced. By the time of the Restoration, however, any doubt as to Whitby's status was thoroughly resolved. It might have rejected, or been deprived of, corporate status, but in every other aspect it was an urban society. Whitby's importance to the Crown as a port was recognised by the determined capture of the town by Fairfax. The fleet was growing both in size and in penetration of other larger ports; Whitby's new extraction and processing industry was of vital importance both nationally and, increasingly, abroad; its population was expanding.

The most interesting aspect of all was the town's occupational structure, which had become decidedly both urban and maritime. The post-Restoration parish registers began to record a number of occupations, chiefly of those who were buried. If to those are added such occupations as a random search has uncovered in wills, then, by 1700, some seventy different occupations had been recorded in Whitby.

However, the use of parish registers as a source for occupations before Rose's Act of 1812 is flawed.[5] Whether occupations were recorded at all was a whim of the parish clerk or of the incumbent. At best they were only partially recorded, very often according to their perceived 'importance' to the community. Because registers are documents recording events over time, there is clearly a risk that some people will be recorded more than once, though as, at least in Whitby, most occupations are recorded in the burial register, this is perhaps less of a distortion than it might otherwise seem. Over a long period there was often a family succession of holders of a particular office or of workers in different crafts. Therefore counting these successive representatives may distort the evidence. Thus, as a means of examining the preponderance of certain occupations over others, parish registers are less than perfect.[6] Nevertheless,

---

4   WLP/Chapman Papers, unfoliated volume containing various financial and manorial documents.
5   25 Geo. III, c. 146 (1812); this Act required the recording of occupations of the deceased and of the fathers of baptised children.
6   Far better for this purpose are the freemen's registers of incorporated boroughs, which can give a much more accurate picture.

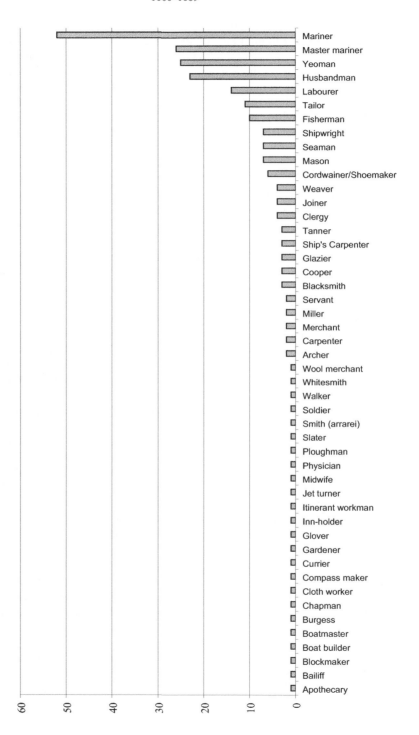

Figure 4.1: Occupations recorded in Whitby Parish Register, 1651–1680

the registers can show the gradual predominance of certain occupations and groups of occupations, as Figure 4.1 shows. It is a table of trends rather than an exact record.

Figure 4.1 shows, not unexpectedly, that in this parish of some 14,000 acres, of which only 48 acres could be classed as urban, yeoman and husbandmen were a large group, but the most important urban grouping is that of the seafaring trades.[7] Mariners were the largest group, indicating, of course, the growth of the port, and apparently differentiated from seamen or sailors, to indicate an especially skilled status and their potential for becoming masters. This was an important distinction which prevailed throughout the seventeenth and eighteenth centuries. Master mariners, who had already reached the pinnacle of their profession, were frequently recorded, and the proportion, roughly one master to two mariners, fits the known crew patterns. Apart from the mate, who could take the master's place if the master died or was killed, there was probably at least one other seaman on the larger vessels who had served his time as a servant-at-sea, and was therefore capable of navigation and watch-keeping.

Of the 249 occupations recorded in this period, other shipping-associated tradesmen were ship's carpenters, coopers and a solitary compass-maker. This was clearly a town with a strong seafaring bias. Ten shipwrights are mentioned in all, some more than once, so that it is clear that in the 1670s there were at least five yards working. Thus, despite the crude nature of the evidence, it is possible to link the dominant recorded trades to the dominant industry.[8]

Figure 4.2 shows the interlinking of various trades and crafts to the shipping industry. Some links are obvious, but others need explanation. Inn-keepers were essential to a sea-port, not just to provide recreational facilities for sailors, but because of the need for lodgings by the merchants, traders and passengers, as well as masters and mates, and their wives, of vessels being repaired at a strange port. Curriers were important to shipping because leather was used for bellows, especially of pumps, and to sheath parts of the rigging likely to chafe. Sail-cloth was woven, of linen, and behind every sailcloth weaver were at least seven flax-spinners.[9] Glass in vessels was very vulnerable; the cabin windows were often broken by following seas in bad weather, and lanterns used below decks were glazed. Another hazard to glass was that the pine from which such windows were made contained a chemical which attacked lead glazing bars, loosening the glass and making it liable to fall out and break. In many cases glaziers were also plumbers, and every vessel contained a good deal of lead, especially in the scuppers, and in any conduits through which unwanted seawater had to flow. Approximately ten per cent of any vessel's building costs

7   The ecclesiastical parishes of the north of England tended to be very extensive, partly reflecting post-Conquest land-holdings. The largest was Halifax in the West Riding of Yorkshire, some 100,000 acres. Whitby's 14,000 acres was modest, but the parish was still much larger than most in the south-east of England.

8   C. Phythian-Adams, 'The Economic and Social Structure' in *English Urban History 1500–1780*; Course A322, Open University, 1977, pp. 12–14.

9   I am grateful for the personal communication of the late Hervey Benham, of Colchester, of information culled from his long research into the sailing fleets of Essex and East Anglia.

were for metal-work, whether 'black' or 'white', including specialist anchor-smithing.[10] Even the archer had his place, since guns were expensive, and a skilled archer would have been useful for keeping smaller privateers at bay, especially if he carried a cross-bow.

Figure 4.2 Occupations relevant to seafaring, listed in Whitby parish registers during the seventeenth century

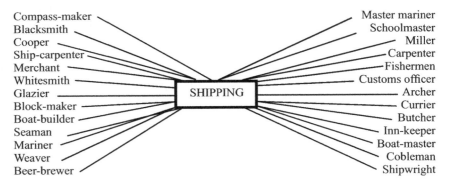

Contemporary with this evidence of a growing shipping industry there were the professions associated with a sophisticated town; surgeons, physician, schoolmaster, scrivener, clergy. There were also the merchants and trades-men who served the whole community, and the pedlar, pannierman, huckster and chapman who traded with the wild rural hinterland. There was even a *luda maiester* (effectively a 'master of entertainment') who perhaps presaged Whitby's twentieth-century emergence as a seaside resort.[11] This was, without a doubt, a substantial town, and the presence of the gentry and the group of yeomen and husbandmen simply serves to emphasise the status of Whitby as a very tightly-knit urban township set in a very large, scattered rural parish.

It is one of the unusual characteristics of Whitby as the town of a former abbey of some note that, although the abbey is known to have had an educational function, and in particular a song school, no compensatory grammar school was endowed at the dissolution. Neither Henry VIII nor Edward VI felt moved by conscience to endow a school in this remote and declining town, nor did the Cholmleys, lessees and later purchasers, do anything for education.[12] The town was dependent on schoolmasters who set themselves up, some of them in due course licensed by the archbishop of York. Although a test of orthodox religious views, the archbishop's licence was in no way prescriptive

10 Those surviving voyage accounts of the seventeenth and eighteenth centuries which record the building costs of the vessel all make this clear.
11 J. Charlesworth (ed.), Register of Whitby, 1600–1676, Yorkshire Parish Register Society, 1928.
12 Many towns of similar size acquired grammar schools of royal or other foundation following the dissolution. Examples were at High Wycombe, Buckingham, Chester, Berkhamsted, Bath, Birmingham, Worcester, York, Bradford and Leeds.

of curriculum, unlike the rules of many grammar school foundations, so it is probable that the absence of such a royal or other foundation from the sixteenth century was to Whitby's great advantage. Hence the schoolmasters could, and did, teach the required navigation and 'mercantile accompts' without interference, to the enormous benefit of the shipping community.[13] It is rarely possible to trace the qualifications of the schoolmasters who come to light in the seventeenth century, but at least two were Cambridge alumni. Some may well have been alumni of the Scottish universities. For potential students in the north-east of England, Edinburgh and St Andrews were much easier to reach than the inland Cambridge and Oxford.

The inhabitants of other towns were beginning to feel that the prescriptive endowed grammar schools of Tudor times were failing the needs of the community, and many private schools were set up to offer an alternative form of education. Some of these were of high quality while others were simply means of making a living. In his volume of the New Oxford History of England series, Paul Langford devotes a useful section on the development of middle-class schooling, and of its successes and limitations, describing the growing misgivings about the inherited endowed schools and universities.[14] Whitby, smaller in population and assumed importance, had in a sense a head start, in that there was no competition for enterprising schoolmasters from an existing system. In neighbouring Scarborough, on the other hand, the master of the contemporary grammar school stayed forty years, till he was both deaf and blind, before releasing his hold on the post.[15]

Within the shipping archive itself there are further glimpses of the changes in the urban environment in this period as the town gained economic confidence. A series of Port Book entries in the period 1664–78 records the importation of large quantities of pottery pantiles, presumably for rebuilding, as well as household equipment and even children's toys. It is clear from the large trade in timber, hemp, iron and other raw materials for ship-building and repair, carried in Whitby-owned vessels, that Whitby's ship-yards were also busy.

Even at this stage in the seventeenth century the Port Books, while detailed where they survive, are also deficient. The picture is further confused by the practice of making all four of the port officials keep separate books to provide checks and balances, and to prevent corruption as far as possible.[16] It is thus easy, when more than one survives, to fall into the error of exaggerating the extent of the various trades, especially if the books are in poor condition and it is not quite clear which book was kept by which official. However, the overall picture of the post-Restoration harbour is of prosperous bustle, and of

---

13 It will become clear in subsequent chapters that Whitby became a magnet town for the training and education of mariners; one school was run by Lionel Charlton, a surveyor, mathematician, and historian of Whitby; another, 16 miles up the Esk valley, left surviving pupil lists at the end of the eighteenth century.

14 P. Langford, *A Polite and Commercial People: England 1727–1783*, Oxford University Press, 1989, pp. 79–90.

15 I am grateful to Dr Jack Binns for this information.

16 The offices were those of the Surveyor, the Searcher, the Collector and the Customer.

a port still partaking of entrepôt activity, trading all over northern Europe, both inward and outward, and even carrying previously imported goods to Virginia, in 1664. Alum was a major export, as was butter, with a steady trade which is confirmed by the voyage book of *Judith*, 1677–82.[17]

Links into the great European trading networks are revealed by the surviving letters of one of the great trading houses of the late seventeenth century, the Marescoe-David company. As well as the larger ports, such as Hull and Bristol, which supplied vessels for the Marescoe-David house, Whitby is specifically mentioned among the smaller ports in the published letters.[18] *Thomasin*, and its master, John Chapman, one of the founders of the firm from whose papers the voyage book of *Judith* comes, are mentioned with great respect in five of the selected letters.

It must have been a strength of the town at this stage in the seventeenth century that it was comparatively healthy, since that would have led to a population growth which relied less on inward migration than did that of some other growing ports.[19] The eleven-year moving average for the period shows an upward trend in baptisms indicative of growth.[20] Figure 4.3 shows that the trend is for a levelling-off of growth at the end of the period, and the failure of the marriage rate to rise may well be due to a rise in the age at marriage, such as might be found in a town settling down rather than growing aggressively. It may also be indicative once more of a seafaring community marrying 'outside', and probably also losing some brides to seafarers from other ports, but it is apparent that the birth-rate was rising quite quickly, and was well above the death rate. It is also important to note that Quakers were allowed to conduct their own marriages after 1689, so that their marriages are missing from the parochial record.[21]

There were, of course, losses at sea, some of which are to be found in the registers of ports with which Whitby traded, but even so, when compared with the moving average of the linked, and very unhealthy, port of Harwich in Essex, Whitby's natural growth rate was high. What is of greater interest in this period is the fact that Whitby was showing a natural increase above that of the national scene, again reinforcing the belief that this was a vibrant, booming town.

Some of the clearest evidence that the boom was economic can be found in the returns for the Hearth Tax in the 1670s. The best evidence for Whitby is to be found in the returns for 1673, which are the most complete for the Liberty

17  WLP/Voyage Accounts of *Judith*, Thomas Rogers, master, 1677–1682 (Chapman Papers).
18  H. Roseveare, *Markets and Merchants of the Late Seventeenth: The Marescoe-David Letters 1668–1680*, British Academy Records of Social and Economic History New Series vol. 12, 1991, p. 579.
19  Harwich, in north-east Essex, had a constant deficit of births in relation to deaths; see Figure 1.2.
20  Eleven years is a standard period over which moving averages of vital events can be calculated to show trends. Shorter periods, while still valid, place more emphasis on the short-term fluctuations caused by epidemic disease or other catastrophic events.
21  E. A. Wrigley and R. S. Schofield, *The Population History of England*, Cambridge University Press (paperback), 1989, pp. 162–179, indicates that there was a national downturn in the ratio of baptisms to burials, and a drop in marriages, possibly indicating a later age of marriage.

Figure 4.3: Whitby vital events, 1658–1690

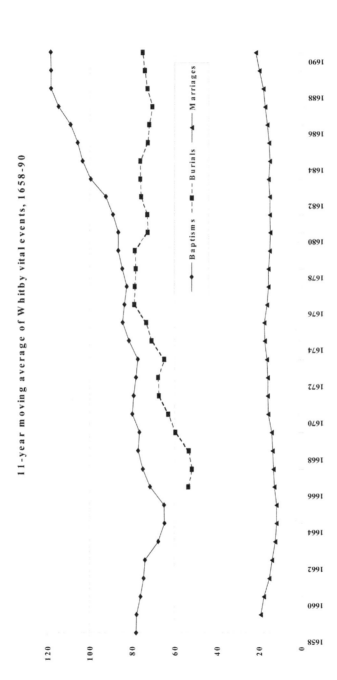

11-year moving average of Whitby vital events, 1658-90

of Whitbystrand and for the surrounding wapentakes, especially in their record of exemptions.[22] For other urban areas, different years are best, so that it is not possible always to compare year with year. However, the publication of various listings has enabled some comparison to be made. The lists for Whitby reflect its non-incorporated state, in that there are no separate wards, and no intra-urban parishes. Whitby was a single township in a large rural parish whose other townships were separately enumerated and exhibit quite different patterns from those of their central town.

Nevertheless, the listing does differentiate between the two banks of the river, and it is clear that both banks had developed to an equal extent. This is an important feature of Whitby; the town was divided equally by its river, and this gave a much greater degree of access to that artery and main 'highway' out of the town, and moreover gave it to a wider range of tradesmen and merchants. The proportion of burgages with direct access to the river was double that of a more conventionally placed port, such as Ipswich which was built on one side of the River Orwell, with only its poorer suburb of Stoke across the river. It is probably a contributing factor to the wider distribution of the benefits accruing from Whitby's seventeenth-century success which can be clearly seen in the Hearth Tax returns.

The taxation schedules provide useful indications of the quality of housing and of levels of wealth within communities. However, some records omit exemptions from the schedules for some parishes. That matters most in towns made up of several parishes, where the experience of one may differ from that of its neighbour. For example, in Colchester, in two parishes of similar size, 61.5 per cent of households in one were exempt from payment, while just 18 per cent were exempt in the other.[23] It has, however, been possible, from a wide range of published sources, to consider a number of examples of other towns, in order to put Whitby into some kind of context. Figure 4.4 shows the distribution of houses of various sizes on either side of the Esk. The very largest houses were on the east side, dominated by the Cholmleys' mansion of thirty-nine hearths on the cliff top. Apart from that, there is a slight predominance in each category on the west side. There was slightly more room for building there, but little other significance.

Two indicators of wealth may be derived from the hearth tax returns. First, from the numbers of hearths per household, it is possible to arrive at some evidence of the quality of the housing of the wealthier members of the community in the late seventeenth century, a period associated with the transition of English towns, when many stagnated while others rose.[24] In some East Anglian towns, with a high level of larger housing stock from their days at the apex of

---

22 Whitbystrand was a liberty rather than a wapentake during the life of the abbey, and the title remained after the dissolution. The name of Whitbystrand was until recently retained by the bench of justices.
23 ERO/Q/RTh 5, 1674.
24 P. Clark and P. Slack, *English Towns in Transition 1500–1700*, Oxford University Press, 1976, pp. 30–2.

Figure 4.4 Hearth Tax data: Hearths per household, Whitby east and west, 1673

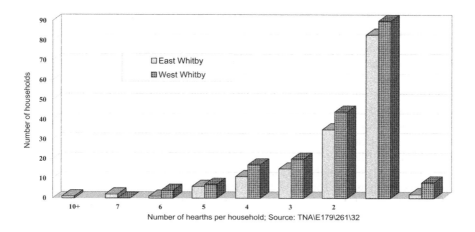

the wool trade, considerable numbers of houses with more than a single hearth were actually assessed as being too poor to pay. In Whitby, where wealth was lately come, the number of hearths per house was more modest, although there is other evidence of wealth. Using the numbers of hearths recorded, it is possible further to refine the discussion, to show the proportions of households at various levels.

It is also possible to compare a rising port such as Whitby with a declining port such as Ipswich, for which estimates of tonnage over time are also available, thus linking this evidence of economic status with the development of shipping. There is a further interest, since the Scarborough Pierage Accounts of 1614–36 show Ipswich to have been the principal coal-carrying port at that time, while Whitby's involvement with the Tyne coal trade was very small.[25] However, as the importance of Whitby, and of other north-east fleets, grew, so that of Ipswich declined, as can be seen in the returns for the Winterton Lights, which show that Ipswich's share of the coal trade had declined to under a third of that of Whitby. Ipswich has also a unique and very long series of Coalmeter's Accounts, through which it is possible to trace the extent to which the Whitby fleet penetrated this once principal coal-carrying port from 1665 onwards, but particularly in the eighteenth century.[26]

25  NYCRO/DC/SBC Pierage Accounts, 1612–36.
26  M. Reed, 'Economic Structure and Change in Seventeenth-Century Ipswich', in P. Clark (ed.), *Country Towns in Pre-Industrial England*, Leicester University Press, 1981 pp. 87–142; NYCRO/DC/SBC/Pierage accounts; SRO/C9/27 et seq. Ipswich Borough Records, Coalmeters' accounts.

The average number of hearths per household in Whitby, which had 361 households in 1673, is 1.98 hearths per household. However, in the smaller Harwich in Essex, a dependent port of Ipswich, with many characteristics similar to those of Whitby, in 1671 there were 2.78 hearths per household, almost 30 per cent more. The same proportion, 2.78 of hearths to households, existed in Ipswich in 1664, but in 1674 that had risen to 3.45 per household.[27] It would appear, therefore, from the quality of the housing stock that Whitby lagged far behind the more southerly ports. However, both Ipswich and Harwich had undergone severe epidemics of plague in 1665/6. Plague tended to affect the more congested and poorer sections of the community, and the overall number of households in Ipswich fell by 20 per cent, accounting for the increase in the number of hearths per household, as there was less pressure to sub-divide housing stock. Plague probably visited Whitby in those years but gained little hold. This analysis may be further refined in a direct comparison between the two years for Ipswich, 1664 and 1674, and the year 1673 for Whitby. Although there was disparity between the two towns as far as size, corporate status and geography were concerned, as well as proximity to London, they were beginning at this time to become 'networked' together, and on their way to becoming rivals. Ipswich, indeed, allied itself with Scarborough to oppose Whitby's petition to Parliament for a Harbour Act in 1696.[28]

Whitby's mansion, Abbey House, owned by the lord of the manor, Sir Hugh Cholmley II, had thirty-nine hearths, but that was an exception, although in the township of Ruswarp, just outside the burgage lay Bagdale Hall, the Newton mansion, with eight hearths. The great Tudor mansion of Christchurch in Ipswich had thirty-seven, and there was a far higher percentage of large houses in Ipswich than in Whitby, suggestive of earlier wealth. In 1664, 8 per cent of houses in Ipswich had between six and nine hearths, and in 1674 that proportion had risen to 13 per cent. At the same time Whitby had only three houses with six to nine hearths, less than one per cent of the total. Of the 'middling sort' of house, with between three and five hearths per household, Whitby's proportion was 20 per cent, while in Ipswich it was 16 per cent in 1664 and had risen to 29 per cent in 1674, a numerical as well as a percentage increase. In Whitby 53 per cent of those who paid Hearth Tax lived in houses with a single hearth, while in the two quoted years in Ipswich, the proportions were respectively 9 per cent and 1 per cent.

It is this, when compared with the towns of East Anglia and Essex, with their failing economies, that shows how far down into the population of Whitby the new prosperity went. These houses may have been small, as is likely in a cramped site, but their occupants were sufficiently well-off to pay the two shillings *per annum* that the tax demanded. In Ipswich, the much larger but declining port town, in both the quoted Hearth Tax collections, under 10 per cent of occupants of single-hearth houses could afford even that. It is at this

---

27 *Ibid.*
28 Gaskin, pp. 334–5.

Figure 4.5: Rates of exemption from Hearth Tax in the seventeenth century

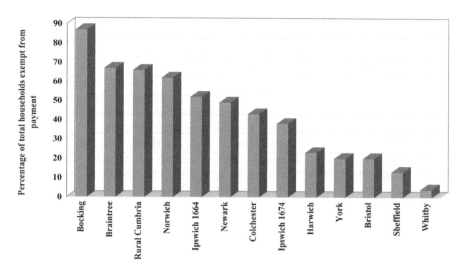

point that the prosperity of the two towns diverged. There was apparently much greater large-scale wealth in Ipswich at this stage, so much nearer the continent and the capital, but in Whitby the growing wealth of the community went all the way down the scale. It is in the exemption rate, shown in Figure 4.5, that Whitby's growing prosperity is to be seen, with only thirteen households exempt, each named, and eight of them headed by women, a level of under 4 per cent. In practice it is likely that these 'households' were of elderly people, perhaps living alone and in straitened circumstances. Harwich, on the other hand, despite its growing prosperity as a result of naval ship-building, had an exemption rate of 25 per cent.[29] If a comparison is made with other towns, this represents a very high level of urban prosperity, and confirms Ogilby's comments that Whitby 'drove a considerable trade' and had a 'well-stored' market.[30] This suggests a community involved in a new prosperity, possibly a youthful community, since there were so few households exempt from Hearth Tax, with expanding shipping and service industries.[31] It also suggests that the profit from these new industries was being spent largely within the town.

The Hearth Tax schedules for the whole of the Liberty of Whitbystrand were well kept and show that the rural subsidiary townships, whose business was not

---

29  The 'Navyard' at Harwich tended to be reopened whenever there was any kind of international conflict. At the time of the most complete Hearth Tax, of 1674, it was still feeling the economic benefits of the Third Dutch War.

30  Woodward, p. 36.

31  In many cases the households which were exempt would be those of persons past work, but with inadequate means of subsistence.

with the sea, had levels of exemption much more in line with those of other rural counties.[32]

Figure 4.5 shows a wide disparity between the town with the highest rate of exemption, Bocking in Essex, and Whitby, at the other end of the scale. Bocking was a close neighbour to Braintree, and the two towns had been affected both by the decline of the woollen industry and by a severe attack of plague in 1665. Indeed, the decline of the woollen industry was a principal cause of high exemption in many East Anglian towns. Harwich, at 25 per cent exemption, had at least its growing port and naval shipyard to support it, and by 1674 Ipswich was beginning to recover from the 'great plague' of 1665/6. Of the other places with published returns, York and Bristol were growing provincial capitals, both with shipping trades. Sheffield was a newly developing cutlery town. Whitby was growing rapidly as a ship-owning port, and had the lowest rate of all. All these variables meant that the national average exemption rate from the Hearth Tax was 30 per cent.[33]

The extant Hearth Tax returns for Yorkshire and Durham ports (Table 4.2) reflect the experience of the region to which Whitby, as a creek port of Newcastle, belongs, and which would be expected to undergo similar economic experience as Whitby. Of these ports, four – Bridlington, Hull, York and Scarborough – belonged to the headport of Hull. The others looked northward to Newcastle, at least in their dealings with the Exchequer.

Hull and York were both involved with extensive river trade, via the Humber estuary and the River Ouse, while the others were exclusively sea-going ports, except for traffic within the harbour via keelboats, cobles and ferries. However, all were involved with the north-east coal trade, and most built boats and ships. In size, Hull and York had around double the number of households of their nearest rivals, and as more important regional and mercantile centres, had a very much higher number of houses with ten or more hearths. With the exception of Whitby they were also the only towns which had an exemption rate of 20 per cent or below, reflecting perhaps a degree of diversification of sources of wealth while the other ports were probably almost entirely dependent on the sea for their incomes. Regrettably, there are no comparable returns for Newcastle upon Tyne. Yet, as with the survey of Hearth Tax returns from around England (Figure 4.5), Whitby whose seafaring was augmented to some extent by the alum industry had by a long way the lowest rate of exemption in 1673. The highest was that of South Shields, downriver from Newcastle, and probably suffering from the restrictive practices for which Newcastle was well known.

Growth in wealth does not mean that there was no distress at all in Whitby. Hidden even within the tax-paying households would be people unable to work, and it is significant at once of that fact, and of the town's growing importance as a port, and confidence in its own economic well-being, that in 1675 a charity and hospital for 'distressed and decayed seamen' and their widows and orphans

---

32  TNA/E179/261/32, Hearth Tax Returns, Wapentake of Whitby Strand.
33  J. Hoppit, *A Land of Liberty? England 1689–1727*, Oxford University Press, 2002, p. 81.

Table 4.2: Hearth Tax for Durham and Yorkshire Ports, 1672–1674

| Durham and Yorkshire Ports: Hearth Taxes for 1672/3/4 | Houses | | | | | | | | | | Exemptions (italics if possibly under-recorded) | Four or more hearths | % with four or more hearths | Total hearths | % exempt |
|---|---|---|---|---|---|---|---|---|---|---|---|---|---|---|---|
| Number of hearths | 1 | 2 | 3 | 4 | 5 | 6 | 7 | 8 | 9 | 10+ | | | | | |
| Stockton | 79 | 12 | 5 | 4 | 3 | 4 | 0 | 0 | 0 | 0 | 67 | 11 | 6 | 174 | 39% |
| Sunderland | 43 | 62 | 37 | 17 | 11 | 8 | 2 | 2 | 3 | 0 | 101 | 43 | 15 | 286 | 35% |
| Bridlington | 100 | 59 | 32 | 23 | 10 | 3 | 1 | 2 | | 2 | 96 | 39 | 12 | 326 | 29% |
| Whitby | 173 | 79 | 35 | 28 | 13 | 5 | 2 | | | 1 | 13 | 49 | 14 | 349 | 4% |
| South Shields | 119 | 46 | 21 | 20 | 17 | 13 | 3 | 2 | 0 | 0 | 204 | 55 | 12 | 445 | 46% |
| Scarborough | 121 | 87 | 48 | 38 | 16 | 6 | 5 | 1 | 2 | 4 | 186 | 72 | 14 | 514 | 36% |
| Gateshead | 200 | 102 | 52 | 49 | 38 | 29 | 10 | 10 | 3 | 8 | 226 | 147 | 20 | 727 | 31% |
| Hull | 238 | 316 | 156 | 138 | 94 | 57 | 44 | 15 | 8 | 34 | 261 | 390 | 29 | 1361 | 19% |
| York | 297 | 447 | 277 | 215 | 120 | 98 | 69 | 45 | 34 | 85 | 434 | 666 | 31 | 2121 | 20% |
| All Ports | 1637 | 1356 | 777 | 601 | 382 | 259 | 155 | 90 | 69 | 174 | 1892 | 1730 | 178 | 7392 | 26% |

was established, to be funded from dues exacted on Whitby vessels.[34] This also indicates that Whitby's fleet was large enough to sustain such an enterprise from its own resources and that these resources were likely to be able to maintain the charity for the foreseeable future. Thomas Rogers, master, paid *Judith*'s charges for 'the poor' between 1677 and 1682, the first record of such payment in Whitby's voyage and other accounts.[35] Rogers was a subscriber to the original proposals, as were most of the leading masters and owners of the day.

There are other more ephemeral glimpses of Whitby's wealth. Timothy Wiggoner, gentleman, made detailed bequests of real estate in 1662. He was childless, but made a number of bequests to relatives and friends and left detailed instructions about his wife's jointure. He owned '1/8th part of Thomas Oliver's new ship now building at Newcastle', '1/8th part of Ralph Toes' vessel, with its stock', '1/6th part of the *Charity*, of which Isaac Lay is now master', to be sold and divided amongst his legatees, and '1/4th part of Richard Grainger's ketch and 1/4th of the stock'.[36]

Jonas Haggas, to whom, an orphan at the age of seven, his grandfather left 5/16ths of *Welcome* in 1637, himself died, widowed and childless, in 1689. His will and inventory survive and give a glimpse, for the first time, of the complexity of shipping investment.[37] He became a master mariner, signed the election of the Register in 1653, and joined the Society of Friends. His share in *Welcome* in 1637 had by his death become a share in ten vessels, of varying sizes, and he was able to leave considerable sums of money to his sisters, all of whom had survived, as well as to nieces and nephews. He had three hearths in 1673, in his house in Baxtergate, which was, as the table of hearths above shows, one of the middling sort.

The Hearth Tax, together with the Compton Census of 1676, provides one of the few times, pre-decennial census, when it is possible to establish an estimate of population size, and this can show approximately where, in the 1670s, Whitby fell in the ranking of small towns.[38] It is likely that in the 1670s Whitby had a population of around 2,500. It is thus clear that it had still not reached a population level anywhere near that of the eleven outports which had more than 5,000 inhabitants in 1600, yet it was clearly an important port which would, over the remainder of the century, achieve sixth rank in an estimate of national outport ship-owning levels.

---

34 Weatherill, pp. 393–9, describes the setting up and development of the charity, which enjoined the payment of various dues from every vessel of above 20 tons. It specifically included voyages to any alum works, thus emphasising the importance of these works to the development of Whitby's fleet and town. It also subscribed to the education of their children, and may well have laid the foundations for the navigational training which was to make Whitby a magnet town for apprentices in the eighteenth century.

35 WLP/Chapman Papers, foliated volume of miscellaneous accounts; fos 4–56, voyage accounts of *Judith*, 1677–82.

36 Borthwick/Microfilm 962, proved February 1662.

37 Borthwick/Archdeaconry of Cleveland, will and inventory of Jonas Haggas, 1689.

38 Named after Henry Compton, Bishop of London, who devised the census.

Amongst the 'small towns' shown in Figure 4.6 are several ports, some of which were on earlier lists of major English ports noted by Davis.[39] The inland towns are those whose Hearth Tax returns serve as examples for comparison with Whitby's exemption rate. Scarborough, Whitby's near neighbour, and Boston are ports, both harbours of refuge and incorporated boroughs. The former apparently rose to great heights at the beginning of the eighteenth century. The latter, while an important market town as well as a port famous for its connections with the Pilgrim Fathers, never reached the heights to which Whitby aspired. Among the most interesting totals is that for Whitehaven, a port being developed by the Lowthers to export their own coal reserves, and which ranked as a ship-owning port at a level similar to that of Whitby during much of the eighteenth century.[40]

Figure 4.6: Population estimates for Clark and Hosking's 'small towns' shown by the Compton Census and the Hearth Tax[41]

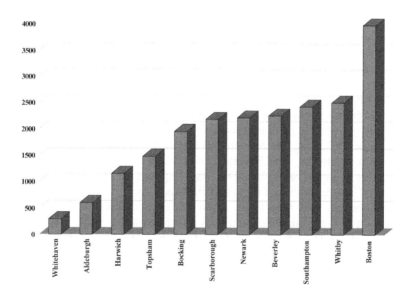

The earliest of the seventeenth-century travel writers to visit Whitby was Richard Blome, who had clearly been pleased with the town.[42] He described it as well built, and commented on the preservation of the abbey.[43] Whitby abbey

39 Davis, p. 35; Harwich was at times enumerated with its headport, Ipswich.
40 D. R. Hainsworth (ed.), *The Correspondence of Sir John Lowther of Whitehaven, 1693–1698*, British Academy Records of Social and Economic History, New Series vol. 7, 1983; various items indicate an interest in the alum industry as a sideline to their developing coal trade.
41 Clark, C. and Hosking, J. (eds), *Population Estimates of English Small Towns, 1550–1851*, revised edition, University of Leicester Press, 1993.

is still a notable sea-mark, and this may well have protected at least the ecclesiastical buildings from the fate of the domestic buildings as a source of stone, even in an age of rebuilding. Blome also commented on a flourishing market, which would have drawn both produce and customers from the River Esk catchment area. The one hundred vessels on which Blome commented were still involved in a mixture of entrepôt, local exports and coal-carrying. His only criticism was that the pier was unfinished. This is the only extant reference to pier works in this period, and does not make clear whether this unfinished pier was Sir Hugh Cholmley's pier, built to protect his east side wharves, or some later construction. Perhaps the harbour, like the town, was busy with rebuilding to protect its '100 sail of vessels'.

Despite high mortality in 1674, double that of a normal year, especially during the months from December 1673 to the late spring of 1674, Ogilby, whose account was published the following year, reinforced Blome's comments.[44] His observations may have been made before a bad winter, but he also saw a well built town with a thriving market and about one hundred vessels which carried the 'considerable trade'. This impression, like Blome's, was gained from looking at a town which it was possible to see from above in its entirety. It was compact, busy and easily scanned from the east or west cliff, which looked down on it, including any apparent slums. This compactness to the viewer makes the extremely low exemption rate in 1673 seem quite probable. Experienced travellers like Blome and Ogilby would have noticed any less prosperous parts, or down-at-heel suburbs.

These accounts report a considerable rise in the number of vessels belonging to Whitby since the forty recorded by Vicars. The Port Books record fewer Whitby vessels after the Restoration, but that seems to reflect a similar diminution of source material. The Second Dutch War (1665–67) may have played a part in this apparent reduction. The State Papers Domestic for 1665/6 show a pattern of impressment of men and blockade by Dutch and French ships between February and July 1666, when Thomas Shipton, himself a Whitby merchant while at the same time acting as agent for the young Earl of Mulgrave, wrote a series of letters to the Navy Commissioners begging for help in dealing with these problems.[45]

However, it more likely indicates the increase in the shift away from purely local trade to that which involved the penetration of other, hitherto more important, ports.[46] After the Restoration this penetration, similar to that of the 1630s, is shown by the surviving Port Books of other outports, which record that in 1662 Whitby vessels were trading between either Tyne or Wear, and

42  Woodward, pp. 28–30.
43  This confirms that the steady importation of pantiles in the 1660s signified rebuilding.
44  Woodward, pp. 31–5.
45  This Earl of Mulgrave was John Sheffield, later Duke of Normanby and Buckingham.

Scarborough, Grimsby, Kings Lynn and Ipswich, all, with the exception of Grimsby, ports which had themselves had a far greater penetration of the coal trade than that of Whitby during the period (1613–36) of the Scarborough Pierage accounting.

The voyage accounts of *Judith*, 1677–82, reinforce the evidence that Whitby's fleet was becoming more and more a service fleet. Of forty-four voyages recorded in detail that the vessel is known to have made over six years, twenty-four, or 55 per cent, did not involve any more than calling at Whitby for victuals and, presumably, orders. When that happened, there was no entry in the Port Book, since there were no customs duties to collect. *Judith* appeared in the Port Books only when was bringing in coal or exporting alum, fish and butter from Whitby.

## Thomas Rogers and *Judith*

It is to Thomas Rogers, master of *Judith*, that we owe a greater understanding of the progress made by Whitby's fleet during the seventeenth century. His detailed and dated accounts, from the building of the vessel in Shields in 1676/7 to sale, probably in London, six years later, reflect the patterns, and problems and solutions, of Whitby's shipping activity in the last quarter of the seventeenth century. The owners, some from among the London merchant community, were named, unlike the accounts of the earlier Browne Bushell, owner of *John*, from 1632; so were many of the merchants with whom he dealt, both in England and overseas. The advantages of having investors from outside Whitby's narrow community can be seen from Rogers' dealings with the Huguenot Thomas Legendre of Rouen, one of the most important seventeenth-century merchants of France.[47]

Thomas Rogers epitomised all the elements that had developed both fleet and town to the condition commended by both Blome and Ogilby and by later travel writers. He was highly literate (though his spelling was occasionally erratic) and numerate, and solvent enough to enable him to buy a one-eighth share in *Judith* when it was built on the Tyne in 1676/7.[48] His investors, gentry and merchants, with strong London connections, had sufficient faith in him to entrust him with the fitting out, the rigging and the precious stock.[49]

---

46 The surviving Port Books for Whitby, E190/193/10, Searcher, Christmas 1665/6, Overseas; E190/193/2, Collector of New Impots, T R Ch I, Overseas; E190/193/4, Controller, Christmas 1663/4, (In) Overseas; E190/194/3, Customer, Christmas 1667/8, Overseas; E190/194/5, Controller, Christmas 1667/8, Overseas, indicate that the coastal books are missing for this period. This would reduce the chance of finding Whitby vessels, but also reduce the chance of estimating the exact penetration of other ports. The Port Books for 1662 are deficient for all ports.

47 H. Roseveare, *Markets and Merchants of the Late Seventeenth Century: The Marescoe-David Letters 1668–1680*, British Academy Records of Social and Economic History New Series vol. 12, 1991, pp. 184, etc. One of Legendre's sons settled in the Whitby area towards the end of the century; I am grateful to Mrs Wendy Bennett of the Huguenot and Walloon Research association for that information.

Thomas Rogers could clearly hold his own with both gentry and extremely wealthy merchants, such as Thomas Legendre, as could John Chapman with the Marescoe-David house. His line of credit was good enough and he himself was sufficiently respected to allow him to factor his own coal, but at the same time he was opportunistic enough to accept a 'freight' of a cargo of apples or anything else that would cover costs.[50]

Since some of his trade was with Rouen, a river-port on the Seine, one would expect that the amount of cargo carried would have been less to compensate for the lower buoyancy level of fresh-water navigation.[51] However, there is no evidence of this, so either Rogers was confident of making this difficult navigation when deeply laden, or there was less difference in the salinity than might be expected. When the impost for the rebuilding of St Paul's Cathedral became too serious a burden, Rogers abandoned the London coal trade and took to the River Colne, more saline, because shorter than the Seine, and sold his cargo there at a lower but less heavily taxed price.[52]

Rogers kept his books meticulously, in the same format as those of the earlier *John*, showing not only every purchase, however small, but also the time each voyage took, so that extra stores could be accounted for by unfavourable winds. He dealt competently with foreign exchange, trading in Russia, the Hanse towns, France and the Netherlands.

He listed his crew by name, down to the smallest boy. He reduced wages, including his own, when profits fell. He bought the kind of supplies that gave as varied a diet as was possible in the difficult conditions of a small sailing merchantman. Vegetables bought included cabbage, turnips, onions and carrots. They were from the same range of supplies that appear in the voyage books of the eighteenth century, on the kind of vessel that trained Captain James Cook, whose later circumnavigations uniquely lost not a single man to scurvy.[53]

48  TNA/PROB 11/447; Will of Thomas Rogers, senior, of Northshields, has recently come to light, and suggests that the Thomas Rogers who was a one-eighth shareholder in *Judith* may have been Thomas senior. Thomas junior, listed in the will as one of his sons and as owning property in Whitby, seems to have been the master. Certainly Thomas senior had shares in other, named Whitby vessels.

49  The stock in *Judith* was £24, making it larger than *Welcome*, even allowing for 40 years' inflation, but still smaller than the John. Judith measured at 74¾ tons.

50  The account for 1678 records: 'November the 10th then received for freight of a butch [sic] of apples from Rouen to Topsham, the sum of thirty pounds, £30:0:0'.

51  A ketch such as *Judith* drew less than the maximum nine feet that was available to shipping in the Seine, provided that any difference in displacement was allowed for in the amount of cargo carried. E. A. Stokoe, *Reed's Ship Construction for Marine Engineers*, Reed, 1964, pp. 114–15, contains the modern formulae.

52  Whether this is an example of either forestalling or regrating, that is, the purchasing of goods destined for a recognised market, and keeping them back in order to create a shortage and artificially inflate the final price, both illegal practices, probably did not concern Rogers. He was avoiding the hated impost. J. Hoppit, *A Land of Liberty? England 1689–1727*; Oxford University Press, 2002, p. 342, explains the contemporary objection to forestalling.

Within the town itself, Rogers was one of the masters and owners who established the Whitby Seaman's Charity which built the hospital houses for distressed and decayed seafarers and whose existence led to much of the record of seamen's lives in the next century, as well as providing an education for seamen's orphans. That he was not above a little opportunism on the edge of legitimacy appears in Whitby's only extant 'lagan' case, in the Admiralty Cause papers for 1680, when Rogers lost a cause brought by a Yarmouth master for taking up an anchor whose cable had been cut and buoyed, and failing to report it.[54]

When vessels anchored to ride out a storm, often on sandbanks, the anchors did not always hold, and the vessel was therefore, if it was an onshore gale, in danger of drifting on to a lee shore and being destroyed. The crew would quickly attach a buoy to the expensive cable and then cut the cable and anchor free of the vessel which could then try to stand out to deeper water and ride out the storm. The buoyed cable and anchor then became 'lagan'.

The sandbanks of East Anglia were a particularly fine source of such treasure and Whitby colliers, as they increased in number, were frequent 'victims', especially of Yarmouth's specialist salvagers, who rowed out into the surf, retrieved the buoyed cable and anchor, and sold the whole, by foot of cable and hundredweight of anchor, to the Receiver of Wrecks. The vessel which had cut its cable then had to send a boat into port at Yarmouth to recover its lost cable and anchor, at a premium which included reimbursement of the Receiver as well as of the salvagers, and later often additionally of an agent who acted as intermediary to save time. Alas, Whitby, with its shale reef, where vessels were unlikely to try to anchor to ride out a storm, was not a good source of lagan for enterprising local boatmen, and salvaging does not seem to have been a major enterprise in the port, although there are occasional references. In any case, 'wreck of the sea' belonged to the manor. When such a chance came his way, it probably seemed to Thomas Rogers a satisfactory irritation to impose upon a Yarmouth vessel.

Figure 4.7, showing the shipping owned in the port of Whitby, can do no more than show vessel numbers. There is little evidence of size of individual vessels, save *Judith* at 74¾ tons. However, the Port Books show that cargoes were increasing in size, so it is a safe assumption that the rise in the size of the fleet was in both number and tonnage. If that is set alongside Figure 4.8, showing Whitby's probable population levels during the seventeenth century, then it can be seen that both have grown together.

In calculating the population estimates in Figure 4.8, two figures have been used in each case. Where the baptismal record has been used, then the upper

53 Foods Standards Agency, *Manual of Nutrition*, 10th edition, HMSO, 1995, pp. 132–143, Table 3.1, gives the composition of 100gm of edible portions of food, including all the vitamins and minerals necessary for health. Given that 30mgms of Vitamin C is the recommended daily requirement, and given that the difficult manual work undertaken by seamen would have necessitated a higher intake of food, then the fresh food bought by Rogers would have kept scurvy at bay. The voyage book takes no account of anything individual seamen may have bought in port, or to eat on board.

54 Borthwick/Admiralty Cause Papers, 1680.

Figure 4.7: Estimated size of the Whitby fleet, 1600–1675

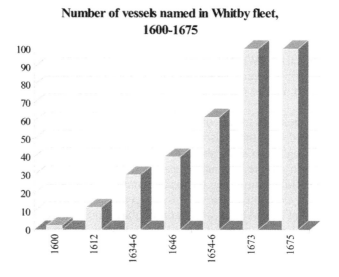

Figure 4.8: Estimated population of Whitby, 1600–1689

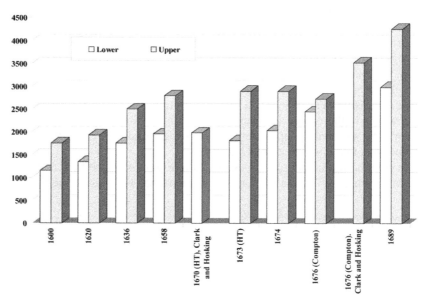

total is based on a fertility rate of 2.8 per cent, and the lower of 4 per cent, the extremes suggested by Wrigley and Schofield. In the case of the Compton Census, the range is created by using Whiteman's suggested figure of 33 per cent below the age of sixteen, and Gregory King's suggestion of 40 per cent, more likely in a young and fertile community, in a relatively healthy town. For the Hearth Tax the range is between 5 and 8 per cent per household, the accepted range for urban societies. Clark and Hosking's figures, though flawed for reasons discussed earlier, have also been included.

It is not to be expected that such disparate calculations would produce an even result, but when viewed in the context of the graph showing the growth of the fleet, then the two support each other and show the similarities that might be expected. By the end of this period the population had probably increased by 300 per cent; in the same period the number of vessels had grown by 5,000 per cent, suggesting, as is borne out by Figure 4.1, on occupations, that the percentage of the population that was in some way involved with the fleet had multiplied greatly. In 1608 a population of some 1,100 had supported two known vessels, roughly one vessel to 650 people. By the end of the period, there was one vessel to every forty people, a dramatic change. However one might have defined Whitby in 1600, by 1689 it was very clearly a seaport of some importance.

In the decade in which *Judith* was sold, Whitby was already well established as a ship-owning port. Thus far Whitby had found a new extraction industry and built on that a fleet to carry both its own goods and, increasingly, those of other ports, both in the coasting trade and overseas. It had experimented with entrepôt trade and had been building ships since the 1620s. It had attracted a reputation for being a well built town, and it seems to have left behind the residual problems of being seigniorally governed. It even seems to have made reasonable peace with Newcastle. Trade with the Tyne had begun to increase once more.

# 5

## Overview of the Seventeenth Century

### The first ninety years

During the first ninety years of the seventeenth century Whitby had established itself as a thriving port and town. It had weathered the catastrophe of the dissolution of the monasteries, and had found and exploited a new source of wealth in the alum industry. Within that industry its inhabitants had either learned new skills or recalled to mind skills existing only in the collective memory of the older residents. They had seen further opportunities tangential to the alum industry, and from them in turn had discovered a talent for networking which gave an impetus to the development of a fleet serving many distant and even international ports rather than the limited horizons of the north-east coast of Yorkshire.

While there is no evidence for the response of individual townspeople to the loss of the abbey, it is quite likely that there was a sense of freedom from the constraints it had imposed on this seigniorial borough. However, there would also have been a sense of loss of its several centuries of managerial skill, and of its links to the wider world. These skills had to be rediscovered and redeveloped, and it is clear that the alum industry played a major part in this. The industry, eventually a Crown monopoly, was leased to a series of 'farmers' who ran it on behalf of the Crown. Since many of these had experience of large-scale investment and of complex trading patterns involving such stratagems as bartering when there was a slump in demand, these skills would have rubbed off on local employees.

In 1633, for example, Timothy Johnson, and Martha, his wife, who was 'sole heir and Administratrix of the estate of Richard Johnson deceased, Merchant and Alderman of the Citie of London' made a return to the Exchequer for the year 1619.[1] In it they recorded the total amount received from the alum vend both overseas and in England; it came to £17,534.33, which would have seemed a colossal sum when the details were whispered to men used to working in an economy of often casual work, in which even a skilled tradesman could earn only 13d (5½p) a day.[2]

In addition the Johnsons had bartered some of the vend for cochineal and brazil wood to make red dye. The whole document epitomises the importance of the industry to the burgeoning port and its fleet. Timothy and Martha had taken over the 'farm' of the alum works from Martha's father. The connection

---

1    TNA/AO1/2487/354.
2    D. Woodard, *Men at Work: Labourers and Building Craftsmen in the Towns of Northern England, 1450–1750*, Cambridge University Press, 1995, pp. 188–9.

with London merchants which was to form such a fundamental part of Whitby's trade with the capital during the next two centuries is here established. So too is the ability to comprehend and handle enormous sums of cash, far beyond those of the proto-industrialists of inland Britain, such as small-scale cutlers and other metal-workers.[3] Moreover, Whitby's growing fleet continued the trade with the great European entrepôt of Amsterdam. There is no record in this particular alum account of the vessels that carried the overseas vend, and the Port Books for this period are lost, but as early as 1612 Luke Foxe, later to become an explorer of Hudson's Bay, was already carrying cargoes of alum in his vessel *Allome An*.

The Port Books, for all their deficiencies, do show that alum was a constant thread in the early development of Whitby's fleet. After the initial stages, it ceased to dominate the trade of the fleet, but the growth of the fleet is mirrored in the growth in the number of cargoes of exported alum throughout the period.

There were fluctuations, due to external events such as the Civil War, but the five-Port Book moving average of shows a steady increase.

The alum industry was heavily dependent on shipping to bring the other raw materials, coal and urine, with which to process the alum shale, and initially this had been provided by the Scots and Dutch fleets. As Whitby vessels gradually infiltrated this rôle, and then entered the greater network of the London coal trade, they were in a position to fill the vacuum caused by the Navigation Acts which did so much to establish a monopoly of trade for the English fleet, especially with the colonies.[4] Whitby, firmly placed on the 'wrong' coast of England, even essayed a venture to Virginia after the Restoration and continued to trade with America throughout the eighteenth century.[5]

Once the fleet had started to grow, the need for infrastructure in the port would have become important. Building and repair yards are known to have existed in the early century, though specialist caulkers had been brought in to caulk *Great Neptune*.[6] Chandlers and victuallers would also have followed, despite the fact that Browne Bushell's victualling in 1632 still involved buying meat on the hoof and corn on the ground. In the forty years between the accounts of Bushell and Rogers a complete infrastructure had grown up and Rogers was able to victual his *Judith* with ready-salted beef and pork, as well as 'bread' in the sense of ship's biscuit. As Rodger's account of the problems of victualling the seventeenth-century Navy shows the provision of preserved meat, mainly beef and pork, in a period without refrigeration was a complex one, whereby the fresh meat had to be obtained and salted down for preservation, during the cold weather months, if the result was to be viable during the

3   M. Rowlands, Lecture at Local Population Studies Conference, 1987.
4   Davis, pp. 305–10, gives a good account of this complex legislation.
5   TNA/E190/194/3, Voyage of *Isabella* to Maryland and Virginia.
6   D. (*sic*), 'Records of the Council for New England', *Proceedings of the American Antiquarian Society*, 1867, Vol. 2, No. 6.

Figure 5.1: Alum Voyages in Whitby vessels, 1612–1678, from Whitby Port Books

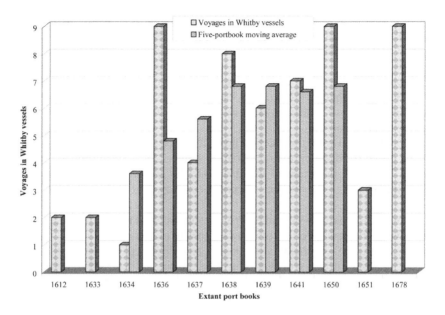

following summer.[7] It was a struggle for the institutionalised Navy; how much more difficult it would have been for relatively 'small' butchery businesses to calculate how much to preserve for a growing fleet subject to the vagaries of an uncertain economic climate. However, it was yet another opportunity to be seized in a town whose economy was growing as fast as Whitby's during the middle of the seventeenth century.

The port and its fleet had weathered the various wars of the century, and in particular the civil wars and the Dutch wars. It had absorbed the shocks of blockade, privateering and downright piracy, and had continued to grow. As the number of vessels increased, so too did the number of citizens with shares in the fleet and therefore in its prosperity, and so the wealth of the town had increased, especially after the decline of the manorial influence in the later part of the century.[8] This prosperity, observed in the Hearth Tax returns discussed in

7   N. A. M. Rodger, *The Safeguard of the Sea; A Naval History of Britain, 660–1649*, Harper Collins, 1997, pp. 372–4.
8   Since there was little marine insurance outside London, risk was shared by dividing ownership into small portions. Early probate evidence shows the existence of very small parcels of investment in what was an industry requiring a heavy capital investment. This is supported by evidence from the Admiralty Cause papers for the seventeenth century, which also show the hazards of failing to have share transactions properly dated and notarised.

the previous chapter, shows that Whitby had apparently achieved that elusive goal of the late twentieth century, the 'trickle-down effect'.

The comparatively healthy site, bisected by a fast-flowing estuary, and with abundant springs in its steep slopes, had also enabled the population to evade the worst economic consequences of the recurrent epidemics of plague which so badly damaged the ports and towns of Essex and elsewhere in the seventeenth century, although such plague as came to Whitby may well have been transmitted by the rats from returning colliers.[9] This had made it possible to maintain its population by natural increase, with all the advantages of a long-standing 'core' population of families used to the town, its geography, its isolation and its opportunism, to be enhanced by the inward migration of families drawn not by the vacancies left by successive mortality crises, as happened in many East Anglian towns, but by the growing prosperity of this well established if remote town. Such migration was driven by a distinct pull, rather than by suction.

In most plague-ridden or threatened towns of East Anglia, it was the borough council, in its various forms – the Headboroughs, Common Councils, Assemblies or 'Four-and-Twentys' – that took quarantine and other precautions. For Whitby, run by its manor court and Select Vestry, it was the North Riding Quarter Sessions that fulfilled the same rôle. In 1665 the Quarter Sessions established quarantine and ordered that no goods or men should come ashore. On fishing boats there was no room for men to live, so the Quarter Sessions ordered that pesthouses were to be erected for fishermen. Because of the lack of building land in Whitby's narrow site, if necessary these were to be built in the surrounding townships. One can imagine how unpopular that suggestion would be with the people in the outlying townships. In addition all boats had to be cast off from larger vessels and secured by the constables, and watches were set to ensure that no infringements took place. A levy was imposed on the town to pay for these precautions. Not only does this order give a good account of the kind of precaution deemed necessary in a port, it also gives unwitting evidence that Whitby was already a congested town, squeezed, despite its prosperity, into the confines of its medieval burgage.

However, the most important factor for this study is the gradual increase in the range and depth of the sources during this period. The increased range enables both events and protagonists to be studied in more than one document, so that it is easier to rely on the accuracy of assumptions made from that evidence. For example, there is a 'cause' in the Whitby Admiralty Court in which the husband of the owner of a single share in a ketch sued the ship's managing owner for profits from the coal and alum trade which he had been assured, when he married the widow, would be forthcoming.[10] The plaintiff's

---

9 R. R. Barker, *Plague in Essex*, Essex Record Office, 1982, records the dreadful visitations in Harwich and Colchester, both trading partners with Whitby in the 1660s; R. R. Barker, 'Comparing Demographic Experience: Harwich and Whitby', *Local Population Studies*, vol. 46, 1991, pp. 32–38, contains a detailed account of the differences between the two towns; NYCRO Quarter Sessions Orders 2/10/1665.

10 Borthwick/Admiralty Cause Papers, 1675–77, re *Sarah* of Whitby.

suit failed, because there *were* no profits, a fact which is confirmed by the four-teen disastrous voyages of *Judith* from which Thomas Rogers recorded a total of fourteen shillings profit in all. The effect on the plaintiff's relationship with his wife is not recorded.

### 'A very skilful and competent master'

It is to the first of Whitby's long-running voyage account books, that of Thomas Rogers for *Judith*, that we owe so much. The book offers details of the vagaries of wind and weather, crew lists, information on the crew's diet, and records of the master's struggles with bureaucracy, skill with foreign exchange, and accounting. It gives us a template against which we can study later voyage books, and by which, with its adherence to the laws and customs of the sea, we can look backwards, taking in and accepting Browne Bushell's incomplete accounts for 1632, to the High Middle Ages. We can be confident that this is part of a continuum and that Whitby is not exceptional in its seafaring practices, but only in the survival of its records.

*Judith* was a ketch, the most common vessel in the northern trades in the latter part of the seventeenth century. Too many harbours had become badly silted up for vessels with a deeper draught to enter, and there were other harbours that were, like Sunderland, 'barred', with sandbanks blocking the channel except at high water, and even then dangerous. Scammell noted the decline in vessel size from the Middle Ages onward.[11] Even the vessels bought for the new Hudson's Bay Company were ketches.[12]

*Judith* measured out at 74¾ tons when it was built at North Shields by Robert Page under the supervision of the new vessel's master, Thomas Rogers. One of the eight investors in the ketch was also called Thomas Rogers, possibly the father of the master. His will survives in The National Archives, dating from his death in Smithfield in 1698. In it he describes himself as 'Thomas Rogers senior', and the will refers to his son Thomas, who had property in Whitby, and to the testator's other interests in Whitby shipping.[13]

*Judith* was built to take high-bulk, low-value cargoes, such as alum, coal and timber. Between 1677 and 1682 she made forty-seven voyages, venturing into the Baltic, through the English Channel as far as Guernsey and up the River Seine to Rouen. It probably, therefore, drew less than nine feet. Rogers recorded the dates of entering and leaving various ports on most voyages, noting the cost of 'help out of' them. This probably meant hiring boats to tow the ketch into the offing where the wind could take over. It is therefore easier than

11  G. V. Scammell, 'English Merchant Shipping at the End of the Middle Ages: Some East Coast Evidence', *Economic History Review*, vol. 13, 3, 1961, p. 334; this evidence is reinforced in R. Unger, *Dutch Shipbuilding before 1800*, van Gorcum, 1978, p. 4, and by the lower cargoes recorded in the Port Books for *John*, despite its capacity for about 126 tons of coal, TNA/HCA30/638, Voyage Book of *John*, of Whitby, Browne Bushell, Master, 1632.

12  The best-known of these was *Nonsuch*, built in the Essex port of Brightlingsea, which made the first voyage.

13  TNA/PROB 11/447; Will of Thomas Rogers of Northshields.

Plate 5.1: An eighteenth-century drawing of a ketch

for any of the other vessels for which voyage books survive to obtain some idea of the impossibility of making accurate forecasts of times of arrival. The accounts show clearly the problems encountered when faced by variable, or absent, winds, or when storms caused hasty flight into the nearest port both for shelter and for repair.

It is the regular trips that show the extremes of voyage time. A round trip from the north-east to London and back could involve anything between sixteen and forty-three days at sea, and even the short leg from Whitby to Sunderland could take from one to six days. From London back to Whitby, round the perilous coast of East Anglia, might be done in seven days, but it might also take twenty-two, and the trip averaged twelve days at sea. The problems of victualling for such elastic voyages often reduced the already narrow profit margin of costs over earnings to shillings, or even turned it into a loss. There was no question until the nineteenth century of calculating profit as a percentage of fixed capital.[14]

Thomas Rogers paid his crew at the end of each voyage or of each month, and the names, though not the posts on board, are almost always given. Apart from Rogers's own wages, the level of wages is the only indicator of status. The names, however, show clearly the already established stability which is so much a feature of the crews of Whitby's sailing vessels. Thomas remained master until the vessel was sold in 1682. Of the remaining crew no-one stayed for fewer than two trips. Two young men, Paul Wakefield and Israel Blackburn, probably apprenticed to one of Whitby's growing number of merchants, joined *Judith* in 1679. In the seventeenth century, boys were often apprenticed to merchants who then sent them to sea with favoured masters to gain experience at sea. They were also apprenticed or 'articulated' to masters themselves or to managing owners. The distinctions between these three categories were in any case often blurred. Thomas, factoring his own cargo and either an equal shareholder in the ketch or the son of a shareholder, certainly qualified in all three respects. Both Paul Wakefield and Israel Blackburn were with *Judith* until the vessel was sold. For most of the time they received the same rate of pay, until in 1682 Blackburn's pay rate passed that of Wakefield. Israel Blackburn rose to be a master, and probably a shipowner, in his own right, living well into the eighteenth century. Paul Wakefield, whose wage rate probably indicates his value as a crew member, died young, possibly of the chest ills which were such a killer of the less robust male population in their early twenties.[15]

The wages paid to the individual members of the crew, and the careful dating of each voyage, make it possible to calculate the daily wage paid for each day at sea for each man. Without information about the posts occupied by each named crew member, apart from the master and the 'boy', probably an apprentice or 'articulate', the descending order of the wage rates listed, and the evidence for the hierarchical structure in Whitby's other voyage accounts, make it probable that the third crewman listed was the carpenter. It is possible, therefore, to compare his wage with that of a master carpenter ashore.

Since voyages varied considerably in length, mainly due to unfavourable winds, and queues to enter major ports, the daily rate fluctuated, since the men seem to have been paid for the notional voyage. Thus a trip to London with the wind 'on the quarter', the most favourable point, could be so quick as to produce more than thirty pence per day, but a long slow haul could reduce income to twelve pence per day. Whichever sum, of course, included victuals, and there was a perquisite, mainly invisible, but enshrined in the law and custom of the sea, in that individual seamen could carry personal freight, provided that it did not interfere with the working of the ship, and the more provident would

---

14 The first such assessment for a Whitby vessel is for *Liberality*, burned to the waterline in the Atlantic in 1824, where the capital lost is calculated in the vessel's accounts.

15 R. Barker, 'A Demographic History of Six Contiguous Parishes in the Tendring Hundred, Essex, 1538–1838'; unpublished SSRC Report HR5014/2, 1980. The phenomenon was confirmed by the Wellcome Institute for the History of Medicine.

Table 5.1: The daily rate of pay at sea on the ketch *Judith*, 1679

| Voyages | Days at sea | Wages (old pence) | Daily rate (old pence) |
|---|---|---|---|
| London | 21 | 540 | 25.71 |
| London | 21 | 516 | 24.57 |
| London | 13 | 516 | 39.69 |
| Hamburg | 36 | 720 | 20.00 |
| Saltwick | 10 | 180 | 18.00 |
| Saltwick | 6 | 180 | 30.00 |
| London | 17 | 516 | 30.35 |
| London | 43 | 516 | 12.00 |
| Totals | 167 | 3684 | 22.06 |

*(The post on board, to which these rates of pay apply, appears to be the ship's carpenter)*

doubtless have carried re-saleable goods whenever possible. The total number of days at sea reflects in part the shortness of the North Sea sailing season, though at times Thomas Rogers continued through the winter.[16] The remaining 'working' days of the year meant that there were at least 135 other days when work ashore for a skilled carpenter could be found. Indeed during 1679 a carpenter was paid separately for work done in harbour. Some of the days at sea were Sundays, so that the number of potential working days ashore would have been higher. Donald Woodward gives the daily wage for a master carpenter ashore in Hull in 1683 as twenty pence, so it becomes clear that the pay rate for a carpenter, working at sea for twenty-two pence per day, with victuals, was a considerable improvement, even if he had to move to a lower rate during the close season.[17] However, these calculations both for shore-based carpenters and for ships' carpenters must be set against the difficulty of finding work or a berth for every single day of the year. There would be many who had to live on savings or charity in lean periods, but at least *Judith's* carpenter could hope for a little help from the Seamen's Hospital.[18]

16 Winter voyages in the North Sea tended to be undertaken only when a cargo was urgent, or when a master wanted to try out a new vessel. Sometimes they were undertaken in a poor year, in the hope of capitalising on the demand for winter coal in London.

17 D. Woodard, *Men at Work; Labourers and Building Craftsmen in the Towns of Northern England, 1450–1750*, Cambridge University Press, 1995, 188–91.

18 N. A. M. Rodger, *The Command of the Ocean: A Naval History of Britain, 1649–1815*, Allen Lane, 2004, p. 620, gives rates of pay in the Navy in 1686. At that time the carpenter on a 'large yacht', probably about the size of a merchant ketch, earned a monthly rate equivalent to 17d per day. C. R. Boxer, *The Dutch Seaborne Empire 1600–1800*, Penguin, 1990, pp. 80, 337–8, gives monthly rates for the Dutch East India Company in the second half of the seventeenth century. A ship-carpenter in the Company's service would have earned between 30 and 48 florins a month. The florin was roughly equivalent to the English florin (2 shillings), so the daily rate would have been between 26d

Most of all, *Judith's* books show that the severe victualling problems met by *John* in 1632 had been overcome. A proper infrastructure, of victualling, chandlery, and of course bureaucracy, had been established. No-one had to buy corn on the ground or beef on the hoof. Masters still called each time they passed the port, for supplies, orders or small repairs, and it is clear that systems to cope with these demands existed. Vessels were laid up in Whitby, where the important 'winter-work' was done. Sails were lofted and mended, ropes and cables were checked, seams were caulked and the hull was scraped free of weed. This winter-work was of great value to the port; 7 per cent of the costs over the whole of *Judith's* life went on repairs and winter-work, an average of £22 per year. At the time *Judith* sailed from Whitby, there were, according to the travel-writers who visited the town, between eighty and one hundred vessels of the same kind and capacity. That meant an income to the port from repairs of between £1,760 and £2,200, a considerable sum at the time. To put it into perspective, in six years of arduous, complex work, trading all round northern Europe, handling considerable sums in foreign exchange and dealing directly with the most important merchant in northern France, Thomas Rogers himself was paid a total of £131.20. His lowest paid seaman earned in the same period £43.68.

Of course, some of the work was done in other ports, especially the straightening of dragged anchors and the purchase of new bowsprits or oars.[19] However, every vessel that sailed in the north-east coal trade to London had to pass Whitby, and although it did not acquire the coveted status of 'harbour of refuge' until the Harbour Act of 1702, the port was still a safe haven, provided vessels did not try to enter during a north or north-easterly gale.[20] Masters of vessels from other ports would have recourse to the same victuallers, chandlers and repair yards as did Thomas Rogers and *Judith*. There may have been known advantages to using Whitby's facilities. Scarborough, although a harbour of refuge, had a formidable force in its borough council, whose early seventeenth-century records show the existence of a municipal pitch kettle.[21] A monopoly over a pitch kettle could have been a very lucrative privilege. Whitby, with its loosening manorial ties, and its competitive and independent repair facilities, might have seemed a good place to call in an emergency. Without a pitch kettle, seams which had opened in bad weather could not be sealed. In a wooden ship, that meant disaster.

---

and 41d. However, an East Indiaman was a much larger and more exotic form of transport than a workaday North Sea ketch, so the difference is not surprising. In any case, Rogers paid his able seamen between 20 and 25 shillings a month while the VOC (the Dutch East India Company) paid only the equivalent of 20–22 shillings a month for the far more dangerous and disease-ridden voyages to the Far East.

19 A new bowsprit was bought in London in April, 1679; the old one was sold; presumably to a smaller vessel to which the remains of the broken spar could still be useful. The anchor was straightened several times, including in Sunderland in September 1681.

20 1 Anne, cap. 19 (8); Despite the longer piers, and the extensions built in the early twentieth century, charts still carry the warning about north and north-easterly gales.

21 M. Y. Ashcroft (ed.), *Scarborough Records 1600–1640*, North Yorkshire County Record Office Publication No. 47 (Draft) 1991, pp. 60–1.

The repair yards provided an outlet for an unlikely product of the moorland behind the town. The accounts of *Judith* for September 1681 record: 'Whins to burn the bottom', and in practice they are a regular purchase. Whin or gorse was sold to vessels to be used in 'graving' the hulls.[22] A vessel was beached and then pulled over on to its side at low tide, and gorse was piled high around the exposed hull and ignited. It burnt very hot and very fast, hot enough to destroy the weed on the bottom, and melt the pitch with which the hull was 'payed' or coated, but not for long enough to ignite the timbers. Fresh pitch was then applied. The pitch itself was distilled from the Stockholm tar, derived from pinewood, with which the standing rigging was coated.

The exercise was repeated at the next low tide to clean and re-pay the other half of the hull, so that the vessel was once more watertight and free from the drag which the curtain of weed produced when under way. Gorse must have been a hideous crop to harvest and transport, and the graving would have been an awe-inspiring sight while it was done.

One mystery emerges from the pages of Thomas Rogers's voyage book, which gives some idea of the use that might be made of merchant shipping for other purposes than the transhipment of goods, or as naval transports in time of war. Most of Rogers's cargoes were factored, bought by the master at the port of outset, and sold at the port of destination. However, sixteen of his forty-seven voyages involved 'freight', whereby he was chartered to carry goods from one port to another. In most cases the nature of the cargo, often 'mixed', is made clear, and the rate of payment given. However, there is one exception, which reveals an insoluble puzzle.

In 1681, on a trip with unspecified 'freight', *Judith* spent 107 days at sea on a voyage from Whitby to Jersey, calling at Sunderland, Deal, Cowes and Guernsey en route, for victuals. The return trip to Dover, presumably with the wind on the quarter, took eight days. The long trip outward, possibly 'tiding' and beating against a wind recorded as being strong and westerly, took well into the winter, when the vessel would normally have been laid up.[23]

It is known from the reconciliation of the accounts at the end of the voyage that *Judith* was working under 'freight', chartered by the Earl of Mulgrave, whose seat, Mulgrave Castle, is some four miles north-west of Whitby. While a continuing westerly wind, recorded for that period, might have made the voyage difficult, it could not by itself account for the duration of the voyage, and the whole episode is surrounded in mystery. *Demurrage* was recorded as

---

22 The voyage accounts of both *John* and *Judith* list the purchase of whin-kids or bundles.

23 H. H. Lamb and K. Frydendahl, *Historic Storms of the North Sea, the British Isles and North-west Europe*, Cambridge University Press, 1991, is a useful resource for maritime historians. Tiding meant being carried along by the flowing tide, in the desired direction, and lying to during the ebb, in order not to be carried in the opposite direction. This was often required when navigating the English Channel, where the prevailing wind was south-westerly, so that vessels going in a south-westerly direction travelled very slowly on a combination of tacking into the wind and moving with the tidal flow. However, even tiding should not have delayed Rogers to the extent that appears from the accounts. Something else was happening; in the words of an experienced modern master mariner, 'He was possibly up to no good!'.

due to the Earl in Jersey. Demurrage was a payment made to a vessel whose 'booked' cargo was not ready in time, or which took too long to load. It was supposed to recompense the crew for loss of wages, or for dangers, due to the delay. Whatever the expected cargo was, it was certainly not available when *Judith* arrived, despite the length of the voyage.

At no time was the nature of the 'cargo' explained. Ballast was loaded in London after *Judith's* previous voyage down with coal. The ketch had been taken into Whitby and 'graved' immediately after its previous coal voyage and the ballast taken on board in London was still there when it reached Sunderland. To anyone watching at Whitby there would be no surprise when *Judith* was 'helped' out, and turned north-west for Sunderland, and therefore no questions asked of the crew. There a damaged anchor was straightened, a victim, perhaps, of equinoctial gales, and the tiller was 'stoned' or smoothed to avoid splinters, and some 'discharges' were sent in, perhaps from *Judith's* previous cargo delivered in London. A man was sent to Whitby for an unspecified reason, though the Earl of Mulgrave's seat, Mulgrave Castle, was four miles from Whitby, and the Earl's agent was a Whitby merchant with whom Rogers had dealt in the past. On the other hand, he might have been sent to fetch John Rogers, probably Thomas's young son who would have been eight or nine, whose name appears for the first time on the crew list at the end of this voyage.[24] He was certainly very young, since his rate of pay was only five shillings per month, half that of the other youngsters.

The year 1681 was a turbulent one, and John Sheffield, Earl of Mulgrave, was a man who lived somewhat 'on the edge'.[25] During the Exclusion Crisis in that year, Mulgrave was a supporter of James, Duke of York, whose daughter Anne he had tried, unsuccessfully, to court. He had as a result been summarily banished to Edinburgh with the Duke. The same year also saw the start of Louis XIV's pressure on the Huguenots in France, and the ban which was imposed to stop them from fleeing the persecution. Thomas Rogers was on good financial, and possibly social, terms with Thomas Legendre, the most important merchant of northern France. Legendre was a member of a strong Huguenot family, though he himself finally recanted in 1685, as did many, perhaps to buy themselves time to arrange an escape. Rogers, therefore, was perhaps sympathetic to the Huguenot cause. Mulgrave, while a strong supporter of the Catholic James of York, may well have felt strongly about the plight of the Huguenots, especially of the gentry. His support for James in any case quickly evaporated into loyalty for William and Mary after 1688. The Huguenot diaspora was enormous and an enthusiastic interest in its progress was shown by Charles II himself. Some of the first refugees left from St Malo, the nearest major French port to Jersey. Someone brought them to England.

---

24 The parish register records two baptisms of a boy called John Rogers, one whose father was one Henry Rogers, in 1672, and the second, to Thomas Rogers in 1673. Baptism is not, of course, the date of birth.
25 He later became Duke of Buckingham and Normanby, and married the illegitimate daughter of James II.

On the other hand, the mysterious and delayed cargo could have related to the Earl's involvement with James, Duke of York. Alliances were being forged, and no doubt money passed. The cargo might have been a politically sensitive passenger or a sum of money in *specie* or promissory notes. Neither would have taken up space in sufficient volume to require the compensatory 'shifting' of ballast. And young John Rogers had been suddenly added to the crew for this winter voyage. At eight or nine he would have been of little use on deck, especially in cold weather. Perhaps he was to be a cabin boy for an unnamed passenger or passengers. The Earl of Mulgrave was himself an experienced sailor, but one has to doubt whether he would clean his own shoes or wash his own clothes. John, probably well-brought up by a father who was used to mixing with gentry, and educated by one of Whitby's schoolmasters, would have made a very acceptable cabin-boy or even page, and of course, whatever was going on was thus kept within the long-established crew and within the family.

Finally, in that very long voyage, *Judith* entered no harbours, but sat in the roads outside, in turn, Sunderland, Deal, Cowes, Jersey, Guernsey and Dover, Rogers presumably sending a boat in for the supplies he bought at each port. He paid no harbour dues at all after leaving Whitby, and thus appeared in no official records which might be scrutinised for 'intelligence'. There is no evidence that can solve the mystery, but mystery it is.

Table 5.2: The ports visited by *Judith* between September and December 1681

| Date | Port | Action |
| --- | --- | --- |
| 10/9/1681 | London | discharged cargo, loaded 45 tons of ballast, victualled |
| 17/9/1681 | Whitby | graved bottom, victualled |
| 25/9/1681 | Sunderland | straightened anchor, sent to Whitby, victualled |
| 4/10/1681 | Deal | bought biscuit and turnips |
| 24/10/1681 | Cowes | bought two oars, victualled |
| 6/11/1681 | Jersey | victualled |
| 16/12/1681 | Guernsey | bought bread and beef |
| 24/12/1681 | Dover | bought beef, bread and beer |
| unknown | Whitby | paid crew |

Thomas Rogers was a competent and well organised master of wide experience, and with a stable, well paid crew. Every other voyage in the accounts was detailed. So was this one, but in such a way that his fellow share-holders would see the exact cost of the voyage, and the 'freight' received and due, but would have no idea what the voyage had been about.[26] A sad little postscript

26 I have been extremely grateful for the advice and comments of Captain Peter Roberts, master mariner, and sometime Harbour Master at Whitby, on this voyage, and for his general comments on

lies in the Whitby parish burial register for 1683. It records the burial of 'Jane Monsieur, a French child, of Whitby'. To be described in the register as 'of Whitby' means that her father had been in the town for over a year, under the terms of the Settlement Act of 1662.[27] 'Monsieur' was clearly a pseudonym, but one that was the equivalent, then, of 'My Lord'.[28] Perhaps this family was attended by small John Rogers on the voyage back to Whitby.

Evidence that there were previous examples of perhaps non-mercantile activity in Whitby vessels can be found in 1642, when Admiral Trenchfield reported to the Speaker of the House of Lords of the interception of 'a packet of letters' carried by a Scotsman in an unnamed Whitby bark. Ironically the letters were forwarded to Sir John Hotham, cousin to Sir Hugh Cholmley of Whitby, and at that time Governor of Hull for Parliament, though later to revert, as did Sir Hugh, to the King's cause.[29]

The travel writers who visited Whitby towards the end of the seventeenth century all spoke well of the town, of the houses, of the size of the fleet, and the excellence of the market.[30] Seigniorial borough it might be, but it had clearly 'arrived' in economic and social terms.

The Hearth Tax returns had shown that Whitby stood well amongst other ports, particularly in the north-east, for the low rate of exemption, although the percentage of houses with three or more hearths, at 20 per cent, was lower than that of Scarborough (27 per cent) or York (45 per cent). The tax for 1673, from which these returns are taken, is contemporary with the earliest of the visits of those travel writers who commented on the 'well-built town'. The Port Books for 1678/9 record the importation of several cargoes of pantiles.[31] The houses might still be confined within the bounds of the medieval burgage, but their owners and occupiers were busy improving what was to be described by Blome in 1673 as a 'well-built' town.[32]

Tables 5.3 and 5.4 show the houses with three or more hearths in both east and west Whitby. Both Bagdale Hall and Whitby Abbey House have been included because they are literally just over the township boundary. Bagdale Hall lies in the suburb of Ruswarp, and Abbey House is technically in Hawsker-cum-Stainsacre, though actually it lies within the abbey precinct. Other houses farther afield in Ruswarp, such as the Bushell mansion of Ruswarp Hall, have not been included, since they were not part of the townscape.

---

Rogers, whom he described as a very skilful and competent master, and very organised. He pointed out the absence of any payment of dues, and the significance of the unchanged ballast. Passengers (or papers or *specie*) do not require ballast-shifting.

27  14 Car II cap 12.
28  I am grateful to my colleague Professor Graham Chesters for this comment.
29  J. R. Powell and E. K. Timings, *Documents Relating to the Civil War 1642–1648,* Navy Records Society, vol. 105, 1963, pp. 32–3.
30  Woodward, various.
31  TNA/E190/197/8.
32  Woodward, p. 31.

Table 5.3: Houses with three or more hearths in West Whitby

| Surname | Christian name | Number of hearths | Gender |
|---------|----------------|-------------------|--------|
| Weames | James | 9 | m |
| Newton | Isaac | 8 | m |
| Harrison | Robert (Mr) | 6 | m |
| Shipton | Thomas (Mr) | 6 | m |
| Tomlinson | Mr | 6 | m |
| Wigginer | Mrs | 6 | f |
| Blenkhorne | John | 5 | m |
| Conyers | Joseph | 5 | m |
| Grainge | Richard | 5 | m |
| Knaggs | Clement | 5 | m |
| Lawson/Wawne | | 5 | u |
| Megginson | George | 5 | m |
| Wawne/Lawson | | 5 | u |
| Wilson | Marmaduke (Mr) | 5 | m |
| Annison | Joseph | 4 | m |
| Chapman | Ingram | 4 | m |
| Fairfax | Captain | 4 | m |
| Fotherley | Robert | 4 | m |
| Fotherley | James | 4 | m |
| Gill | William | 4 | m |
| Hill | James | 4 | m |
| Jefferson | William | 4 | m |
| Lotherington | George | 4 | m |
| Newton | William | 4 | m |
| Potter | Henry | 4 | m |
| Readman | John | 4 | m |
| Rogers | Henry | 4 | m |
| Rymer | John | 4 | m |
| Scarth | Isack | 4 | m |
| Wakefield | John | 4 | m |
| Wilson | Francis | 4 | m |
| Ableson | Richard | 3 | m |
| Bagwith | Widow | 3 | f |
| Blades | James | 3 | m |
| Bradshaw | William | 3 | m |

| Surname (cont.) | Christian name | Number of hearths | Gender |
|---|---|---|---|
| Daile | John | 3 | m |
| Fotherby | Thomas | 3 | m |
| Grainger | Widow | 3 | f |
| Haggas | Jonas | 3 | m |
| Harland | Henry | 3 | m |
| Hill | Richard | 3 | m |
| Hirde | John | 3 | m |
| Linskill | William (senr) | 3 | m |
| Marsingall | Widow | 3 | f |
| Marsingall | Richard | 3 | m |
| Nellis | Samuel | 3 | m |
| Newton | Elizabeth | 3 | f |
| Osburne | Samuel | 3 | m |
| Readman | Elizabeth | 3 | f |
| Snawdon | Henry | 3 | m |
| Waster | Dorothy | 3 | f |
| Newton | Isaac | 8 | m |

Fifteen of the houses were occupied by widows, some of whom were the relicts of known investors in shipping, and one of whom, Widow Bagwith, was the widow of a shipbuilder. Of the other houses several were owned by families who had profited from the efforts of Sir Hugh Cholmley to pay his compositions during the Commonwealth. Although these were not very large houses, they were the homes of some of Whitby's most substantial and important people, although Spital Bridge House was the house for the poor. There were enough of them, however, to impress the various travel writers, especially when they had probably been re-roofed with the imported pantiles, and as the town became more populous, they would eventually pave the way for newer houses for the wealthiest. Whitby's elegant Georgian buildings, both inside and outside the township, would attract artists and photographers, and architectural historians, but not until after the 1750s. Until then, garths would be filled in with extensions, and extra storeys might be added, but for the whole of the early modern period the town contained the wealthier and the poorer in its bounds.[33]

33 A. White, *The Buildings of Georgian Whitby*, Keele University Press, 1995, gives an excellent account of the eighteenth-century buildings in Whitby; T. English, *Whitby Prints*, 2 vols, Horne, Whitby, 1931, contains a good selection of engravings and prints of many of Whitby's Georgian buildings.

Table 5.4: Houses with three or more hearths in East Whitby

| Surname | Christian name | Number of hearths | Gender |
|---------|----------------|-------------------|--------|
| Cholmley | Hugh (Sir) | 39 | m |
| Barnarde | Widow | 7 | f |
| Comminges | Mr | 7 | m |
| Wade | Thomas (Mr) | 6 | m |
| Jackson | William (senr) | 5 | m |
| Knight | Mary | 5 | f |
| Lislee | Joseph | 5 | m |
| Meed | Edward (junr) | 5 | m |
| Sutton | Isabell | 5 | f |
| Wilkinson | Margaret | 5 | f |
| Auther | John | 4 | m |
| Comminges | Major | 4 | m |
| Craven | Andrew | 4 | m |
| Fairfax | Mr | 4 | m |
| Hart | Elizabeth | 4 | f |
| Jackson | Daniel | 4 | m |
| Linskill | Thomas | 4 | m |
| Lotherington | William | 4 | m |
| Peighns | Thomas | 4 | m |
| Russell | James | 4 | m |
| Salmon | Robert | 4 | m |
| Aire | Widow | 3 | f |
| Clarke | William | 3 | m |
| Frankland | Richard | 3 | m |
| Harrison | Thomas | 3 | m |
| Hill | Francis | 3 | m |
| Jefferson | Marmaduke | 3 | m |
| Johnes | Mr | 3 | m |
| Johnson | Ingram | 3 | m |
| Lambert | Ann | 3 | f |
| Liell | Henry | 3 | m |
| Linskill | William (junr) | 3 | m |
| Lislee | Henry (Mr) | 3 | m |
| Noble | Roger | 3 | m |
| Spital Bridge House | | 4 | |
| Trewhit | Elizabeth | 3 | f |
| Woode | Mr | 3 | m |

In 1689 the Bill of Rights would serve the whole country, and, despite the wars of the early eighteenth century, Whitby would benefit from the stability it introduced. The next step was to see to the status of the harbour, but meanwhile Whitby must send its men to serve in King William's War, the first time the use of Whitby men and vessels to serve the Crown becomes overt, and start the long parliamentary process of becoming a designated harbour of refuge.

# Part 2

1690–1750

# 6

## The Established Port

### Consolidation and growth during the eighteenth century

Whitby and its fleet grew and thrived during the wars against France and Holland, the Civil War and the so-called 'glorious revolution'. The accession of William and Mary led not to peace but to involvement in the grand alliance with Austria, the Netherlands and Spain against the invasion of the Palatinates by Louis XIV of France, and thus to the war known in England as King William's War, which in itself led at the start of the next century into the War of the Spanish Succession. Little is known about Whitby's direct involvement in these new external upheavals except that the indexes of Wills in the Prerogative Court of Canterbury contain the names of men who died at sea in naval ships and include a considerable number of Whitby seamen.[1] Whether any Whitby shipping was hired to be used as naval transports is not clear. The Navy had at this stage by no means solved the problems of victualling at sea, as Rodger explains in his *Command of the Ocean*.[2] It is not until well after the accession of William and Mary, and King William's War, that Whitby's long, but arm's-length, association with the Navy can be understood in detail. From 1747 onwards, there is ample evidence of the hire of Whitby vessels as 'Armed Ships' or as transports, whenever there was a European or Atlantic war.

Such involvement as there was with the Navy early in the eighteenth century could have been as a result of impressment. However, in some cases the names and designation of the vessels named in the early eighteenth-century wills are ambiguous, and some may well have been vessels hired from Whitby.[3] In any case, the number who served would have been far in excess of those who died, and even among the dead, not all would have left wills, or indeed possessed anything other than the clothes they wore. Whatever the exact nature of this naval connection, the presence of Whitby men in the Navy would have enlarged Whitby's horizons and extended the town's contacts with other ports. Moreover, if men had indeed been impressed to such an extent then there must have been, by that period, a very large pool of competent seamen and mariners in the town to serve both the Navy and the already large merchant fleet, which apparently carried on with its normal mercantile business.

---

1 A recently discovered will of 1698 suggests that Whitby shipping was involved in naval transport service; TNA/PROB 11/447, will of Thomas Rogers senior of Northshields. Among his bequests was the sum he was owed for 'transport service'.
2 N. A. M. Rodger, *The Command of the Ocean: A Naval History of Britain, 1649–1815*, Allen Lane, 2004, pp. 168 and 174.
3 Wills of Prerogative Court of Canterbury.

After 1689 the increased survival of the locally-held archives makes it much easier to understand clearly the mechanisms by which the town and fleet were changing. For the first time, there are almost complete parish registers, which make analysis of the demographic events much more likely to be accurate. At the same time there are probate inventories and wills made during the eighteenth century which have not only been published, but are also much more detailed about wealth and about investment in shipping.[4]

Instead of two voyage books, forty years apart, of which the earliest is very brief, there are a good number of such books in the Whitby Museum archives, several of which are simultaneous, so that it is possible not only to aggregate economic calculations, but also to look in more detail at ship-owning practices over time. There are also the records of the Whitby Monthly Meeting of the Society of Friends, which make it possible to study a particularly important group of masters and investors in shipping and to see how their kinship patterns highlight the importance of networking to Whitby's fleet.[5] There are even some educational materials and, above all, the first few volumes of some sixty years of muster rolls for Whitby shipping, which make it much easier to understand the working of the eighteenth-century merchant fleet. Unfortunately the letters to Orkney which shed so much light on the latter years of the eighteenth century come too late for this study.[6]

In other local and national archives there are official records of most English ports, albeit flawed, especially the various attempts by government to calculate the size of fleets belonging to various ports and the number of seamen available for impressment in time of war.[7]

The previous chapters dealt more or less sequentially with the rise of both port and town from almost anonymity in 1600 to well established success and reputation by c. 1690. This chapter has to deal with rather more complex concepts, with changes within the town and the fleet rather than a straightforward progression to a more eminent position. The introduction referred to Phythian-Adams 'societal' view of local history, and his contention that not all the societies or social groupings which went to make up a community functioned in the same time-scale. As a result, it is not possible for this chapter to deal with the changes that occurred during the eighteenth century in a purely chronological framework, since different 'societies' within the community of Whitby changed in different ways and at different speeds. This chapter will also show that within the undoubted success of both fleet and town there lurked, hidden, the seeds of its eventual decline long after the period of this study.

By 1689 the Whitby fleet had become firmly established as an industry and had acquired a considerable entrepreneurial momentum. The last decade of

4    N. Vickers (ed.), *A Yorkshire Town of the Eighteenth Century: The Probate Inventories of Whitby, North Yorkshire, 1700–1800*, Brewin, 1986.
5    These are largely held in the archives of the University of Hull.
6    OA/D3, Papers of Watt of Breckness, and OA/D2, Papers of Balfour.
7    BL/Musgrave Papers, Add Mss 11255–6, 69087 and 61579 (see Appendix 1: The Size of the Fleet).

the seventeenth century confirmed the consolidation of that fleet as a major part of the national merchant fleet. Yet, when added to the first half of the eighteenth century, the last years of the seventeenth century make a kind of fulcrum in which the mechanisms of growth were replaced by a refinement of ship-owning and working practices which led to dramatic changes in the relationship between the fleet and the society which it supported and from which it mutually derived support.

During the long eighteenth century there are many manifestations of Whitby's widening influence, and also of the fact that the Whitby fleet was sustained by its involvement with two high-bulk but low-value trades. These two trades were in coal from the north-east and in timber and other supplies for ship-building from Norway and the Baltic. Both trades, from early in the eighteenth century, were largely between ports other than Whitby. These trades were at times augmented with opportunistic ventures, often high-risk, into other, sometimes regular, often occasional, and higher value, trades, such as the whale-fishery, or trade with the Americas or the White Sea.

## The development of the harbour: The Harbour Act of 1702

During the autumn and winter of 1696/7 the citizens of Whitby made a determined effort to obtain an Act of Parliament which would enable them to repair or replace Whitby's crumbling piers by means of a charge made upon passing shipping engaged in the coal trade. It was a process that was to take some thirteen years, before a completely satisfactory arrangement was made.

According to the House of Commons Journals of the time, it began with a petition read to Parliament on 8 December 1696, 'of the Ship-masters, Seamen, and other inhabitants, of the ancient town of Whitby'.[8] The petition described Whitby as 'one of the most commodious harbours in the North of England, being capable of receiving 500 Sail of Ships, that may go out or in with any Wind fit to go to Sea in, either Northerly or Southerly'.[9] The harbour mouth was said to be silting up, making entry impossible. Emphasis was also placed on Whitby's position as 'a Nursery for Seamen', a status usually irresistible to a government at war. Leave was given to 'bring in a Bill', and Sir John Kay, one of the two members for Yorkshire, was asked to prepare and present the Bill. The Bill passed to a second reading and was sent to the committee stage.

At that point, other petitions appeared; one came from neighbouring Scarborough, a long-time rival in the coal trade, and the nearest 'harbour of refuge' on the seaway from the Tyne and Wear to the Thames. That petition was led by the Bailiffs and Burgesses of the ancient Corporation, and cast serious

---

8   *House of Commons Journal*, vol. 11, 14 January 1697.
9   The remark about 500 ships looks like a rather wild estimate, but was probably technically correct, given that the whole harbour is about a mile in length to its upper limit at Ruswarp, and counted as the exchequer port. It would, however, have been difficult to put to sea if one were in a small ketch hard up against the weir at Ruswarp, with 499 vessels between that and the harbour mouth, even at a high spring tide.

aspersions on Whitby harbour. It ended with the 'prayer' that the Bill may not pass, 'it being to the Petitioners Prejudice'.[10] That at least was honest. Not surprisingly, given Whitby's long history of animosity with its headport, a petition arrived from Newcastle upon Tyne, supported by all the might of a 'Town and County', and the 'Fellowship of Hostmen'. Their complaint was blunt. A charge on shipping carrying coal and other goods from Newcastle would be 'very injurious to the Coal Trade, and a Discouragement to Navigation'. Both petitions were referred to the committee. Sadly for Whitby, after the committee stage the Bill was put to the House on 10 March 1697, and defeated by 108 votes to 78.

Four years later, after another petition to Parliament put the same arguments, this time, despite more opposition from ports such as Newcastle and Scarborough, the Bill passed. The struggle did not end there, since insufficient money came in from the tax on the coal trade. In 1708/9 a further petition amending the Act and agreeing a tax in perpetuity was sponsored by Hugh Cholmley, and the *House of Lords Journal* for 10 February 1709 records the passing of 'An Act continuing' the Act of 1702.[11] This Act continued until 1861, when the Passing Tolls Act of that year abolished all such support systems. In the end it gave the Trustees of Whitby Piers an income of some £5,000 per annum. Whitby henceforth had enviable piers, as it still has. The present piers are higher and longer than those of 1702–09, but they follow the same lines.

The size of the piers must have astonished ports such as Newcastle and Scarborough which had objected so strenuously to the proposal to build them, especially as their shipping had to pay the dues towards their building and upkeep. That the piers were so impressive is perhaps the most overt evidence from the period of Whitby's growing importance. It certainly reinforces the documentary evidence from the Winterton Lights accounts. The harbour, nonetheless, was still tied to the manor, and was not ceded to the local government until 1906, when the harbour and franchise of the port were conveyed to Whitby Urban District Council by authority of Parliament.[12]

In 1734 the piers were extended by another Harbour Act, funded on the same basis as the earlier ones, by a charge on the coal trade.[13] Map 3.1 shows the curved end to the west pier, and the photograph and drawings above (Plate 6.1 and Figure 6.1) show the dimensions of these later extensions.

It must be borne in mind that this harbour was not extended to provide facilities for additional trade with the town itself. Although there was a steady harbour trade during the long eighteenth century, well analysed by Stephanie Jones in her thesis of 1982, the lack of a populous hinterland, or a viable river system, meant that the main customers for the harbour trade were the ship-

---

10  *House of Commons Journal*, vol. 11, 28 January 1697.
11  *House of Lords Journal*, vol. 18, 10 February 1709.
12  R. T. Gaskin, *The Old Seaport of Whitby*, first published Forth, Whitby, 1909, Caedmon reprints, 1986, p. 326; dues were presumably still being paid to the manor until this time.
13  Whitby Harbour Act of 1734 (8 Geo II cap 10).

builders and chandlers.[14] The urban population, whose size peaked by 1821 at some 15,000, increased by only a factor of four during the whole century, while the tonnage of the fleet probably increased by a factor of ten.[15] The primary need was to provide shelter for Whitby vessels coming into Whitby harbour as part of a Whitby-owned fleet which was increasingly serving other ports, and indeed heavily encroaching on the trade of East Anglian coal-ship-owning ports such as Ipswich, another objector to the Bill.[16]

The construction of the new piers must have brought work to the town and may well have increased the population, and therefore the housing stock, although much of that would have been by sub-division, since it is clear that little building land was available outside the probable limits of the medieval burgage.[17] Since the town was still a seigniorial borough and the land outside was largely owned by the Cholmleys, there would be prohibitions on building outside the burgage, and in any case the traditional desire to remain within the 'town' rather than in the suburbs would still hold good.[18]

## The Whitby fleet at the turning of the century

When Edmund Gibson visited Whitby about 1695, he made a comment that is important from the point of view of this study:

> Upon the same coast [as Scarborough] is Whitby ... [which] hath a very fair and commodious Haven. There are about sixty ships of eighty Tuns or more belonging to the Town.[19]

This was the first comment since the return of 1544 on the tonnage as well as the number of vessels in the fleet owned in Whitby. Moreover, Edmund Gibson was commenting on Whitby's 'fair and commodious haven' in the year before the abortive first Harbour Bill. This must have been music to the town's ears, for Gibson, having seen in his travels many other ports, including the neighbouring Scarborough whose Corporation was blocking the Bill, could make comparisons of worth. Gibson only recorded the number of larger vessels, but 60 vessels of at least 80 tons burthen means a fleet of over 4,500 tons. The total of all vessels had been estimated by Blome and Ogilby twenty years earlier at 100, and indeed when the Act was passed, in 1702, there were said to be 120

---

14  S. K. Jones, 'A Maritime History of the Port of Whitby 1700–1914', unpubd PhD thesis, University College, London, 1982.

15  It is difficult to be certain of the increase in tonnage because of the differences in methods of calculating tonnage; see Appendix 1.

16  Table X.X.

17  A map of 1740 shows only limited expansion in the suburbs, and considerable amounts of garden space, much of which was later turned over to congested tenements.

18  Maps of other towns, such as those of John Speed of Ipswich and Colchester, show little substantial building 'outwith' the town. P. Clark and P. Slack, *English Towns in Transition 1500–1700*, Oxford University Press, pp. 144–5, shows Speed's map of Southampton, c. 1611, and comments on the poverty of suburban housing.

19  Appendix 3.

The original medieval east pier

The mid-17th century west pier

The limit of the 1702 east pier

The limit of the 1702 west pier

The 1734 extension to the west pier

The 1734 extension to the east pier

The lighthouses were built in the nineteenth century.

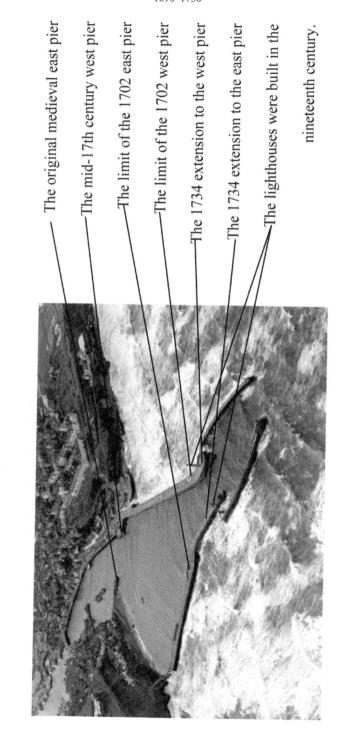

Plate 6.1 Whitby piers from the air in rough weather

Figure 6.1: Engineering drawing of Whitby piers (Drawing from Scarborough Borough Council)

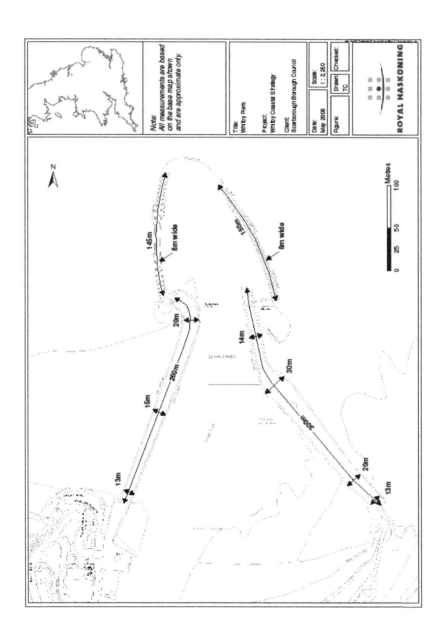

vessels, of up to 320 tons burthen, so the tonnage in 1695 was probably already well above 4,000.[20]

Patrick Crowhurst's work on the defence of British trade provides some interesting comparative figures about the number of vessels, and the type and tonnage, owned in the ports of France, particularly the privateering port of St Malo, which he describes as the principal entrepôt, and as owning the largest number of merchant vessels of all the French ports. In 1687 St Malo had 117 'large sea-going vessels'. Dieppe and Havre, both ports with which Whitby traded, had respectively 96 and 114, while the privateering port of Dunkirk, with which Whitby vessels also traded, had only 69. Given that the average tonnage of merchant vessels at this time was about 100 tons burthen, by the end of the seventeenth century, Whitby's fleet was already beginning to rival those of major European ports.[21]

While it is important to try to set Whitby's fleet within a European context, it was with the fleets of other English ports' that the town was competing for trade. Ralph Davis published the total of tonnage for Whitby and other ports for the year of the Harbour Act, 1702, and for the first time comparison with other major ports can be made. Davis abstracted his figures from returns to the Commissioners of Customs, and although Davis questions the accuracy of the returns, they show Whitby's position in a national context.[22] Since the total for Whitby matches quite well the estimate given in the submissions to Parliament in relation to the Harbour Act, and there is no reason to assume that the returns for Whitby were any more or less accurate than those for other ports, they are worthy of consideration. Table 6.1 shows the tonnages owned in the principal outports. London was estimated to own 140,000 tons burthen, 43 per cent of the whole national merchant fleet. Smaller outports owned a further 24 per cent, leaving the largest ship-owning ports to share 32 per cent of the fleet.

It is clear from Table 6.1 that most of the important ship-owning outports of England now lay on the east coast, with a total of 60,000 tons of shipping. If London were included in the totals for the east and south-east, then two-thirds of all English shipping belonged to that coast. Whitby was thus geographically well placed for continued growth.[23] The east coast ports were most conveniently sited for exports to northern Europe, and therefore anything that was going to be re-exported there would pass to the east coast for onward transit. London remained the largest of the entrepôts and fed imports to the coastal trade as well as to Europe. At the same time London itself, expanding rapidly as a great European capital, made enormous demands for imports such

---

20  Gaskin, p. 335. The Bill had suggested that there was room for upwards of 500 sail in the commodious harbour, and that it should become a harbour of refuge as well. The 500 sail would have been a very tight fit, with many of them very small. When the tide was out, and all were listing on the mud, their masts and rigging would have become very easily entangled.

21  P. Crowhurst, *The Defence of British Trade 1689–1815*, Dawson, 1977, pp. 17–22 and notes.

22  Davis, pp. 401–3; arguing that the method of calculating these returns, for each port, was flawed.

23  Davis, p. 33, analysed all the figures, and not just those of major ports.

as coal and foodstuffs, exactly the kind of cargo in which the east coast fleets, including that of Whitby, specialised.

The growth in trade with the Americas should have favoured the west coast fleets, but the Navigation Acts and Ordinances (1660–1672) decreed that goods exported from the colonies, to whatever country, must be carried in English vessels, and therefore the English fleets nearest to Europe could and did absorb much of this trade. It was not until 1707 that even Scots vessels could trade with the colonies.

Table 6.1: Tonnage owned in leading outports in 1702

| Outport | Tonnage owned |
|---|---|
| Bristol | 17,000 |
| Ipswich/Harwich | 11,000 |
| Newcastle | 11,000 |
| Great Yarmouth | 10,000 |
| Liverpool | 9,000 |
| Whitby | 8,000 |
| Hull | 8,000 |
| Whitehaven | 7,000 |
| Exeter | 7,000 |
| Kings Lynn | 6,000 |
| Sunderland | 4,000 |
| Southampton | 4,000 |
| Aldeburgh | 2,000 |
| Total | 104,000 |

(Source: Davis, p. 35.)

Thus Whitby, a creek port, dependent both on Newcastle and on a manorial court, apparently remote and isolated, with little primary produce other than alum and butter, stood sixth among English outports at the start of the eighteenth century, despite starting the previous century with only two known merchant vessels and a fishing fleet. The members of Whitby's shipping fraternity had built on the success of the alum trade and on the networks derived from it. These had enabled them to branch out into coal and other trades and most importantly to break into the trade of other ports and thus achieve their rich reward.

## The town at the turning of the century

In the terms of Clark and Slack's definitions of the characteristics of pre-industrial towns, Whitby now qualified overwhelmingly on all counts, especially since the rather simple status of a seigniorial borough had been augmented by the new grant of a Harbour Act, with its important Board of Trustees. This engendered a new strength which enabled the town to challenge its headport and to continue to bypass the manor, a process which had begun with the sale of Cholmley holdings in the seventeenth century.

It is likely that by this time a Select Vestry was in place, probably made up of the same men as were the Burgess Court or Fifteen, and the homage, or members of the Court Leet; the founding of the Seamen's Hospital had added to the political complexity, providing yet another pressure group within the town. By the middle of the eighteenth century there were other societies, and the Seamen's Hospital had become the centre of bureaucratic seafaring activity, especially after the Act of 1747 enabled the charity to benefit from the Seamen's Sixpence collection. Moreover, the town's position as sixth in the ranking of ship-owning outports gave it a 'distinctive influence beyond its immediate boundaries'.[24]

Furthermore, although this is a period usually defined for most of England as pre-industrial or proto-industrial, with low capitalisation of individual enterprises, Whitby had been for some time exhibiting an industrial development that is characteristic of a later age. Extraction industries, as well as shipping and ship-building, were always highly capital-intensive, in terms of both plant and operating costs and Whitby, with its alum industry and shipping, was clearly showing at this early period the entrepreneurial and management skills that would develop in other centres much later in the century. The town was becoming particularly adept at handling the complexities of multiple investors in single enterprises and in capital-intensive industry, as will be shown in the following sections.

### Ship-building

The town was becoming expert at ship-building too, although little direct evidence survives.[25] That these manifestations of competence and success were remarkable achievements was also acknowledged by outsiders, as is confirmed by Daniel Defoe's comment, made c. 1720:

> At the entrance of a little nameless river, scarce indeed worth a name, stands Whitby, which, however, is an excellent harbour, and where they build very good ships for the coal trade, and many of them too, which makes the town rich.[26]

Defoe, that indefatigable traveller and commentator, with his apparent insult to the Yorkshire Esk, had spotted the anomaly of Whitby's geographical position as a major ship-owning and ship-building port. Interestingly, he attributed

---

24 P. Clark and P. Slack, *English Towns in Transition 1500–1700*, Oxford University Press, 1976, pp. 4–5.
25 Various Whitby secondary sources, based on primary material no longer extant, refer particularly to the yard of Jarvis Coates at the turn of the seventeenth and eighteenth centuries, and assert that the great Thomas Fishburn of the mid-eighteenth century was his apprentice.
26 Woodward, pp. 59.

the wealth of the town only to ship-building, with his comment on the good ships that it built for the coal trade, although in fact it is likely that it was also the trade itself which was contributing to the town's wealth.

There are two surviving documents, however, which support Defoe's contention; one is the probate inventory of Francis Knaggs, who died in 1701.[27] Unusually, the inventory includes 'realty', or real estate, as well as 'personalty' or goods and chattels, to the total of £380.[28] The rest of his £935 estate consists of his 'raffins yard with all oak and fir wood and book debts and other debts', worth £160, his household goods, and his shipping, totalling £300. A *raffins* or *raff* yard was a timber yard, and one might attribute his large stock of timber to house building, or to the building of the new pier, but in view of the earlier glimpses of seventeenth-century ship-building, and the number of shipwrights mentioned in the late seventeenth-century parish register, this inventory would seem to confirm the importance of ship-building, with its great demand for timber, at the turn of the century. A second document has recently come to light which transfers land in Baxtergate, leading down to the river, to two named shipwrights in 1698.[29] Secondary evidence talks of Jarvis Coates as a ship-builder in the late seventeenth century.[30]

## Share-holding

However, the overwhelming evidence throughout the eighteenth century is that it was ship-owning and investment which produced Whitby's great wealth, and it is to the earliest eighteenth-century voyage book that we turn to see clear evidence of the methods of investment and disbursement which pertained in this period.

It was the custom for the ownership of vessels to be divided into shares, as property in common.[31] Usually these shares were in factors of four; eighths, sixteenths, thirty-seconds or sixty-fourths. Shares in shipping are still divided into sixty-fourths. Some vessels, like *Hannah* (see below) might have as many as forty share-holders. For each share-holder, his or her share of any profit or

27  N. Vickers (ed.), *A Yorkshire Town of the Eighteenth Century: The Probate Inventories of Whitby, North Yorkshire, 1700–1800*, Brewin, 1986, p. 38.
28  The inventory recorded two dwelling houses or tenements in the Market Place, one new dwelling house and yard and one dwelling house in Grape Lane. It does not record which one Knaggs himself occupied. As it listed the contents of 'the forehouse', this may well be the new dwelling house with a yard, worth £200; on the other hand that might have been built as an investment and he may have lived in a forehouse at the raffins yard. Knaggs is not listed as a purchaser in the sales of land by Cholmley.
29  S. Lewis-Simpson, 'Sources of Whitby History Pre–1700', collated for the Friends of Whitby Abbey, 2005, PB274, 28/04/1692; land off Baxtergate transferred to Henry Vasey and John Vaughan, shipwrights.
30  Table X.X *et seq.*
31  Tenure in common was the normal means of owning vessels; each share-holder had the right to sell or mortgage his share without reference to his fellow share-holders. So well ingrained was the custom that when a new church was built in 1778 as a proprietary chapel of ease, it was set up as a ship, with thirty shares as tenancies in common. The ramifications of this still exercise the twentieth-century congregation.

loss had to be calculated and either disbursed or reclaimed. Surviving probate inventories from the early eighteenth century which list holdings in shipping give the size of each share, in fractions of the whole, its value, and the name of the ship's husband, or managing owner.

In 1701 Francis Knaggs had almost twice as much invested in shipping as in his yard, which supports the view that wealth was coming from shipping investment rather than shipbuilding. Probate provides other evidence of Whitby's activities at the turn of the seventeenth and eighteenth centuries. It is clear from surviving inventories that, in the absence of a banking system, there was a great deal of money-lending involved in the financing of Whitby's fleet. While there was a clear pattern of investment in each others' vessels, there was also money lent out in the form of bonds, and of mortgages in real estate, which could then be used to finance shipping.[32]

The complexity of the capitalisation of Whitby shipping in the early years of the eighteenth century can be seen from Table 6.2, on share-holding in *Hannah*, 1716–18. The voyage accounts of *Hannah* are to be found among the Chapman Papers at Whitby Museum, and give the building details, and four years' voyages, of a collier of unknown tonnage.[33] At the end of three of those years the annual disbursements to share-holders are listed. As far as can be seen, only those who appeared in person collected their profits, so that in no single year did all share-holders appear. Thirty-three are named altogether, including the master, Peter Barker, who appears to have acted as ship's husband. The term 'ship's husband' is used for the managing owner. He may be the master, who might hold a share in the vessel, or he may be a shore-based shareholder willing to undertake the financial management of the vessel. Confusingly, as in the case of women such as Anne Carnaby or Dorothy Benson, both of whom took over their late husbands' shipping, a ship's husband could be a woman. Four women can be identified who ran fleets of ships in the eighteenth century.

In no year is disbursement made on every share, suggesting that some share-holders did not attend the meeting. Exactly how the profits were disbursed is not known, save that all who collected money signed for it. There must have been some way of notifying, perhaps by a public notice, those with an interest in a certain vessel to attend on a certain day. The custom of being able to dispose of shares without reference to other share-holders must have added to difficulties in contacting share-holders, even in a small community. In fact 91 per cent of the share-holders in *Hannah* can be traced as living in Whitby. There seem to be sixty-seven shares in all, but in two cases it is likely that a total of three shares passed from one member of a family to another between disbursements, so that the aggregate is actually sixty-four, as it should be. It is known that in other, more loosely knit communities, more shares were sold than actually existed. Davis gives an example of this abuse.[34] It must have been

32  Borthwick/Archdeaconry of Cleveland, will and inventory of Jonas Haggas, 1689; this document shows clearly two kinds of investment, some in shipping, and some in money lent on bonds.
33  WLP/Chapman Papers, *Hannah*, 1714–18.
34  Davis, pp. 107–8.

a strength of Whitby's shipping interest that within a remote and close-knit community such abuses would have been much more difficult to arrange.

Table 6.2: Shareholding in *Hannah*, 1716–1718

| Years | All | 1716 | 1717 | 1718 |
|---|---|---|---|---|
| Share-holders attending | 33 | 23 | 28 | 28 |
| Women share-holders | 2 | | 2 | 2 |
| Shares for which disbursement was made | 67 | 46 | 48 | 51 |

## Profits in the early eighteenth century

Table 6.3 shows the profit on *Hannah's* voyages at this critical point in the study. The profits recorded were simply operating profits, returns after all expenses had been paid and the stock made up, since, as shown earlier, the concept of profit recorded as a return on invested capital did not appear in any document from Whitby's shipping, or indeed in documents from other ports, until the start of the nineteenth century.[35]

Table 6.3: Profits from *Hannah*, 1715–1718

| Year | Profit as percentage of receipts | Receipts | Perceived profit |
|---|---|---|---|
| 1715 | 4% | £1,883.33 | £70.36 |
| 1716 | 3% | £2,564.04 | £79.91 |
| 1717 | 13% | £2,131.16 | £278.85 |
| 1718 | 13% | £2,469.83 | £321.66 |

For the first two years profits were low, but still worth having, while 1717 and 1718 saw a huge increase in profitability, and give the first real insight into the reasons for the popularity of shipping as a form of investment in Whitby. The disbursement, if some kind of invitation or public notice had been issued, also meant that the level of the profit would be known, and when the level for *Hannah* in 1717/18 was calculated, then this would seem to be a good inducement to further investment, and therefore to an increase in the size of the fleet. Table 6.4 lists all the shareholders known for *Hannah*, that is, all who attended the disbursement in one or more years, either in person or by proxy. It also shows how many sixty-fourths each shareholder owned.

---

35 S. P. Ville, *English Shipowning during the Industrial Revolution: Michael Henley and Son, London Shipowners 1770–1830*, Manchester University Press, 1987, pp. 120–1.

Table 6.4: Share-holders in *Hannah*, 1716–1718

| Surname | Christian Name | 1716 | 1717 | 1718 |
|---|---|---|---|---|
| Armstrong | George | | 1 | 1 |
| Armstrong | Joseph | 1 | | |
| Bagwith | Christopher | | | 2 |
| Barker | Peter | 2 | | |
| Clark | Cornelius | 2 | 2 | 2 |
| Clavering | James (by proxy) | 8 | | |
| Coates | Jarvis | 2 | 2 | 2 |
| Cowston | William | 2 | 2 | 2 |
| Creighton | Francis | 1 | 1 | 1 |
| Dunn | Jane | | 2 | 2 |
| Dunn | William | 2 | | |
| Grahame | Charles | 1 | 1 | 1 |
| Heron | Michael | 1 | 1 | 1 |
| Huntrodes | Francis | 1 | 1 | 1 |
| Jackson | John | | 1 | 1 |
| Jackson | William | | 1 | 1 |
| Jefferson | William | | 2 | 2 |
| Johnson | Hannah | | 4 | 4 |
| Johnson | John | 2 | 2 | 6 |
| Linton | John | 1 | 1 | 1 |
| Newton | John | 2 | 2 | 2 |
| Noble | George | | 1 | 1 |
| Parnell | John | 2 | 2 | 2 |
| Pearson | Henry | | 1 | 1 |
| Pearson | William | 2 | 2 | |
| Pursglove | Robert | 1 | 1 | 1 |
| Ridout | William | 1 | 1 | 1 |
| Swainson | John | 2 | 2 | 2 |
| Trott | Thomas | 2 | 2 | 2 |
| Walker | John | | 1 | 1 |
| Watson | John | 2 | 2 | 2 |
| Wood | Joseph | 4 | 4 | 4 |
| Yeoman | James | 2 | 2 | 2 |

The accounts for a second Whitby vessel, *William and Jane*, show a similar shareholding pattern. Table 6.5 shows the list of known shareholders, that is, those who attended for the disbursements.

Table 6.5, like Table 6.4 for *Hannah*, lists each individual share-holder by name. Comparison with the table for *Hannah* shows that there was a wide range of share-holders within the town. Although some surnames are repeated, they belong to different individuals. It is clear from these examples that the pattern of widespread benefit from the growing shipping industry in Whitby shown by the Hearth Tax returns seems still to have been prevalent some forty years later.

## Changes in practice and their effect on the port

In the seventeenth century, as far as we can make out from the limited sources extant, Whitby vessels entered the port en route for their destinations, whatever the trade in which they were involved. However, this acted as a brake to their efficiency, in that Whitby is a tidal harbour, with the estuary bridged by what was probably then a drawbridge. Recent excavations discovered seventeenth-century foundations for a bridge, but there was nothing left to indicate how the bridge was opened to allow shipping to enter the inner harbour. The bridge had a bridge-master, who collected tolls. Even with today's high standards of dredging, bridge opening is only available two hours either side of high water, every hour and half hour, and that is with a electro-mechanical facility for opening what is now a swing bridge. In the past the bridge mechanism would have been worked by muscle-power, a slow and painful process. Better by far to have anchored in the Roads and sent a boat in for supplies, instructions and anything else that was needed.

That is exactly what seems to have been happening by the end of the second decade of the eighteenth century. Since there are no voyage accounts between 1682 and 1714, there is no way of telling at what point at the beginning of the long eighteenth century the practice changed. In any case, it would have changed by degrees, with some vessels continuing to be victualled in Whitby right up to the end of this study.

The artist of the engraving (Plate 6.2) was looking upstream. Buildings on piles seem to have encroached on the bridge itself. There are several surviving engravings of the various bridges of Whitby. As the shipyards were above the bridge, in the safety of the upper harbour, the gap between the main piers, which were built of either brick or stone, had to accommodate the hulls of newly-built vessels, as well as those which had over-wintered in the upper harbour. One solution was to taper the piers downwards to accommodate the widest part of the hull. Great care would have been taken, with crew ready to fend the sides of the vessel off the solid piers, as a vessel passed through the bridge under the supervision of the bridge-master and the master of the vessel itself.

Table 6.5: Share-holders in *William and Jane*, 1718–1726

| Surname | Christian name | 1718 64ths | 1719 64ths | 1720 64ths | 1721 64ths | 1723 64ths | 1725 64ths | 1726 64ths |
|---|---|---|---|---|---|---|---|---|
| Allanson | James | 1 | 1 | 1 | 1 | 1 | 1 | 1 |
| Anderson | John | 1 | 1 | 1 | 1 | 1 | 1 | 1 |
| Benton | John | | | | | 2 | | |
| Binks | Jane | 2 | 2 | 2 | 2 | 2 | 2 | 2 |
| Brand | Edward | 1 | 1 | 1 | 1 | 1 | 1 | 1 |
| Brown | John | | | | | | 2 | 2 |
| Clarke | Henry | 4 | 4 | 4 | | | master | master |
| Clarke | Ann | | | | | 1 | 1 | 1 |
| Dawson and Wikinson | | 4 | 4 | 4 | 4 | 4 | 4 | 4 |
| Dickinson | William | 2 | 2 | 2 | 2 | | | |
| Harland | Ann | 2 | 2 | | 2 | | | |
| Harrison | Christopher | | | | | 2 | 2 | 2 |
| Hook | Edward | 2 | 2 | 2 | 2 | 2 | | |
| Johnson | Thomas | | | | | 1 | 1 | 1 |
| Kitchingman | William | 1 | 1 | 1 | 1 | 1 | 1 | 1 |
| Lascelles | Peregrine | | | | | | | 1 |
| Lascelles | Mary | 1 | 1 | 1 | 1 | 1 | 1 | |

| | | | | | | | | |
|---|---|---|---|---|---|---|---|---|
| Liddell | Sir Henry, Bt | 4 | 4 | 4 | 4 | 3 | | 3 |
| Liddell | George | 2 | 2 | 2 | 2 | 3 | 3 | 3 |
| Liddell | exors of Sir Henry, Bt | | | | | | 3 | 3 |
| Linskill | Robert | 3 | 3 | 3 | 3 | 3 | 3 | 3 |
| Linskill | Henry | 2 | 2 | 2 | 2 | 2 | 2 | 2 |
| Linskill | John | 1 | 1 | 1 | | 1 | 1 | 1 |
| Linskill | Joseph | | | | | | | 1 |
| Pearson | William | 2 | 2 | 2 | 2 | 2 | | |
| Pearson | John | | | | | | | 2 |
| Robinson | John | 2 | 2 | 2 | 2 | 2 | 2 | 2 |
| Rudston | | | | | | 2 | | 2 |
| Trewhitt | Robert | | | | | 2 | | |
| Trewitt | Elizabeth | 2 | 2 | 2 | 2 | | 2 | 2 |
| Vasie | Henry | 2 | 2 | 2 | 2 | 2 | 2 | 2 |
| Vasie | Mary | | | | | | | 2 |
| Watson | John | | | | | | 1 | 1 |
| Wilde | Leonard | 2 | 2 | 2 | 2 | 2 | 2 | 2 |
| Total | | 39 | 39 | 37 | 34 | 38 | 36 | 41 |

Plate 6.2: Engraving of one of Whitby's eighteenth-century drawbridges

## 'Winter-work'

Despite the loss of the regular visits to the port by passing Whitby vessels, there was still one major part of the shipping business which benefited the town. At the end of each sailing year, which in the North Sea came about the beginning of November, vessels 'were laid up', or 'lay up' – both phrases are used – in their home ports. While they were laid up, small repairs and routine maintenance were undertaken; rigging was checked, graving and caulking were done and ropes were checked for wear and replaced if necessary. Sails were dried, 'unbent' and lofted, laid out in airy sail-lofts to avoid mildew and rot. Several surviving buildings on the east side of the river were once sail lofts.

Repairs were made, patching sails, and renewal of the bolt-ropes with which each sail was framed. Lead scuppers were replaced, window glass mended, and the vessel was scrubbed clean and if necessary, painted. The crew was discharged, but the master would supervise the work if necessary. The servants, or apprentices, went to school, and helped with the repairs.

In some of the extant accounts, the tasks undertaken are described as 'winter-work' and accounted separately. In others they can be deduced from the much greater than normal costs of the first voyage of the new sailing year. All the Whitby and Scarborough vessels whose accounts start before 1756 show these patterns of winter-work done in the home port. Above all, winter-work represented an opportunity for sail-makers, ropers and other skilled craftsmen to make a living from the fleet without themselves going to sea. The work ended with the re-victualling of the vessel, thus providing business for the dedicated victuallers who had made their appearance during the latter part of the seventeenth century. Smaller vessels would still call regularly, as well as those delivering goods for the town itself, so that chandlery and victualling were very much a part of the town's success.

However, changes were beginning to occur, as shown in the two surviving voyage books that cover the period between 1718 and 1728, overlapping the accounts of *Hannah* for 1716–18. These are the accounts of *William and Jane* of Whitby, 1718–28, and *Blessing* of Scarborough, 1715–26. Both show winter-work as separate items at the end of each year, though added into the accounts for the next year. The work on both *Hannah* and *William and Jane* appears to have been done in Whitby, while *Blessing* twice had its winter-work done in Sunderland, presumably because the master was anxious to start the new coaling season early, although in the other years it was done in Scarborough.

*Hannah* was newly built when the voyage books begin in 1715, and carried around 220–280 London chaldrons of coal. *Blessing* carried about 250–270 London chaldrons, while *William and Jane* was much larger and carried between 340 and 360 chaldrons. Before the registration of shipping began in 1786, it is usually difficult to make any kind of accurate assessment of the size and capability of any given vessel. The only information available may well be the amount of cargo carried. If the building costs are extant, that might give the measured tonnage, but more often the only figures available represent the capacity in terms of coal. That seems to have been an accepted way of evaluating vessels in ports where the coal trade was dominant. Nevertheless, even that is only available in circumstances where coal is actually being carried from the north-east coalfields to London. Other ports, such as Plymouth in the south-west, dealt in quarters, which in themselves could vary from port to port.

A London chaldron at this time was about 27cwt. The figure for chaldrons can be multiplied by 27 and divided by 20 to convert it into tons. Thus 360 London chaldrons represent a cargo of around 480 tons. It is not until a later voyage book, that of *Three Sisters*, George Galilee master, 1761–88, that it is possible to understand the relationship between London and Newcastle chaldrons, as Whitby masters saw it. They factored their own cargo, buying it in Newcastle or other coal ports, where it was measured on board in Newcastle chaldrons. They then sold it in London, or other ports, even as close as Whitby, in London chaldrons. Several pieces of regulation were passed defining the capacity of both kinds of chaldron, but, as Smith explains in *Seacoal for London*, there was never any regulation linking the two kinds of chaldron together, so that masters were in the end forced to assume that one Newcastle chaldron equalled two London chaldrons.[36] In practice, a London chaldron, like that of Newcastle, was a measure of capacity rather than weight, adding to the problem of calculation. However, as Smith explains, something between 25 and 27cwt came to be the assumed weight of a London chaldron of coal.

36 R. Smith, *Sea-coal for London: The History of the Coal Factors in the London Market*, Longman, 1961, pp. 363–4, 'Glossary'.

Figure 6.2 shows the relationship between Newcastle and London chaldron as George Galilee had to deal with them over 13 years as owner of *Three Sisters*.

Figure 6.2: The ratio of London to Newcastle chaldrons (carried by *Three Sisters*, 1775–1787)

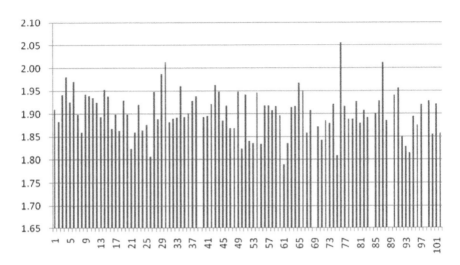

In some 100 voyages carrying coal from Newcastle to London, only in three trips did the ratio of the London chaldron to the Newcastle chaldron reach the assumed total of two. The average was 1.90 London chaldrons to one Newcastle chaldron, and on several voyages the ratio was less than 1.85 to 1. George Galilee was a highly respected Quaker-influenced owner, who used a fellow-shareholder to 'deliver' or unload the cargo. If there was sharp practice involved either at the Tyne or the Thames, then many less wary or less respected masters and owners must have suffered much more.

Table 6.6 shows the costs incurred for winter-work on *Hannah, Blessing* and *William and Jane*. These vary considerably both from year to year and probably according to the age of the vessel and the way in which it was handled. There is no figure for 1715 for *Hannah*, because it was newly built, and presumably newly equipped.

The variation in winter costs is considerable, and does not seem to relate to size. *Hannah's* average cost, for the first three years of a new vessel's working life was £26. *William and Jane*, the largest, paid £26 on average, while *Blessing*, about the same size as *Hannah*, paid twice as much, £52 per annum. This averages out for the three vessels at £35 per annum at this period. We know from several sources that Whitby had around 120 vessels at this time, so the total income to the town from winter-work, much of it done not in the large and highly capitalised ship-yards but by smaller victuallers and chandlers, sail-makers and ropers, and by individual tradesmen, must have been well over £4,000 per annum, twice as much as in the days of *Judith*, 1677–82. That *Blessing* appears to have been a Scarborough vessel does not imply that the cost of its work cannot be included in the calculation for the average. Exactly the same provision would be available in Scarborough as in Whitby, with the possible exception of Scarborough's municipal pitch-kettle. Any monopolistic implications that may have had would not substantially affect the costs. However, the Borough may have had other restrictive practices whose absence in Whitby may have made the town more competitive.

Table 6.6: Charges for Winter-work

| Year | Hannah | Where done | Blessing | Where done | William and Jane | Where done |
|------|--------|-----------|----------|-----------|-----------------|-----------|
| 1716 | £16.77 | Whitby | £19.24 | Scarborough | | |
| 1717 | £34.65 | Whitby | £29.69 | Scarborough | | |
| 1718 | £26.15 | Whitby | £16.53 | Scarborough | | |
| 1719 | | | £78.91 | Scarborough | £23.71 | Whitby |
| 1720 | | | £20.97 | Scarborough | £20.28 | Whitby |
| 1721 | | | £57.03 | Scarborough | £29.06 | Whitby |
| 1722 | | | £84.93 | Scarborough | £26.19 | Whitby |
| 1723 | | | £113.11 | Scarborough | £21.22 | Whitby |
| 1724 | | | £37.23 | Scarborough | £23.99 | Whitby |
| 1725 | | | £67.98 | Scarborough | £32.93 | Whitby |
| 1726 | | | £48.13 | Sunderland | | |
| 1727 | | | | | £32.83 | Whitby |
| 1728 | | | | | £37.38 | Whitby |
| *Totals* | £77.57 | | £573.75 | | £263.85 | |
| *Mean* | £25.86 | | £52.16 | | £26.39 | |

## The difficult years

Whether *Hannah* was lost or sold is not known, so that the short run of accounts of its life does not extend into a period which Davis reports as being a time of a major slump in the shipping industry. Various things appear to have contributed to this slump; the first Jacobite rebellion, various minor conflicts, a levelling-off of the population of London, and therefore of its demand for coal and other imports, and of course, the bursting of the South Sea Bubble. To some extent it is the failure of the national fleet to increase in size, and reductions in the number of entries of goods into the country which indicate this slump, but the accounts of *William and Jane* and of *Blessing* provide new evidence of how these factors affected shipping at the level of the individual owner, master and crew. They shine clear light on a hitherto unclear situation. Both vessels suffered heavy trading losses during the third decade of the eighteenth century, though their overall performances were very different.

Figure 6.3: Profitability of *Hannah*, *William and Jane* and *Blessing*, 1716–1728

Three-year moving average of profitability 1716–28

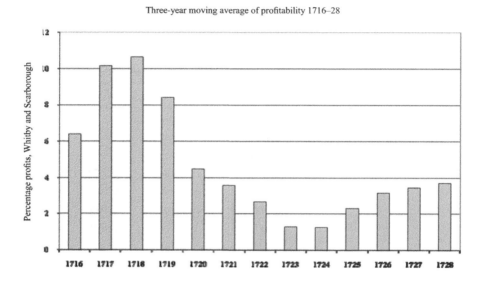

Figure 6.3, a chart of the three-year moving average of profit in all three vessels, *Hannah, William and Jane* and *Blessing*, shows clearly the decline in profitability of shipping during this period, reinforcing Davis's evidence.[37]

Most of *William and Jane's* voyage losses were in the first voyage of the year, which included, of course, the expenditure on winter-work. The accounts are meticulous and detailed, neatly written, if occasionally eccentrically spelled. However, the ability to write standard English, if such a concept then existed, was not of particular value in avoiding sandbanks and rocks on the difficult coastal run from the Tyne to London. The master was certainly highly numerate, and at least consistent in his spelling. However, despite the difficulties of the period through which he sailed, he managed at the end of each year, the stock having been made up to its proper sum, to declare a profit. Over all the years of the book, there was a turnover for the thirteen years of £27,887, averaging £2,145 for each year, and a profit of 5.2 per cent. These carefully

---

37  Since the run of years is so short, the number on which the moving average is based is necessarily small, just sufficient to iron out anomalies, but still demonstrating the trend.

entered details show two things (apart from the skill and competence of the master); the extremely large amount of working capital which was tied up in the shipping industry, on top of the fixed asset capital consisting of the value of the vessel itself, and its equally important capital asset, the stock. Again, multiplied by the huge cloud of shipping which daily passed the entrance to Whitby harbour throughout the sailing season, this might not represent, as did the East Indies fleet, or the Spanish treasure fleets, imagined untold riches, yet this fixed and working capital, notwithstanding the value of cargoes, was an immense, yet unsung, contribution to the national economy.

*William and Jane*, as we saw earlier, was owned by a large body of shareholders, spreading the risk, and well aware of the importance of the precious stock, to be made up before they saw a penny of the profit. But not all masters were like Henry Clark of *William and Jane*. The accounts of *Blessing* indicate that it was commanded by Allatson Bell, of Scarborough. There is a Latin flourish on the fly-leaf that labels the accounts book, *Allatson Bell, ejuis (sic) Liber*. On the front page the inscription is repeated in English in another hand, with the addendum, *Scriptum per me Johannes Bell*. Alas this literary flourish is then surrounded by desperate scribblings of sums, which, if it were possible to relate them exactly to the relevant pages of the accounts, probably record the relentless onslaught of disaster.

When the book starts, it soon becomes clear that rather than the large, risk-sharing group of share-holders favoured by both *Hannah* and *William and Jane*, *Blessing* had but seven, and one, Richard Allatson, owned 32/64ths of the vessel. Even if he had found insurance in the early London markets, of which there is no sign in the accounts, it would not have availed in the end. It has already been shown that the cost of winter-work for *Blessing* was twice as high as that of its two contemporaries. This cannot just have been due to sharp municipal practices in Scarborough, for the most expensive lay-up, which cost £113, was in Sunderland in 1723. As with *William and Jane*, the first voyage was usually loss-making due to the cost of winter-work, but in the years from 1723 to 1725 *Blessing* made large losses on the whole year's trading. In the last year, 1726, the master declared only a 1.2 per cent profit.

Legally, that was not a profit at all, for *Blessing* was unable to make up its stock. It had been reduced from its declared value of £117 to just over £10. Maritime law declared that the stock should exist, as much a part of the vessel as the hull, the mast, the anchors or any other vital piece of equipment. Without it the vessel was insolvent. Had Richard Allatson been insured, trading losses would not have been covered, however bad the slump. Had there been sufficient part-owners, each with a small share, it might have been possible to keep going another year or two to see if 'things improved'. But the loss of income from his 32/64th shares, half the value of the ship, made him responsible for replenishing half the stock. The acquisition of the thirty-two shares, possibly from a base of three or four, could be described as typical 'bubble' economics. The early profits were high, so Bell took on more of the risk, until the almost inevitable crash found him completely exposed. It may be that the high average cost of winter-work indicated a poorly-built vessel. That in itself may mean that Bell was not a perceptive purchaser, or it may have meant inefficient masters and crew, and dishonest winter-work. However, the cost of one year's winter-work done in Sunderland at twice the normal cost, suggests that *Blessing* was not the best-built vessel in Scarborough's fleet.

The resolution of the problem is unknown. The voyage book ends with the sorry statement about the stock. Presumably the vessel was sold, and the stock replenished out of the purchase price before it was handed over, for it could not then be sold without a stock. *Blessing* was presumably bought by some cannier souls, and its book came to Whitby and ended up among those of a highly successful shipowner, Nicholas Piper. Piper moved his growing fleet from Scarborough to Whitby later in the century, together with the voyage accounts of *Swallow* of Scarborough for 1756 to 1763, and *William and Anne* for 1751. These, with the accounts of *Blessing*, are the only Scarborough shipping accounts to survive, but they serve to emphasise the importance of the accounts that all vessels were expected to keep, and which could be demanded in court if there was a dispute, and above all, the importance of the stock.[38]

### Changes in shareholding at the end of the period

It is to a larger group of vessels beyond the period of this study that we must look to see how shareholding practice gradually changed. It would be simplistic to appear to show that the practice of multiple ownership persisted far beyond 1750. It did not.

The graph in Figure 6.4 is somewhat skewed at either end by two particular vessels. At the start there is no profit to be seen from the vessels concerned because one, *William and Anne*, whose voyage accounts only survive for one year, found itself, as did *Swallow*, struggling with a steep increase of wages due to the imminent war against France. The woes of *Swallow* were compounded by a perceived need to arm the vessel, whether to ensure being hired as a transport or to acquire Letters of Marque. This exercise took over a year, and cost £111. At the other end of the chart the whole is distorted by the extremely expensive refit of *Three Sisters*, which cost its owner, George Galilee, over £550.

Between these extremes, the chart shows steady profits, never falling below 6 per cent and rising considerably during time of war, when the demand for shipping was huge, both in the Seven Years' War and the War of American Independence. However, it is not purely for their productivity that these voyage books are remarkable, although that of *Three Sisters* contrasts sharply the ability of George Galilee to afford to cover apparent catastrophe with the failure of Richard Allatson to survive the slump.

By this stage in the eighteenth century the days of multiple ownership of individual vessels appear to have been over. Nicholas Piper seems to have been,

---

38 There are references within the voyage accounts of the *Blessing* to their being shown in court, presumably in some lawsuit after the collapse.

Figure 6.4: Profitability of various vessels, 1756–1786

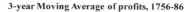

3-year Moving Average of profits, 1756-86

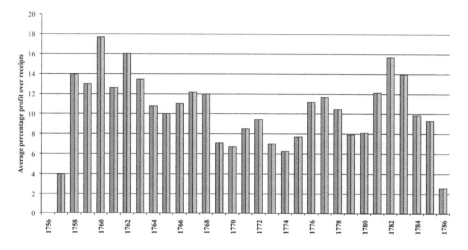

if not the sole share-holder in his two vessels, *William and Anne* and *Swallow*, by far the majority share-holder. The Galilee brothers, John and George, were virtually sole owners of their two vessels, *Three Sisters* and *Four Brothers*. At first John owned both, until he sold *Three Sisters* to George, who had been its first master. Both had minor partners, owning less than 15 per cent of the shares. The stock still existed, but its importance was vanishing along with the concept of multiple ownership. With a single major share-holder there was no longer a need to keep the stock as a 'rod' with which to browbeat reluctant share-holders into paying for major repairs or to share losses. Insurance had become the norm, both with the somewhat obscure mutual insurance clubs of the north-east and with Lloyds Register established in 1776.

There were other changes. No longer did every Whitby vessel come into port in late autumn to be laid up. Instead many were laid up in either the Tyne or the Thames, depending on the plans for the next year. That ensured a flying start in the new season, first call on the coal-keels, or being first to reach the Baltic as the ice melted. However, the downside to this was the loss to Whitby of the winter-work. By 1773 the fleet had almost doubled in number, and more than doubled in tonnage. At the start of the century, with some 120 vessels, the largest of which were about 340 tons, it had been worth over £4,000 per annum. With the figures for tonnage found in the 1773 list, some 56,000 tons, and 241 vessels, the loss of winter-work represented a potential loss to the town of up to £20,000 per annum, allowing for inflation, and probably more in hidden costs. Gone would have been most of the chandlers and victuallers, though the ship-yards and sail-lofts flourished, building from new, and carrying out major refits both for Whitby's own fleet, and for vessels from other towns.

The pull of a speedy start to a particular trade was not the only reason for being laid up for winter in the Thames or the Tyne. Whitby was already feeling the constraints of its comparatively small estuary and therefore the available space for over-wintering. The larger vessels, the full-rigged ships and barques and even some of the brigs, were not easy to manoeuvre in a constricted space. The bow-sprit of each was about a third as long again as the length of the hull, and could cause havoc in a tightly packed area if not well-managed, by cutting through the rigging on neighbouring vessels. There simply would not have been the space or the facilities to manage the almost simultaneous work of making vessels ready for sea and 'helping' them out of the harbour under the pressure of the start of the sailing season at the beginning of March.

The more enterprising chandlers would have diversified, remaining as independent enterprises and providing goods for the ship-building and repair yards. Other businesses would have flourished. As Whitby became a magnet town for training future sea officers for the merchant fleet, so an industry grew up catering for this influx of youngsters. Washerwomen washed 'the lads' clothes'; tailors made not only trousers for boys to wear at sea, but also the breeches they needed for Sunday best in this town where sea officers were the elite. One of the most illuminating probate inventories of the early eighteenth century is that of Robert Stainridge, mercer, whose stock-in-trade was listed in detail, and included extremely expensive fabrics for the wives and daughters of the same elite. His goods and chattels were valued in 1707 at almost £1,000 and he was wealthy enough to have lent out, in Whitby's sophisticated financial web, almost £1,800, some of it invested as far afield as London.[39]

However, the disappearance of the opportunity to become share-holders in one or more vessels rapidly diminished as insurance gradually took over the risks inherent in the industry. That, together with the gradual disappearance of most of the specialist chandlers and victuallers, meant that the 'trickle-down' effect of the importance of the shipping industry which had been so clear in the last quarter of the seventeenth century began to be replaced by an economy polarised between wealthy ship-owning and ship-building families such as the Chapmans, Usherwoods, Galilees, Fishburns, Holts and Walker Yeomans and those whose income from the industry came purely from wages earned from working in the ship-yards, roperies, and sail-manufactories, and at sea during the sailing season.

Certainly there was, during the eighteenth century, a substantial increase in the amount of ship-building and repair. Dry-docks were built, not always successfully, as when hidden springs burst through the massive walls, making it impossible to dry them out completely to enable work on hulls.[40] However, Charlton's map of 1778 (Map 0.2) shows those that were successful, the oldest

---

39  N. Vickers (ed.), *A Yorkshire Town of the Eighteenth Century: The Probate Inventories of Whitby, North Yorkshire, 1700–1800,* Brewin, 1986, pp. 48–57; Inventory of Robert Stainridge, mercer, October, 1707.

40  The effects of such a catastrophe were revealed in recent archaeological works associated with the renewal of much of Whitby's sewerage by Yorkshire Water. A beautifully built dry-dock from the

of which had been built in 1734. There were several roperies in the town, some of them capable of producing the 440-yard cables without which they could not supply the growing demands of the Navy. Sailcloth was made extensively, of all grades of canvas, and this added to the polarisation between owners and wage-earners.

As the town became polarised in this way, so the townscape itself changed. Stuck as the town was within the confines of its twenty-four acres of dry land, it was only the wealthy who could escape. What had been the ignored suburb of Ruswarp suddenly began to seem more desirable, as the town grew more congested. Enterprising investors bought land from the surrounding landowners and new streets were added to the town. Silver Street and Skinner Street were occupied by master mariners and small-business owners. The shipowners had early in the century squeezed their large town houses into the burgage, houses that are still there, like that of John Walker in Grape Lane, and Haggersgate House, built around 1711 in Haggersgate, both cheek by jowl with their poorer neighbours.

The original burgage houses were gradually subdivided to contain more and more tenements, from cellar to garret, five floors in many cases, and often as infill in yards behind medieval frontages, till by 1831 Whitby had the most desperately crowded central township in the north of England, while the wealthy had moved out of the town to surrounding mansions or to the elegant terraces of Bagdale and St Hilda's Terrace.

---

eighteenth century was uncovered, as was the damage caused when a spring broke through the walls within a few years of its construction. (Personal communication from the project archaeologist.)

# 'They That Go Down to the Sea in Ships'

## The Seamen's Sixpence

Between the voyage book of *Judith*, 1677–81, and the Seamen's Sixpence muster rolls beginning in 1747, a picture of the men who manned the growing fleet, of their conditions of service, training and career structure and welfare, begins to emerge. Crews were listed, masters named, and 'posts on board' indicated within some of the surviving voyage books, as were the wages paid, usually by the month.

The 'Sixpence', payable for each month or part of a month at sea for each seaman on board an English merchant ship, was intended for the upkeep of Greenwich Hospital for incapacitated naval seamen. Merchant seamen were not eligible for the hospital unless incapacitated during a naval engagement.[1] After 1747 Whitby and other seaports which had either a Trinity House or a Seamen's Hospital became eligible for some of the proceeds of the local Sixpence collection, and muster rolls were thereafter kept at the port of collection instead of being returned directly to London. The primary use of the muster rolls was as evidence that the money had been deducted, but their existence means that after 1747 a much broader and clearer picture begins to emerge of the manning of the Whitby fleet.

## The muster rolls

In the first two years of the muster rolls, 1747–48, the place of birth of members of the floating workforce which kept the industry going were given, in accordance with the Poor Relief Act of 1662.[2] There was also a column for the ages of individual members, for the dates when they joined the vessel, and for their departure from the crew. From this was calculated the number of months and part-months for the deduction of the 'Seamen's Sixpence'. A final piece of information indicated the manner of leaving, whether by discharge, death, desertion or, in time of war, by impressment. Each vessel carried a muster roll

---

1 TNA/ADM 68; Ledgers of the Receiver of Sixpences, 1725–1830.
2 13 & 14 Car. II, cap. 12, dealt with entitlement to poor relief in the parish in which a man was born, or alternately where he worked, and in which, once he had been there for a year and a day, he and his family could be regarded as settled. With time this entry in the muster rolls came to be left blank, as clerks grew a little less conscientious, and the importance, from the point of view of welfare and assistance, of the poor law system became secondary to the support of the Seamen's Hospital charity to which all those who served in vessels 'belonging to' Whitby, and their legal families, were entitled.

for its crew, which had to be presented to any naval press-tender seeking seamen for the Navy.

The money, and a summary of the information kept in the rolls, was then sent to the Receiver of Sixpences in London. The Whitby rolls were then copied up into ledgers, which were kept at the Seamen's Hospital. This would have made it much easier to find the details of any seaman, or seaman's widow, seeking relief, than if the growing pile of muster rolls had to be searched individually. Whitby, with its large fleet, may be the only port that kept such ledgers. It may be that the influence of the Quaker members of the shipping interest, who were scrupulous record-keepers, suggested the practice. Whitby certainly seems to be the only port for which both rolls and volumes survive. These large volumes also carry indexes for the names of the vessels, and for each vessel the name of the ship's husband and, where relevant, the names of the sub-division of the port of Whitby where the vessel was principally owned. That might be Robin Hood's Bay, Sandsend or Staithes, all of which were regarded for welfare purposes as part of the port of Whitby.

Very occasionally an individual seaman or even a group of seamen would refuse to pay, but if they did they were no longer eligible for relief. There might be more than one reason for this refusal to pay; before the 1747 Act, there was considerable resentment about having to pay the sixpence for Greenwich Hospital, for whose services merchant seamen were not eligible. While they might acknowledge the importance of the Navy's protection in times of war, it was soon forgotten when war was over and the sense of injustice would rise again and remain as a residual objection even after the provincial institutions began to benefit. It is also possible that seamen had good reason for not being recorded on official documents. They might be naval deserters, or escaping from an unhappy relationship, or even evading their responsibilities towards a pregnant girl. However, it is most likely that it was a connivance between master and men to avoid the depredations of the impress service. In such case, the 'refusers' are not listed, and are only known from other surviving documents.[3] A boarding party from the press tender would demand to see the muster roll, and ask for specific crewmen. However, the press was not allowed to remove so many men that the safety of the affected vessel was compromised (see Appendix 2).

If a vessel disappeared without trace, perhaps foundering during a storm, then the ship's husband or his or her representative presented a makeshift list, recording the probable members of the crew and the estimated date of loss, and this was duly entered into the schedules. This was vital to ensure that the dependants of the dead seamen could claim support if needed from the charity. There is, amongst the archives of the Seamen's Hospital, a collection of sad little affidavits, attesting that a named vessel from Whitby crossed the bar of the

---

3   R. Barker, *Prisoners of the Tsar: East Coast Sailors Held in Russia, 1800–1801*, Highgate, 1992, is based on the journal kept by Thomas Etty, a seaman aboard *George* of Whitby, Thomas Coverdale, master. Thomas Etty does not appear on the muster roll, although he kept the journal on behalf of the master.

Tyne, or passed Tynemouth Castle on a certain day, and that a named seaman
was said to be on board, and that a storm was known to have occurred thereafter, and the vessel was never seen again. There are letters from clergy in distant
parishes giving evidence that women had been legally married to named crew-
men of lost vessels. Considerable effort went into the completion of the picture.
The loss of a vessel, however small, was never regarded casually.

A recently discovered document shows the lengths to which a Quaker ship's
husband, Warren Maude, went to unravel the fate of one small brig, whose
incomplete muster for the voyage on which it was lost duly appeared in the
schedules. The document is actually a Protest, by means of which the said
Warren Maude was exempted from debts caused by his failure to deliver the
chartered cargo, in this case to the Crown. It is worth citing the full text:

> Whereas Robson Richardson and Warren Maude became bound unto His
> present Majesty King George the Second in a Coast bond given at the Port of
> Sunderland the thirteenth day of November 1755 for landing at Lynn or some
> other port of Great Britain Sixty three chaldrons of coals out of the *Mary and
> Rebecca* of Whitby Robson Richardson Master.
>
> NB Warren Maude being one of the People call'd Quakers on his Solemn
> Affirmation Saith that on the said thirteenth day of November, The said
> ship being then in Sunderland Road, having only taken on board Thirty five
> Chaldrons of Coals, part of the quantity above mentioned, a Gale of Wind
> arose and blew from the South South East, so strong that [it did] force the
> ship out of the roads to the Northward as far as Fearn [Farne] Island, Where
> this Affirmant verily believes, the ship, together with the Master and Ships
> Company and the said Thirty five Chaldrons of Coals were Intirely lost, the
> next morning being the fourteenth day of November 1755, As this Affirmant
> has never since received any Account from the Master or Ship's Company,
> And further this Affirmant saith, That being informed of some Materialls of
> A wreckt Vessel coming on shore near to Fearn Island aforesaid, He went
> thither and upon seeing them verily believes they belonged to the Aforesaid
> Ship and this Affirmant Lastly saith that he was A part owner of the said
> Ship and Coals and that he has not received, (or any person for him) or ever
> expects to receive any benefitt or advantage whatever from the said Thirty
> five chaldrons of Coals or any part thereof, But that the same together with
> the Ship and Company were intirely lost and perished in the Sea
>
> Affirmed at Sunderland in County of Durham this Eighth day of July, 1756
> before C Hanson A Comm[issioner] etc.
> Signed
> Warren Maude[4]

That the brig had been anchored in the Roads rather than the River Wear
at Sunderland seems at first careless when taking on board coal, but coal was
normally taken on board in the Roads from keels, flat-bottomed boats which
carried the coal from the coal staithes to the waiting collier brigs and ships.
Sunderland was a notoriously barred harbour, with several shifting sandbanks

---

4  I am indebted to Clifford Thornton for sight of this Protest.

in its approaches. These were less of a threat to flat-bottomed keels than to sea-going vessels. However, with only half a cargo on board, the brig would have been riding comparatively high in the water, and would therefore have been much more vulnerable to wind. It would have been a terrifying ordeal, facing certain ship-wreck and possible death on the rocks to the north of the harbour entrance. The vessel must have managed to avoid these, but apparently drove onto the notorious Farnes much farther north. Storm damage to the brig, coupled with probable exhaustion of the crew, would have made the end almost inevitable.

There are several thousand muster rolls for Whitby vessels, from between 1747 and 1818, mustering an average of around twelve crew members per year. Most men are named, and the rolls thus represent a huge resource for historians. They continue the system of crew lists found in the earlier voyage books. The voyage accounts of *Judith*, 1677–82, list by name all those who sailed in it, from the master, to, for the last two years, his young son. The posts are not listed, but it seems from muster rolls and from other sources that there was a set way of listing the crew:

Master
Mate
Carpenter
Cook
Seamen
Servants

No distinction was made between servants as apprentices (or, earlier, 'articulates') and ship's boys.[5] Apprentices might be entering as potential mariners or as potential ship-carpenters. Boys would have been simply there to run errands and eventually become able seamen, without rising to watch-keeping status. There was a differentiation in civil documents such as wills and parish registers between seamen and mariners. Mariners appear to have served their time and to be capable of pilotage and navigation, whereas seamen often stayed at that level for their whole lives. In addition, the men who sailed in the fishing fleet were also classified as seamen and may indeed have served in both trades. Only the skippers or the owners of boats were called 'fishermen'. In the musters all servants apprenticed as potential mariners progressed through the post of seaman, before being promoted to that of mate and then master, if indeed they survived or were competent.

It is much more difficult to trace the boys who became ship-carpenters, and eventually shipwrights. None of the sample of 1,600 or so musters after 1747 which have been analysed in detail mention a carpenter's mate or anything to indicate an interim post. Even in the heyday of Whitby's late eighteenth-century involvement with whaling, there is no way of distinguishing carpenters' apprentices from any others in the much longer and more detailed crew lists

5    So called because they had been 'articled' or indentured as apprentices to shipowners or masters.

which whaling demanded. What is known is that boys were often apprenticed to merchants with an 'interest' in shipping, or to ship's husbands ashore, and then sent to sea with favoured masters. The ship paid a wage for their services. How much of that wage went to the servant, how much to his apprentice-master and how much to the master of the vessel is not clear. In some cases the boy was apprenticed directly to a master who may still have been at sea, but unless a muster roll corresponding to the rare survival of an indenture survives, it is not possible to be exact. It is reasonable to suppose, however, that boys apprenticed to shipwrights would be sent to sea with competent ship-carpenters to learn how to apply their skills in the much more difficult conditions of life at sea. Vessels under construction or being repaired in a dry-dock remain upright and stable while the work is being done. By contrast the carpenter and seamen who hung on a stage over the stern of *Flora* to putty the leak under her counter in a following sea in mid-Atlantic worked in conditions which were both difficult and dangerous.[6]

The carpenter was responsible for the technical side of the vessel, roughly as is the chief engineer in a modern merchant ship. He was a highly-trained specialist, and in the absence of a cooper, did that job as well. Only whalers expended cash on coopers' wages. The carpenter, aided by able seamen, must have looked to the sails and ropes as well. Merchant crews were pared to the minimum and very few Whitby vessels carried bosuns (boatswains), either to take care of ropes and sails or to act as ship's policeman. Marcus Rediker's emphasis on the importance of the bosun in the working of the vessel and the control of the crew finds no parallel in Whitby or Scarborough vessels.

The more complex and numerous crew of a whaler in the Greenland Sea or the Davis Straits at the end of the eighteenth century occasionally included a bosun, since there were whale boats and lines to be maintained as well as the ship itself. On the other hand a seaman who could mend sails, splice ropes and assist the carpenter was a valuable member of the crew. When profit and loss were often so finely balanced and subject to the vagaries of wind, weather and war, there was little to spare for more crew members than were needed. Unlike their naval counterparts, merchant seamen were well paid, but expected to 'work' twenty to thirty tons per man, while the naval rating handled only three to four tons.

Whitby's involvement in the eighteenth-century whaling trade did not begin until 1753. Many north-east whaling ships carried Dutch specialists in their first voyages, but Whitby's early whaling voyages involved largely British crews, and as men became skilled in this new business, local seamen joined.[7] Whether they were Whitby-born, or immigrants to the town has yet to be investigated.

The mate of a merchant vessel of any size would have been a mariner who had served a full apprenticeship to a shipowner or a master, paid at the same

---

6   The log of *Flora*, of Whitby, William Manson, 1764–71.
7   T. Barrow, *The Whaling Trade of North-East England, 1750–1850*, University of Sunderland Press, 2001, pp. 12–14, discusses Whitby's early crewing patterns.

wage as the carpenter. In the modern merchant service, a Mate or First Officer has to hold a relevant master's ticket. He had to be a watch-keeper, trained in both pilotage and navigation, literate, numerate and capable of taking over the running of the vessel in the event of the discharge, illness or death of the master. The sudden need to take over might well be in difficult circumstances, caused by the master's death or incapacity, perhaps in a foreign port or in an accident at sea.

The mate had to be capable of performing all the master's tasks as well as steadying the crew in such circumstances. When going 'foreign', away from the normal northern seas, the vessel might carry a second mate, paid slightly, but not very much, above a seaman's rate. If the mate took over as master, then the second mate moved up to take his place. A competent watch-keeping seaman might then find himself suddenly promoted to the cabin, a privilege shared by the master, the carpenter, and the mate. Here, on some vessels, he might partake of Hoisin tea, rather than the common tea provided for the crew.[8]

One other crew member in larger vessels was routinely paid at a higher rate and that was the cook. This suggests that it was a much more specialised rôle than the pejorative expression 'sea-cook' would suggest. In the Navy his qualification was often the loss of a limb or some other incapacitating injury which might entitle him to a warrant, but the voyage accounts which survive from Whitby and Scarborough, and which record the existence of a cook, suggest that he was actually chosen for his ability to cook. It is difficult to imagine Yorkshire ship's husbands paying good wages above the normal rate to a boy or a man who was going to spoil the victuals which they also provided. It is also difficult to imagine the crew putting up with badly-cooked food. While they were to a large extent under the control of the master, they could leave at the first port of call if the victuals were not to their liking. The stability of most of the crews named in the muster rolls suggests that on the whole the inner man was kept well satisfied.

This stability is shown in Table 7.1, which shows the number of voyages undertaken by each named member of the crew of *Judith*, together with what appears to be his post on board, during the period 1677–82. Those named without a (suggested) post were most likely seamen. Of the 27 men and boys named, 4 men sailed only for two voyages, and 3 for four voyages. Thirteen sailed for eight or more of the forty-five recorded voyages, a high level of stability. Given that most North Sea vessels paid off their crew in November and started the new season at the beginning of March, there was considerable scope for a change of crew or vessel if the previous employment had not been to the liking of either master or man.

Finally, the most important man on board was the master, who commanded the ship. However small a vessel, down to a two-man hoy or a fishing boat, one man held command. It was essential for the safety of the vessels that there should be one with whom should rest the final responsibility for making

---

8   WLP/Voyage book of *Swallow*, of Scarborough, 1755–61.

decisions in desperate situations. He might be supported by the mate, but the master carried the burden on his shoulders.

Table 7.1: Stability of the crew of *Judith*, 1677–1682

| *Number of voyages undertaken by individual crew members in the Judith, 1677–82* | | | |
| --- | --- | --- | --- |
| *Surname* | *Christian name* | *Post (supposed)* | *Number of voyages* |
| Rogers | Thomas | Master | 45 |
| Wakefield | John | (boy, seaman) | 42 |
| Blackburn | Israel | (boy, seaman) | 35 |
| Rafton | Denis | (mate) | 31 |
| White | Miles | (carpenter) | 27 |
| Noble | Matthew | | 23 |
| Massom | John | (servant) | 19 |
| Summerside | George | | 12 |
| Haines | Matthew | (mate) | 10 |
| Rogers | John | (servant) | 9 |
| Woodhouse | Mark | | 9 |
| Haines | William | (carpenter) | 8 |
| Jefferson | Luke | (servant) | 8 |
| Boyes | Richard | | 7 |
| Storr | William | (carpenter) | 7 |
| Ingledew | Roger | | |
| Ripley | Henry | (mate) | 5 |
| Seaton | John | | 5 |
| Douthard | Ralph | | 4 |
| Greetham | Robert | | 4 |
| Widgett | George | (carpenter) | 4 |
| Duck | Thomas | | 2 |
| Hill | John | | 2 |
| Sturtell | Richard | | 2 |
| Theaxton | Richard | | 2 |

The master's duties were varied. He might act as ship's husband and make all the trading decisions on behalf of the share-holders. In that case he probably held some shares himself, as did Thomas Rogers of *Judith*, 1677–82, and Peter Barker of *Hannah*, 1714–18. If he was engaged in the high-bulk, low-value coal trade, he usually acted as his own agent, factoring the cargo on the Tyne, and selling it at London or some other port on the Thames, as did Browne

Bushell, of *John*, 1632, Thomas Rogers and Peter Barker. So too did Henry Clarke, master of *William and Jane*, 1718–29.

The master authorised all the financial transactions himself, using either cash or bills of exchange for an initial cargo when the vessel was new, and thereafter recycling the money he received from its sale to run back to the north-east under ballast and buy another cargo. The master was responsible for the stock, which paid for items purchased for the ship and which was replenished from the profits at the end of the year. He paid the wages and any charges for 'bureaucracy', an increasing amount as better facilities were provided in the way of lightage, buoyage and harbour installations. He also paid out tips and bribes, generally recorded as 'drinks', to facilitate speedier unloading and other forms of queue-jumping. A vessel made no money sitting in the roads waiting for keels or berths.

A further responsibility was payment in support of sick crew-men, who, under the Laws of Oléron, must be put ashore to recover, with the services of a boy and enough money for his care. This sounds as if it would be a law more honoured in the breach than the observance, but in fact both Whitby and Scarborough vessels record such payments and the archives of the Seamen's Hospital contain claims from masters, with witness statements, for such payments. Sometimes it was the master himself who fell sick, and even died, at sea. The mate then had to assume all these responsibilities immediately. Davis estimated that a third of masters died at sea, since it was they who were responsible for getting everyone off the vessel if it was on fire or sinking, being themselves the last to leave. During wartime masters took responsibility for their crews even when they were all prisoners of war, as did Thomas Coverdale for the crew of *George* in Russia, 1801–02, during the Napoleonic Wars, well outside our time-frame.[9] With such a raft of responsibilities for a man in charge of even an average brig of perhaps 200 tons, it is not surprising that his training and education were demanding.

## Servants and apprentices

In 1732 the orphaned son of a master mariner was indentured to John Calvert, master and mariner of Whitby. The indenture was drawn up at Tankerness in Orkney, and a summary is reproduced below as Table 7.2. Strong trading links had been established between Orkney and Whitby because of the need for Orkney's product of kelp for Whitby's alum industry. Alexander, probably about twelve years old, as this was to be a six-year servitude, was the first of many such Orcadian boys of middle-class family who joined the Whitby fleet. It is to the family letters of two of his successors, James Watt, the son of 'William Watt the Jacobite', and William Manson, that we owe much of our

9   R. R. Barker, *Prisoners of the Tsar: East Coast Sailors Held in Russia, 1800–1801*, Highgate Publications, 1992.

knowledge of the lives of Whitby's mariners in the late eighteenth century.[10] William Manson's life was the more exotic of the two; his first wife, the step-daughter of shipowner Jonas Brown, later Viscount Montague, was lost in an Indian raid in Georgia, and his second wife, after his return to Orkney to hold a post as a Collector of Customs, was the sister-in-law of the Earl of Ligonier. These were boys of what they would themselves have called 'the better sort', whose sponsors were able to pledge a premium of £40 in 1726, a considerable sum. They are indicative of the growing reputation of the Whitby fleet and its town for training sea officers for the merchant service. In 1747/8, while the young James Cook was a servant at sea, apprenticed to the Quaker John Walker, there were 1,256 boys entered in Whitby's muster rolls as servants.

Table 7.2: Apprenticeship of Alexander Sibbald
Calendar of apprenticeship agreement, 1732: NAS/GD217/676

At Tankerness, (Orkney), the 2nd of September, 1732.

| | |
|---|---|
| On the one part: | John Calvert, shipmaster of Whitby. |
| On the other part: | Alexander Sibbald, son of Alexander Sibbald, shipmaster deceased, of St Andrews. |
| Cautioner (surety): | Mr Robert Baikie, Merchant, of Kirkwall |

Alexander was apprenticed for six years.

Master to provide bed, board and washing, and teach the art of sailing and navigation, within his and the boy's capability.

Sliding scale of payments in lieu of clothing:

Year 1: 25s

Year 2: 30s

Year 3: 40s

Year 4: 40s

Year 5: 45s

Year 6: 60s (all in sterling), but notwithstanding agreement, because of his non-age (minority), master to buy his clothes and charge to his account.

Bound under *failzie* (consideration in case of failure of the agreement) of £40 to be paid by the 'partie breaker' to the 'partie observer'.

Forty years after Alexander Sibbald, William Barker became a servant to the Galilee brothers on board the brig *Three Sisters* in 1772. Because the voyage account to match the musters survives, it is easier to use it as an example of a career progression than to try to pick one out from earlier musters.

Towards the end of the sailing season in 1782 William Barker left *Three Sisters*. The muster roll gives no reason for his departure, so it must be assumed that he left to take command of a larger vessel than a 240-ton brig. Had he died or been discharged, the roll would have stated that. He may have been taken ill, but, in a young man, the more likely cause was another vessel. Whitby's fleet

---

10  Orkney Archives, OA/D3, Papers of Watt of Breckness; OA/D2, Papers of Balfour.

was expanding at this time to cope with the demand for shipping during the War of American Independence – it reached its greatest size, 318 vessels and 78,000 measured tons, in 1782 – so there would have been ample opportunity for promotion for a bright young master.[11] One can only hope that the inevitable slump which would have followed the cessation of the war in 1783 did not leave young William 'on the beach'.

Table 7.3: William Barker's career on board *Three Sisters*

| Year | Post on board | Months and days |
| --- | --- | --- |
| 1772 | Servant | 8_02 |
| 1773 | Servant | 7_05 |
| 1774 | Servant | 8_05 |
| 1775 | Servant | 8_03 |
| 1776 | Seaman | 7_03 |
| 1776 | Mate | 1_14 |
| 1777 | Mate | 8_18 |
| 1778 | Mate | 8_14 |
| 1779 | Mate | 8_26 |
| 1780 | Mate | 8_22 |
| 1781 | Master | 9_21 |
| 1782 | Master | 7_06 |

William was probably older than Alexander Sibbald when he became a servant, since his servitude seems to have lasted just four years. The duration of an apprenticeship seems to have depended on the age at starting, as a servant would not have been deemed strong enough for a seaman's work, or pay, before the age of eighteen or ninteteen. James Cook served three years as an older entrant, so this was probably assumed to be the length of time it took to learn the skills of seamanship and the mathematics, navigation and accountancy needed ultimately to command his own vessel.

Alexander Sibbald, James Watt, William Manson and William Barker, like all their fellow apprentices, would have spent the sailing season at sea and the winter at school. Some thirty-five active schoolmasters have been identified during the eighteenth century, and among them are known mathematicians and teachers of navigation, such as Lionel Charlton, a polymath of some distinction who flourished from about 1750.

William Barker, unlike the other three boys, came from Marske-in-Cleveland, some twenty-five miles up the coast from Whitby. However, the muster rolls

11 TNA/T1/430, Maps and notes sent to the Board of Ordnance, by Francis Gibson, concerning the defence of Whitby, 1782, 1794.

of 1747/8, with their careful record of the place of birth, indicate the wide horizons of the boys who became 'servants' in the Whitby fleet. Figure 7.1 shows the distance between Whitby and the birthplaces of those of the 1,256 boys listed as servants who did not come from the town or its suburbs, as did just over a two-thirds of their number. A good, but indeterminate, number of those apprentices would not be intending to become mariners, nevertheless, a large number of boys would come to Whitby to learn the 'art and mystery' of seafaring. It used to be thought that James Cook somehow sprang, self-taught and unexpectedly, from a seafaring backwater. The reverse is the case; he was one of the 1,256 servants recorded in these musters, one of some thirty-six apprentices indentured to John Walker. He might well have shown a greater application to his studies and a genius which lifted him above his contemporaries, but he passed through exactly the same system as did his fellow servants.

Figure 7.1: Birthplace, other than Whitby, of servants recorded in Muster Rolls, 1747–1748

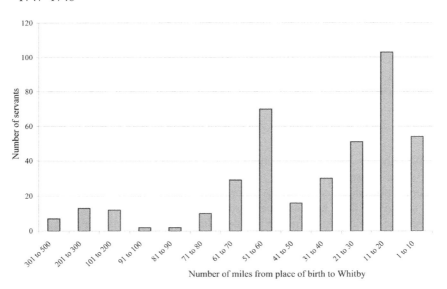

The ports and inland towns from which boys came to serve in the Whitby fleet mirror the ports with which Whitby had strong trading links. Most were on the east coast and likely to have been regularly visited by Whitby masters and merchants. It is of interest that some twenty-five of the servants were born in Newcastle. This was a much larger port than Whitby, with a higher tonnage of shipping, and the apparent preference for boys to be sent to Whitby to train may relate to the high reputation of Whitby's fleet, and possibly to the attraction of Quaker involvement in the fleet. Newcastle had its own flourishing Society of Friends, but the spirit of networking was strong within the Society, and it may have seemed expedient to exploit it for training the young. Moreover, it was known that Quaker vessels captured by the French during wartime were always ransomed, so that their crews did not expect to languish in a prison for the remainder of the current war.

Boys also came to Whitby to train from the other coal-ports of the north-east, and from ports to which coal and other goods might well be delivered. It was all part of the networking which was essential to the shipping industry as a whole. However, the link with Orkney came from the alum industry, since kelp was increasingly required for the process of manufacture, and once the industry outgrew the local supply it was sought from the growing Orkney kelp industry.[12] Letters home from William Manson to his Orcadian parents in the second part of the eighteenth century give some explanation for the Whitby fleet's popularity as a training place for ambitious youngsters, in the quality of the education which could be obtained there.[13] He had clearly been expected home for the winter, but wrote regretfully to say that he could obtain far better teaching in Whitby than anywhere near home.

## Wages

As early as 1677–82, the accounts of *Judith* show that there were clear advantages to service at sea over service on land when it came to wages. A man working at a lowly level on land, say as a labourer, however experienced in his work, was probably hired on a daily basis, with the likelihood of employment based on weather, or even the whim of an overseer or employer.

Once a man had been taken on at sea, then he was assured, at least theoretically, of payment for the whole voyage, provided the vessel was not lost, or that he did not commit some offence which meant he was discharged at the nearest port. Whitby's fairly regular trades, be they Baltic, Norway, coal or alum, meant that in practice an industrious seaman could be reasonably sure of a year's employment. In addition, he would have his meals and the benefits offered by the seamen's hospital in case of injury. He was also protected by the 'law of the sea', which cared for not only the owners but also the workforce and often their dependants.

During periods of war, when there was a shortage of shipping, due in part to losses by enemy action, and to the demands of the transport service, his wages would soar to a level of which a landsman could only dream. The first voyage book that covers periods of war and peace over a long timescale is that of *Three Sisters*, 1761–88. This vessel sailed, largely in the coal-trade, through the last years of the Seven Years' War, and the whole of the War of American Independence, so that, although after the early modern period, it provides the best example of those fluctuations.

---

12  W. P. L. Thomson, *Kelp-making in Orkney*, Orkney Press, 1983, gives an excellent account of the processing of kelp for various industries, including the glass industry for which the north-east was famous.
13  OA/D3, Papers of Watt of Breckness and OA/D2, Papers of Balfour.

Figure 7.2: Annual wages paid aboard *Three Sisters*, 1761–1787

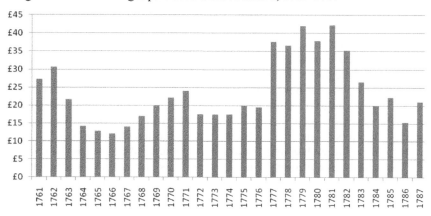

For *Three Sisters'* first three years, Britain was at war with France and wages were comparatively high, although the annual totals do not always show this correctly. The first year, 1761, involved only three voyages, two to the Tyne for coal and one to the Baltic for hemp which was taken to the naval base at Plymouth. The latter is somewhat anomalous for wage rates. For the master, at £8 per calendar month, a rate which never varied, the £56 he received implies a seven-month trip, though he does not date his accounts as clearly as did Thomas Rogers of *Judith*. However, for the mate, carpenter and seamen, the multiplier varies between 5½ and 6½. Other years are also anomalous; 1766 saw a long dry-docking in the middle of the year, during which the master, George Galilee, married in the parish church Mary Richardson, the daughter of a leading Quaker. The Society of Friends 'denied' Mary for this disobedience, but she and George were later welcomed back, though George seems to have remained an 'attender' rather than a member.[14]

It is during the long haul through the American War, with John Paul Jones in his *Bonhomme Richard* harrying the coal trade and blockading the east coast ports, that the greatest increases in seamen's wages are found. At this point Whitby's fleet reached its highest tonnage, and that and the pressures on the pool of seamen caused by the press-gang, together with losses due to capture, injury or death due to enemy action, had a huge impact on wages. In 1786, *Three Sisters* had a major and extremely expensive refit, which shortened its sailing year. At the start of 1788 it sank off the mouth of the Tyne, fully laden, but with all hands saved, together with the accounts, a boat, a gun and her precious stock. By then George Galilee owned the vessel almost outright, having bought it from his brother John.

*Three Sisters* was the last of the eighteenth-century Whitby vessels known

14 Mary's justification for her action is described in private family papers.

*Three Sisters* was the last of the eighteenth-century Whitby vessels known to carry a stock.[15] The growth of insurance meant that ownership was no longer shared out to spread the risk and the costs, so the use of a 'stock', as part of the capital value of the vessel, was probably thought to be no longer necessary. That *Three Sisters* carried on with it to the end of its days is indicative of the slightly conservative practices of the Galilee family, and perhaps those of other less modern-minded firms. *Three Sisters'* last master took the boat into the Tyne, sold gun and boat and reclaimed the money he had paid for light and buoys, on the irrefutable grounds that he had passed none. He spent the recovered cash on transport home to Whitby. Why the vessel sank, or what happened to the insurance, mentioned in Lloyds register for the year, but without a note of the loss of the vessel, was not recorded.

During the life of *Three Sisters*, there is no evidence that any Whitby vessels were involved in the Tyneside strikes of the 1760s or early 1770s. There is nothing in the Whitby archive that even hints at such disturbances. Whether the accounts of the event have not survived, or whether there was a conspiracy of silence, or whether the more pragmatic and Quaker-influenced Whitby ships' husbands simply conceded the demands, is so far unknown.

It is possible, by aggregating the information from all the voyage books, to see how wages gradually rose over the early modern period. While it is not always easy to pick out the wages of individual seamen, it is possible to make sense of the overall picture. Ten vessels contribute to Figure 7.3, some of them the only representative for several years, some overlapping for several years. The totals reflect the average cost per vessel per annum. The *John* has only one incomplete year and is therefore shown only for interest, while between *Judith* and the second decade of the seventeenth century, there had been a considerable increase in both the size of the fleet and the tonnage of its individual members. *Judith* was a ketch of 74¾ measured tons; *William and Jane*, the oldest Whitby vessel to survive into the period of routine registration, was a three-masted ship of almost 237 measured tons.

The high costs of the Seven Years' War are very clear to see. So too is the inexorable rise due to inflation and also the increasing size of vessels. A listing for 1773 states that the average tonnage of Whitby vessels was about 240 measured tons, ranging from the 30-ton sloop *Prosperous Adventure* to the 420-ton ship *Prince of Wales*.[16]

---

15  However, evidence of its continued use into the nineteenth century is being examined. (Personal communication from Stephen Baines, to whom I am grateful for the information).

16  WLP/Burnett Papers, PB5032, the transcript of a now-lost notebook probably kept by the Customer, of all the vessels 'belonging' to Whitby in 1773, when new legislation concerning measured tonnage came into use. This is one of the invaluable transcripts made by the late Percy Burnett.

Figure 7.3: Mean annual wage costs, ten vessels, 1632–1765

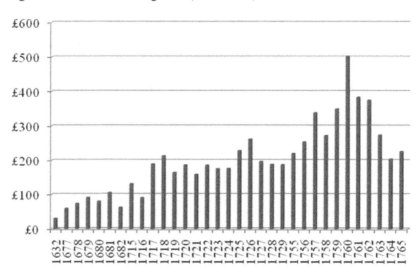

## Horizons

For most of the men serving in Whitby's merchant fleet the horizons of their working lives would have seemed quite exotic to a land-bound worker, whether labourer or specialist. Most seamen sailed at least up and down the east coast, visiting other ports and, more excitingly, the most exotic port of all, London. For a smaller part of the workforce at sea, the horizons stretched to include both sides of the North Sea and much of northern Europe, and even the Baltic and the White Sea. Later the Greenland Sea and the Davis Straits were added by the whaling fleet. From the seventeenth century Whitby and Scarborough shipping ventured across the Irish Sea and the Atlantic, both specialised trades undertaken by a few owners.

However, it was government service that extended horizons farthest, as the Navy and its attendant victuallers and storeships, and the Army and its transports, extended British influence through exploration and war. Though it appears likely that Whitby vessels entered the transport service around the turn of the seventeenth and eighteenth centuries, none of the early voyage books give an indication of this. It is to the muster rolls that we must turn for such evidence, but even they, in their early years, are fairly laconic, simply stating that they were engaged in the transport service, but giving little or no account of their ports of call. Nevertheless, it is known that on Anson's great voyage of 1740–44 in search of the Manila treasure galleon, there was a Whitby-built store-ship.[17] However, one slightly later muster roll, of *Archer*, a 275-ton ship, built in Whitby in 1762, and finally lost in 1796, covers, uniquely among the

17  G. Williams, *The Prize of All the Oceans*, Harper-Collins, 1999, pp. 61–4.

muster rolls, a period of almost fourteen years before the unnamed ship's husband paid the Sixpences due at the Seamen's Hospital. The roll rambles on through the second half of 1775 until the end of 1788. *Archer* returned several times to Whitby after the end of the War of American Independence, but appears to have continued in government service until the end of 1786, when it finally appeared its extensive wanderings were over, and did two years of coal-carrying before submitting its musters.

The roll itself is complex, made up as it must have been from many different sheets of information as one muster ended and another was begun, and it must have sorely taxed the clerk who had to make sense of it and ensure that the requisite sum was paid up in 1788. There are gaps in the information as to where the ship was at certain times, but on the whole it gives a likely picture of the peregrinations of a number of Whitby vessels in times of war. The rolls have been arranged to give the various events in date order. In the original, the order is that of the names of crewmen who came and went at various times. Information technology has enabled that to become an itinerary of a single vessel as it serviced the Army and the Navy during and beyond the American War. That it carried on beyond the Peace of Paris in 1783 simply indicates that there were always troops and equipment to be shipped abroad and back again, and garrisons to be maintained and supplied.

There are several instances of confusion in the dates and times of events and personnel. It must be borne in mind that the sheets from which the clerk was trying to enter the rolls had been across the Atlantic several times, in all weathers. They had been kept, not by a captain's clerk, as would have happened in a naval vessel, but by the master or mate, in difficult circumstances, often using a muster started and kept by several different men during the year, as the unhealthy ports of the southern states of America and the West Indies took their toll of deaths. The Navy would have been hovering, unable to press men from a protected transport, but nonetheless willing to accept volunteers, such as Will White, seaman, who 'entered on board of a King's ship' in March, 1779, presumably lured by the bounty available in wartime. Exotic destinations such as St Lucia and Grenada might be, but complex voyages did not make for stability of crew.

Several men ran at various times, an unusually high number for a Whitby ship. America must have seemed a land of opportunity, and wartime and foreign parts offered far greater openings for change than did the steady trades of northern Europe, in which if a master was fair and conditions aboard were reasonable, there was no great incentive to exchange from one coal-carrier to another except for promotion. One might have a better cook, or have a friend on board, but otherwise crews tended to remain very stable. The North Sea, nicknamed in more recent times 'The Herring Pond', was a closely-knit region, and good or bad masters or vessels were soon known, and ports such as Whitby had tremendous social control.

Table 7.4: The voyages of *Archer* in the Transport Service, 1775–1788

| Master | First name | Port | Date | Event |
|---|---|---|---|---|
| Sippins | John | London | 16/08/1775 | Port of outset. |
| Sippins | John | Portsmouth | 31/12/1775 | End of muster. |
| Coates | William | Portsmouth | 04/01/1776 | Promoted from Mate; new muster. |
| Coates | William | at sea | 03/07/1776 | Death of Second Mate, Will Edmondson. |
| Coates | William | | 07/08/1776 | Peter Carlin and William Atkinson, servants, ran. |
| Coates | William | Jamaica | 12/08/1776 | Robert Ventress, servant, died. |
| Coates | William | Jamaica | 03/09/1776 | James Campbell, seaman, mustered. |
| Coates | William | Portsmouth | 31/12/1776 | End of muster. |
| Coates | William | Portsmouth | 01/01/1777 | New muster. |
| Coates | William | New York | 31/05/1777 | John Little, seaman, discharged. |
| Coates | William | New York | 13/06/1777 | John Swan, seaman, discharged. |
| Coates | William | New York | 13/06/1777 | John Brown, seaman, died. |
| Coates | William | New York | 14/06/1777 | James Blake, seaman, mustered. |
| Coates | William | New York | 31/12/1777 | End of muster. |
| Coates | William | | 01/01/1778 | New muster. |
| Hugell | William | New York | 03/02/1778 | Henry Reed, servant, ran. |
| Hugell | William | New York | 14/02/1778 | John Wing, seaman, mustered. |
| Coates | William | Philadelphia | 03/03/1778 | William Coates, master, died; succeeded by Will Hugell, of London. |
| Hugell | William | Philadelphia | 12/05/1778 | David Stone, seaman, died. |
| Hugell | William | | 01/01/1779 | New muster. |
| Hugell | William | Savannah | 03/02/1779 | Nicholas Dixon, mate, discharged. |

| | | | | |
|---|---|---|---|---|
| Hugell | William | Savannah | 12/02/1779 | John Wing, seaman, ran. |
| Hugell | William | Savannah | 15/02/1779 | James Neat, mate, mustered. |
| Hugell | William | Savannah | 14/03/1779 | Will White, seaman, entered on board of a King's ship. |
| Hugell | William | | 20/04/1779 | James Little, seaman, ran. |
| Hugell | William | | 31/12/1779 | End of muster. |
| Hugell | William | | 01/01/1780 | New muster. |
| Hugell | William | Quebec | 12/07/1780 | James Neat, mate, discharged. |
| Hugell | William | Quebec | 24/07/1780 | James Jenkins mustered as mate. |
| Hugell | William | New York | 20/09/1780 | John Mahong, seaman, discharged. |
| Hugell | William | New York | 25/09/1780 | David Macklin, seaman, discharged. |
| Hugell | William | New York | 05/10/1780 | Will Reed, seaman, mustered. |
| Hugell | William | | 31/12/1780 | End of muster. |
| Hugell | William | | 01/01/1781 | New muster. |
| Hugell | William | Whitby | 15/03/1781 | Return to Whitby. |
| Hugell | William | Whitby | 20/06/1781 | New muster. |
| Hugell | William | | 31/12/1781 | End of muster. |
| Hugell | William | | 01/01/1782 | New muster. |
| Brown | Thomas | New York | 03/04/1782 | Edward Thompson, servant, ran. |
| Brown | Thomas | New York | 12/04/1782 | Joseph Clark, servant, died. |
| Brown | Thomas | New York | 06/05/1782 | James Donal, servant, ran. |
| Brown | Thomas | Portsmouth | 03/08/1782 | James Swan, seaman, impressed. |
| Brown | Thomas | Portsmouth | 03/08/1782 | Carpenter, Robert Scott, and second mate, Will Green, discharged. |
| Brown | Thomas | Portsmouth | 12/08/1782 | John Hunt, carpenter, mustered. |
| Hugell | William | Portsmouth | 01/09/1782 | Master discharged; succeeded by Thomas Brown. |

| Master (cont.) | First name | Port | Date | Event |
|---|---|---|---|---|
| Brown | Thomas | | 31/12/1782 | End of muster. |
| Brown | Thomas | | 01/01/1783 | New muster. |
| Brown | Thomas | St Lucia | 08/03/1783 | Thomas Brown, master, died; succeeded by Henry Reed. |
| Reed | Henry | St Lucia | 06/04/1783 | Richard Pratt, servant, died. |
| Reed | Henry | St Lucia | 10/04/1783 | John Forster, servant, ran. |
| Reed | Henry | St Lucia | 03/05/1783 | James Smithem, seaman, died. |
| Reed | Henry | Grenada | 05/05/1783 | Peter Green, seaman, mustered. |
| Reed | Henry | | 06/06/1783 | Peter Green, seaman, ran. |
| Reed | Henry | | 31/12/1783 | End of muster. |
| Reed | Henry | | 01/01/1784 | New muster. |
| Reed | Henry | Grenada | 06/06/1784 | John Black, Will Wright and Edward White, seamen, mustered. |
| Reed | Henry | London | 02/08/1784 | End of muster. |
| Dunn | William | London | 14/09/1784 | New muster. |
| Dunn | William | London | 12/11/1784 | Discharging and mustering crew; 14 days in port. |
| Dunn | William | Whitby | 04/12/1784 | End of muster. |
| Dunn | William | Whitby | 26/03/1785 | New muster. |
| Rudd | John | | 14/04/1784 | New muster. |
| Rudd | John | London | 29/05/1785 | Discharging and mustering crew; 12 days in port. |
| Rudd | John | Portsmouth | 24/09/1786 | Discharging and mustering crew. |

| Rudd | John | Whitby | 28/11/1786 | End of muster. |
| Rudd | John | London | 01/12/1786 | Two seamen mustered. |
| Rudd | John | Shields | 05/12/1786 | Two seamen discharged. |
| Rudd | John | Shields | 27/01/1787 | End of muster. |
| Rudd | John | Shields | 30/04/1787 | New muster. |
| Rudd | John | London | 07/05/1787 | Discharging crew. |
| Rudd | John | London | 21/05/1787 | Mustering crew. |
| Rudd | John | Cowes | 01/08/1787 | Discharged Thomas Rudd, mate, and Henry Hardy, seaman. |
| Rudd | John | London | 10/11/1787 | Mustering crew. |
| Rudd | John | Shields | 14/11/1787 | End of muster. |
| Rudd | John | Shields | 10/04/1788 | New muster. |
| Rudd | John | London | 10/07/1788 | Discharging and mustering crew; 18 days in port. |
| Rudd | John | London | 02/10/1788 | Discharging and mustering crew; 18 days in port. |
| Rudd | John | Whitby | 31/12/1788 | End of muster. |

Whitby's social control stemmed in part from its relative isolation as a community without near neighbours. The population of the town was relatively stable, with a core of families who had lived there for centuries. The influence of the Society of Friends was another factor; Friends' vessels were well and honestly run. Their rules for themselves were strict, but they were known to be just and fair. Their numbers and success meant that non-Quaker owners also had to be just and fair in order to compete for good crews and good cargoes.

The most important element of social control was undoubtedly the Seamen's Hospital Charity, which would turn away those who were dissolute or otherwise ill-behaved, but who also provided an extra level of welfare for seamen past their working lives and for their dependants, whether they had been incapacitated or had died at sea on a Whitby vessel. It was probably better than the relief provided by the overseer of the poor, especially for seamen on Whitby ships who were not actually resident in Whitby but who were still eligible if the end of their seafaring was on board a Whitby vessel. The disbursement books show many payments to widows and children far from Whitby. In addition, orphans would be apprenticed and could thereby rise up the social ladder. Such benefits were not to be thrown away lightly.

Why did men and boys go to sea? They often went because the opportunities on land or in a town with an impoverished hinterland were few. That was a 'push', as was at times the need to escape from land-based difficulties. However, wages were higher at sea, welfare was deemed better, and there was the excitement of strange places and sights. Even Kings Lynn or Yarmouth with their flat hinterland might seem exotic, and tempting to an older man for whom the inevitable arthritis made the gradients of Whitby's steep streets seem unattractive. He was paid to climb masts, and could use his arms to help him up, but not to climb hills.

London was a great magnet, and so were European ports, with strange tongues, strange dress and customs, and goods to purchase. Even the poorest Whitby homes could contain small items of foreign origin. The food was probably better than was affordable on land-based wages, and it was provided free of charge. There is no record anywhere of deductions from wages for food. And above all there was the comradeship of being part of a crew, entirely dependent on each other for company, and for safety and survival. The work was hard, disciplined and often dangerous, but it was not solitary, unlike much agricultural work in a pastoral landscape. There was even social control over masters, for if they struck and injured a crewman so that he had to have medical treatment, they were not reimbursed by the Hospital. For every claim for expenses witness statements had to be produced from senior members of the crew as to how an injury was sustained. Sometimes such claims were turned down, presumably due to lukewarm witnesses. Bad masters would soon be known and avoided where possible.

The surviving petitions to the Seamen's Hospital demonstrate the risks to which seamen were subject in the merchant fleet, particularly in the North Sea trades. There must have been many more petitions than have survived, and there is other evidence of vessels lost either by wreck or foundering, or even deliberately by being sunk to create a sheltered area close inshore for landing troops and stores, but the extant petitions provide evidence of the individual risk, and the proportion of each kind of injury or loss.

Table 7.5: Seamen's Hospital petitions, by type of injury or cause of death

| Nature or cause of injury | Injured | Dead | Captured |
|---|---|---|---|
| Water immersion | 1 | 88 | |
| Struck by snapped rigging | 5 | | |
| Struck by sails | 1 | 1 | |
| Struck by masts or yards | 3 | | |
| Fall from masts or yards | 3 | 1 | |
| Fall into hold | 2 | 2 | |
| Fall from boat | 1 | 2 | |
| Sickness | 1 | 1 | |
| Injured by implements | 3 | | |
| Gunpowder/shot | 2 | 1 | |
| Enemy action | | 1 | |
| Other | 7 | 2 | |
| Totals | 30 | 99 | 1 |

(Source: WLP/Seamen's Hospital Petitions)

Of the 130 surviving petitions, by far the largest number of requests for aid are for the dependants of men who have been drowned. Nine of the injuries were caused by the rigging, five of them by 'back-lashing' – injury caused by the snapping of a rope under tension, still a high risk in the fishing industry today. Sharp implements such as carpenters' adzes, or axes, or the many knives carried on board, also caused injury sufficiently bad to maim the victim. Handspikes, the most frequently purchased implements listed in the voyage accounts, which were the universal levers on board, were sharp at one end, as were fids made of dense and heavy *lignum vitae*, and could cause considerable injuries.

The muster rolls for 1757–79 show evidence of the importance of Whitby's stable and usually locally-recruited crews, and must reflect the situation that occurred within the unrecorded earlier crews. The depredations of the press-gang show in the sudden high number of foreign crew members, as well as many from other British ports. Crews changed frequently during the sailing year, and accidents happened. Men accustomed to working in a familiar team could be disorientated by language problems, or even sheer ignorance of procedure in emergencies. Far more deaths and serious injuries were recorded in wartime. Men 'ran' as they did from *Archer* in a later war.

A sample of thirteen of the fifty-four Whitby vessels engaged as transports during the Seven Years' War, sailing to Canada and the West Indies, suffered twenty-six desertions and twenty deaths, mainly from fever in the Indies. One death was of the master of the *True Briton*, who died while helping to heave the ship down for cleaning or repairing the bottom of the hull, in Antigua. That would have been an appalling task, without proper facilities, in high temperatures, and probably worse, high humidity.

The weather was another hazard, causing most of the deaths by drowning, but also causing the chest ills which affected seamen. The raw cold of the deck on the North Sea would be followed by the 'fug' which could be created below decks, complete with tobacco smoke. There is anecdotal evidence that in very bad cold weather men would caulk round every fissure below to keep out the draught. This was probably exaggerated, but draught exclusion would be a skill learnt early for use in the bad weather at each end of the sailing season.

Men and boys from Whitby have gone to sea for at least a millennium. Whitby was already a port when the abbey was refounded in 1078. Whitby's is an exemplar for many other fleets, some greater throughout the millennium, and some whose fortunes have risen and fallen, at times in apposition to those of Whitby, fleets such as the great Tudor coal-fleet of Ipswich, or the fleets of ports now silted up, like Chester.

For many men it was a cherished way of life; for others it was all that was available. Men often left the sea in their late twenties or thirties, to invest good wages in some small enterprise or other. The age-range of masters is of interest; they were at the height of their careers, comparatively well paid, with the opportunity to invest, to carry cargo, to make small sums in the money markets of foreign ports. Yet even they came ashore before the toll of rheumatics and chest ailments killed them off; one third of them died at sea, the others rarely served after the age of fifty.

Figure 7.4: The age range of masters, Muster Rolls, 1747–1749

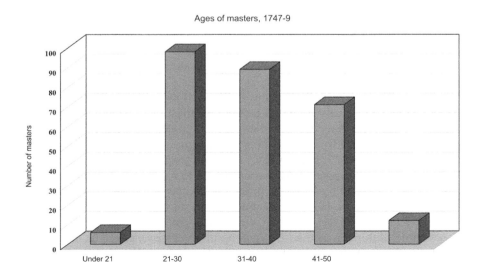

As this chapter has shown, there was much to attract men to sea, and for many the sea remained in their blood, their shipmates perhaps the only family they knew, for all their lives. For others it was a way to spend youth, and find a way to social advancement. It paid more than work on shore, it fed and housed men and gave some excitement to their lives. Above all, perhaps, it set them apart from their fellow men.

# Conclusion

The shipping industry is unlike any other, in that it takes place largely in a very unstable element, far from the land in which its financial investors are based. Like agriculture and horticulture, it is dependent on the weather, but even those ancient means of earning a livelihood are rooted in the land. Mining, as distinct from quarrying, takes place below the surface of the land, and is in its own way an industry whose workforce labours beyond the element on which most of us live. Yet even that is closely linked by geography to the source of capital.

Shipping is unique in that it is absolutely dependent on trust. Its laws are the oldest codified system which protects all the participants, even down to the smallest boy. It protects the owners, the masters, the merchants who entrust their goods to the vessel, and the ordinary men who work in the vessel itself. What other terrestrially-based owner sees the means of earning a living disappearing routinely from view for months on end, yet trusts a group of comparative strangers to bring home not only a profit, but also the vessel, the means of repeating the exercise? Even a medieval tradesman sending his goods by a carrier to a market several days away retained at home the means of making further goods.

A ship makes money only when it is at sea, because it is the voyage itself, as a means of distribution, that generates the income. The owner or owners, who might number as many as forty, could go with the vessel to ensure its security, but the cost of feeding them would make the voyage unprofitable, and in any case an owner at sea is not in a position to do the networking that will ensure future cargoes. Hence, unless the vessel was very small, with one or two owner-masters, the owner must engage a master and crew to undertake the voyage and negotiate for a return cargo and bring the vessel home, wind and weather and enemy action permitting. It was, as far as can be seen from the Whitby evidence, a trust honoured for the most part in the observance. The law of the sea must play a large part in this; the causes for breach of trust which appear in the provincial Admiralty courts often have a strident indignation about them which implies that such occurrences were not routinely expected.

Bartholomew Gill, sailing a Whitby ketch, clearly received a better offer from someone in a European port and did not bother to return either profit or vessel to its indignant owner.[1] That seafaring was a close-knit industry, however, was shown by the reported sightings of Gill in Antwerp and other ports. The gaps in the record fail to show his return. Having once cast himself adrift,

---

[1] Borthwick/Admiralty Cause Papers, 1675, Abel Grant's cause for the loss of his cargo.

Gill would have been unwilling to face the consequences of what was in effect piracy.[2]

That the smaller Admiralty courts contain such causes probably indicates that they were rare, that the pressures of the community kept the trust going, so that breaches were comparatively few, whether in the treatment of crews or in the honesty of transactions. The law laid down the keeping of records of purchases, so that the master of a vessel who starved his crew would soon come to notice, when the state, and the voiced opinions, of the discharged seamen were set against the figures in the accounts.

It is incumbent on the maritime historian to bear this need for trust in mind, along with the strange circumstances in which this industry functioned, out of sight and beyond the control of the entrepreneurs who financed it. For the crews there was always an escape from ill-treatment, by simply 'jumping ship', taking their beds with them to indicate they had done so. There were always other masters in need of crew in other ports.[3] For the investors, there were just the seemingly endless weeks of waiting for the vessel to return.

Of course there would be 'creative accounting'. That most skilled navigator and respected master, Thomas Rogers of *Judith*, 1677–82, kept an immaculate account of every penny spent in several ports on his last voyage in 1681. He had his charter-party, from the Earl of Mulgrave, and *Judith's* owners, including either himself or his father, signed off the accounts, quite satisfied with them all. However, not one of the ports in which he purchased victuals or chandlery has any record of his passage, because he entered none. To have done so would have incurred harbour and other dues, to be written in the ledgers of each port. An anonymous ship's boat, one of dozens rowing purposefully up and down and in and out of the harbour or estuary, could do all the purchasing, while the ketch itself sat quietly, possibly even out of sight, in the offing. Thomas accounted for 104 days at sea, without ever revealing what the charter was for.

Beyond the period covered by this book, Whitby's shipping industry continued to flourish. Its ship-building, ably discussed by Stephanie Jones in her thesis, equalled that of larger ports, and earned it the kind of reputation that led the Admiralty to choose Whitby-built ships for Cook's voyages of exploration, and earlier, the *Anna* for Anson, and to hire a large number of Whitby vessels as store-ships, victuallers and transports.[4] A count of those listed in Weatherill's unique volume shows fifty-four Whitby ships supporting the Navy during the Peninsular campaign in 1814.[5] Two, *Fishburn* and *Golden Grove*, sailed in company round the world with the First Fleet to Botany Bay, though

---

2   G. Morgan and P. Rushton, *Rogues, Thieves, and the Rule of Law*, UCL Press, 1998, pp. 45–6, describes the Sutton case, in which a rogue English master became a French privateer, and captured a British merchant ship. Most noteworthy was the refusal of the government to tackle the problem.

3   The numbers of men recorded in muster rolls as having 'run' during wartime is indicative of this.

4   S. K. Jones, 'A Maritime History of the Port of Whitby 1700–1914', unpubd PhD thesis, University College, London, 1982

5   R. Weatherill, *The Ancient Port of Whitby and its Shipping*, Horne, Whitby, 1908.

as storeships rather than as convict transports. That gruesome trade, however, engaged the ships of the Barry family in the early nineteenth century.[6]

The same Barry family took advantage of the East India Act of 1813 to enter the Far East trade. One of its captains, Captain Edward Theaker, master of *Earl of Eldon*, earned admiration from the public by accomplishing one of the great small boat voyages of the nineteenth century, when his cargo of cotton, loaded under protest in the monsoon, spontaneously combusted over 1,000 miles from land in the Indian Ocean. Captain Theaker saved all the crew and passengers, including a four-month-old baby and brought them safely to Mauritius.[7]

The lure of the Indies, however, started a movement which heralded the eventual decline of Whitby as a major merchant port. Norrison Coverdale bought the 579-ton ship, named *Coverdale*, from Fishburn's yard, and, mindful that the East India Company would only hire ships registered on the Thames, moved himself and his new ship to London. Thence, with a Whitby master, Benjamin Gowland, The Honourable Company's Extra Ship *Coverdale* sailed twice to India, with troops out and a cargo of indigo back.[8]

Coverdale was followed by others of Whitby's ship-owning families, some of whom went north to Newcastle and others south to London. Whitby's harbour was becoming too small, as larger ships were built and bought, and in any case wealth and influence inevitably led to politicisation and gentrification, and the long-established practice of indenturing sons to other shipowners and merchants lapsed. The close networks inherent in membership of the Society of Friends gradually collapsed, as new generations pushed against the constraints of marriage within the Society. The most important Quaker family of all, the Chapmans, reached equal heights in the shipping politics of London. Abel became leader of the ship-owning elite, and William became the first Chairman of the reconstituted Lloyds in 1838.

In the middle of the eighteenth century Whitby entered the whaling trade, sending highly successful ships and skilled masters to the Greenland Sea and later, as the stock of whales declined, to the Davis Straits.[9] Two of its masters, William Scoresby senior, and his son, also William, are still remembered, respectively, for William senior's invention of the crow's nest, and for his son's scientific work on the qualities of snow and on the magnetic compass.[10] The whaling trade lasted eighty years, though it diminished greatly until the last Whitby whaler, *Camden*, came back 'clean' (empty) in 1837.

---

6  J. Howard, *Bound to Van Diemen's Land*, NYCRO, 1995.

7  J. Howard, *Captain Edward Theaker, Master Mariner Extraordinary*, University of Hull, 1993.

8  IOR L/MAR/B/347A and 347B, Logs of the Honourable East India Company's Extra Ship *Coverdale*.

9  G. Young, *History of Whitby*, 2 vols, Whitby, 1817, pp. 562–68, gives a good contemporary account of Whitby's whalers; T. Barrow, *The Whaling Trade of North-East England, 1750–1850*, University of Sunderland Press, 2001, and A. Credland, *The Hull Whaling Trade*, Hutton Press, 1995, give a much more modern overview of the northern whaling trade.

10  C. I. Jackson (ed.), *The Arctic Whaling Journals of William Scoresby the Younger*, vols 1, 2 and 3, Hakluyt Society Series III, Volumes 12, 20 and 21.

The fishing industry, reduced in the eighteenth century to nine vessels, gradually reasserted itself, especially with the advent of steam, and Whitby became a major herring port in the twentieth century.[11] The railway came in 1836, and within twenty years Whitby had become a genteel watering place, favoured by the Victorian intelligentsia, artists and authors. To Whitby we owe Elizabeth Gaskell's *Sylvia's Lovers*, Lewis Carroll's 'The Walrus and the Carpenter', and Bram Stoker's *Dracula*.

Money once invested in shipping went to build the large boarding houses and hotels that covered the West Cliff. Land once in the hands of a few shipowners who built their country houses outside the town, passed into the hands of speculative builders. Whitby still faced the sea, and 'used' the sea, but its nineteenth-century steamships formed a much smaller fleet, both in vessel tonnage and in number, than did those of other, newer ports. Whitby's last registered merchant ship, *Egton*, was finally deregistered in 1983.

Like those of many seaports, Whitby's fleet suffered, throughout the early and late modern periods, particularly as war and peace alternated. Other ports, like Chester, declined because of silting, or were overtaken by their growing neighbours and creek ports, such as Liverpool. In the same way Harwich overtook its headport of Ipswich. Whitby never rose above its headport of Newcastle-upon-Tyne, but its fleet was a force to be reckoned with for two and a half centuries. It was, almost from the start in the seventeenth century, one of the great carrying fleets of northern Europe. Whitby's shipping was Whitby-owned, and as far as possible, Whitby-manned, but its larger vessels rarely came into the port. The port's decline in the end came from isolation on the landward side, from the narrowness of the estuary, when measured against the great estuaries of the Tyne, the Tees and the Humber, Whitby's closest neighbours, but perhaps also from the political and social ambitions of its best and richest entrepreneurs.

This is the history of the rise of the shipping fleet of one of England's small towns. The towns themselves have in recent years begun to emerge from the shadows of historical research, propelled by urban historians and historical demographers. Much is now known of their political structures, their trades and crafts, and their links to their rural hinterlands. Some, such as Manchester and Leeds, have burgeoned into great cities. Others, like Lavenham and Long Melford, cloth towns of Suffolk, are famous for their antique charm, villages rather than towns.

Many such towns were ports on Britain's long seaboard, and similar fates have befallen them. The shipping of many of the smaller ports has declined or even disappeared. In some respects Whitby was lucky. It too had a harbour bar, and a dangerous reef guarding the entrance to the port. Worse than that, the town had little viable hinterland; 800 square miles of moorland cut it off from

---

11  R. Robinson, *A History of the Yorkshire Coast Fishing Industry 1780–1914*, Hull University Press, 1987, and P. Frank, *Yorkshire Fishing Folk*, Phillimore, 2000, both tell the story of Whitby fishing's rise and fall.

the rest of England. Until the alum industry came in the seventeenth century its only products were the output of pastoral farming and fish, and a small trade in 'crooked timber for boats' knees'.

Yet Whitby stands as an exemplar of what can be done with scarce resources, when a tiny opportunity comes. Whitby never became a large town; its population peaked at 15,000 in the middle of the nineteenth century. However, its people had the entrepreneurial and opportunistic cast of mind which enabled them to rise above the town's inherent disadvantages and put to good use the sheltered harbour and their seafaring skills to profit from this new industry. The alum industry was highly capitalised, and the skills of handling such sums were quickly learnt, as were the skills of networking with the Dutch and Scots fleets that initially serviced the alum banks.

The alum industry never dominated the town after the early years of the seventeenth century. That did not matter, however the fleet was functioning in the seafaring trades to which the early alum voyages had introduced it. It had, above all, learnt that a good reputation and good networking skills could help to overcome other disadvantages. It was those qualities which ensured that every shipping historian has heard of Whitby, perhaps of its ship-building, or its presence in the coal and timber trades, or as the source of Cook's ships or in the whaling industry.

This study takes all these glimpses of Whitby's fleet, and, by using the town's own own hitherto unknown archives, reveals the whole of the rise of Whitby's merchant fleet. Whitby's shipping served the entire known world at one time or another. Hopefully this study will stimulate the examination of other ports and other fleets, and enable a much broader view of the shipping industry and the ports which served it. Meanwhile, because of the universality of seafaring, and its broad uniformity of practice, the hidden documents of Whitby's fleet can stand for the lost records of the fleets of so many other ports, especially on the North Sea coast.

Whitby's vessels carried humdrum cargoes for much of their working lives; no spice trade, *specie* or precious silks and stones for them. These were not Masefield's 'stately Spanish galleons' carrying diamonds and cinnamon and gold moidores. They might not have the salt-caked smoke stacks of a later age, but they carried the same cargo of Tyne coal, even through the Channel, in the same mad March days as did his dirty British coasters.

Their crews slaked the dust of coal by feeding bread-and-butter and tea to a thirsty coal-meter; they cleaned up the ships after regiments of sea-sick soldiers; they hung about the Channel Islands in winter storms to rescue refugees; they went to the Indies, east and west, carrying military stores. They carried, and nurtured, horses and donkeys to America, and cleaned up after them.

Mostly they carried coal or timber or butter or alum or urine or lead. There was no gilding on their carving; they wasted no hard-won cash on figure-heads. They patched and mended sails and 'fished' masts and put in new bits of planking when needed. They hung over the stern putting putty in the leaks under *Flora's* cabin-window frames. They bought new vessels, with new rigging, and promptly added old rope and aged canvas to patch the inevitable wear and tear. They learned how to fother holes in the hull – and that hard-learned skill carried a Whitby-built collier captained by a Whitby-trained Lieutenant James Cook off the Great Barrier Reef and safely round the world.

For a small, remote town built on a north-facing estuary at the edge of an inhospitable moor, with few natural resources or primary products, it was indeed a golden fleet.

# Appendix 1

## The Size of the Fleet

One of the most difficult aspects of shipping history is the lack of reliable data for comparative tonnage figures during the period under study. Davis used the figures obtained from Collectors of Customs for 1629 and 1702 with those from the new returns following the Act requiring registration of all shipping in 1786. Penelope Corfield relied, with caveats as to their reliability, on returns to be found among the Musgrave Papers (British Library, Additional Mss 11,255–6). The preamble to this document states that it is:

> An account of the Tonnage of all Ships and Vessels belonging to each respective Port in England that have traded to or from foreign ports or coastwise or have been employed as Fishing vessels distinguishing each sort and each year and accounting each vessel once for the year.

An accompanying letter dated 21 January 1782 from one J. Dalley at the Custom House makes the point that, during war, especially the War of American Independence, there is an apparent decrease in tonnage due to the number of vessels removed from trade as either privateers or transports. The latter counted as King's ships and did not report inwards or outwards.

Table Appendix 1.1 shows Penelope Corfield's interpretation of the figures for the largest ports in the eighteenth century.[1]

As interpreted by Penelope Corfield, who uses the years 1709, 1751 and 1792 as the most reliable for data, Whitby retained its level as a major port. The figures show Scarborough as the most important ship-owning port in both 1709 and 1751, while Whitby had become fifth outport by 1709, but dropped to tenth by 1751. Whitby's ranking had been restored by 1792, when the figures came from the Register of Shipping. The actual tonnages, of course, are subject to the usual problems of conversion from tonnage burthen to measured tonnage.

The table makes quite clear the discrepancy between the two methods of measuring tonnage, and the sudden leap after 1786 casts considerable doubt on the accuracy of all the tonnages before that date, and therefore on the rankings which Corfield has suggested. It also makes it extremely likely that the size of the national fleet at various times before 1786 has been considerably under-estimated. Dalley himself argued that in time of war privateers and transports did not 'report'. Many Whitby vessels carried Letters of Marque and Reprisal during wartime, but only one, during the War of American Independence, ever took a prize.[2] The Letters of Marque were probably for protection against

---

1    P. J. Corfield, *The Impact of English Towns 1700–1800*, Oxford University Press, 1982, pp. 36–7.
2    D. J. Starkey, 'British Privateering 1702–1783, with Particular Reference to London', unpubd PhD thesis, Exeter University, 1985.

bureaucracy. Furthermore, it is clear from muster rolls and other sources that the Whitby fleet was active in the transport trade during many wars in the eighteenth century and probably earlier, and that would have accounted for the apparent drop in tonnage in 1761–63.

Table Appendix 1.1: Tonnage in principal English ports

| Port belonging | Tons burthen, 000s | Port belonging | Tons burthen, 000s | Port belonging | Tons measured, 000s |
|---|---|---|---|---|---|
| Year | 1709 | | 1751 | | 1792 |
| London | 140 | London | 119 | London | 374 |
| Scarborough | 27 | Scarborough | 33 | Newcastle | 121 |
| Bristol | 16 | Sunderland | 24 | Liverpool | 92 |
| Newcastle | 12 | Newcastle | 22 | Sunderland | 58 |
| Great Yarmouth | 11 | Liverpool | 21 | Hull | 58 |
| Whitby | 11 | Whitehaven | 18 | Whitehaven | 56 |
| Sunderland | 8 | Hull | 16 | Whitby | 51 |
| Hull | 8 | Great Yarmouth | 15 | Bristol | 44 |
| Exeter | 7 | Whitby | 14 | Great Yarmouth | 36 |
| King's Lynn | 7 | King's Lynn | 9 | Scarborough | 26 |
| Liverpool | 6 | Poole | 8 | Poole | 19 |
| Whitehaven | 5 | Exeter | 7 | King's Lynn | 17 |
| Poole | 4 | Lancaster | 2 | Exeter | 13 |
| Lancaster | 1 | Bristol | | Lancaster | 11 |
| All others | 59 | All others | 92 | All others | 211 |
| *All English tonnage* | *320* | *All English tonnage* | *281* | *All English tonnage* | *813* |
| *All outport tonnage* | *180* | *All outport tonnage* | *162* | *All outport tonnage* | *439* |

There is, however, a further source of confusion which Dalley does not mention. He states that each vessel was only accounted once in each year. Since there were many duplications of vessel names within the Whitby fleet at any one time, that alone could have reduced the apparent tonnage of the fleet. Returns, particularly when they are suspected of leading to some kind of levy, or of conscription into an unwanted trade, can be notoriously deficient. The muster rolls of the vessels themselves were often deficient, because of fear of the press-gang in wartime, and dislike of paying the 'sixpence' in peacetime.

On 30 September 1782, Dalley wrote further, enclosing

An account of the Total Tonnage of Shipping employed in the Coasting Trade of in the several ports of England, exclusive of Ships employed in carrying coals, lime, chalk, and manure, also fishing boats as far as the same can be excluded, from 1772 to 1781, both inclusive, distinguishing each Year the Ports to which the Vessels respectively belong and reckoning only one Voyage in a year. J. Dalley.[3]

Sadly there are no extant listings of the tonnage of colliers, or vessels carrying lime or salt, or fishing vessels, but it may be that Dalley had access to such now-lost listings, and that therefore his exclusion of such vessels from his calculations was not as ill thought out as might be supposed. However, it must have reduced the tonnage totals for Whitby and other ports specialising in the coal-trade, to the point where the modern tonnage estimates for these ports are grossly underestimated. Table Appendix 1.2 shows this effect clearly for the port of Sunderland.

Table Appendix 1.2: Tonnage burthen for selected ports, excluding that involved in coal, salt, lime and fishing

| Year | Hull | Liverpool | Newcastle | Sunderland | Whitby |
|------|------|-----------|-----------|------------|--------|
| 1772 | 6009 | 2971 | 2152 | 270 | 5985 |
| 1773 | 6673 | 3318 | 2150 | 280 | 6479 |
| 1774 | 6120 | 3105 | 2180 | 480 | 7111 |
| 1775 | 6090 | 3357 | 2150 | 210 | 4758 |
| 1776 | 6923 | 2787 | 2140 | 330 | 4485 |
| 1777 | 6557 | 4413 | 2130 | 140 | 5185 |
| 1778 | 7622 | 4931 | 2150 | 110 | 3790 |
| 1779 | 8610 | 4022 | 2010 | 250 | 3896 |
| 1780 | 8533 | 3662 | 2060 | 130 | 5666 |
| 1781 | 8906 | 3881 | 2080 | 80 | 4466 |

(Source: BL/Additional Ms 11,256)

Whitby had many vessels almost exclusively involved in the coal trade, so the substantial figures given in this table suggest that there was a considerable tonnage of shipping over and above the specialist and, in wartime, 'King's' vessels. The last seven years of the table are the years of the War of American Independence, when Whitby's fleet is known to have been expanding, and when many of its larger vessels would have been involved in the naval transport service.

Acknowledgement of the problem goes no way towards correcting it. However, there are two later, but pre-registration, documents relevant to Whitby which serve to show just how wildly astray the figures for tonnage in

3   BL/Musgrave Papers, Additional Mss 11,255–6.

the eighteenth century can be, and to show just how important Whitby was as a ship-owning port.

The first of these sources relates to the year 1773, after the Seven Years' War and before the War of American Independence. It is a transcript of a notebook, now no longer accessible, which listed each vessel belonging to Whitby, giving its tonnage deadweight or burthen, its measured tonnage and its capacity, in keels of coal (at 20 tons to a keel).[4]

During the mid 1700s several subscriptions were raised for fighting funds, to fight either government regulation or the supposed intransigencies of Newcastle-upon-Tyne, but of the two listings which survive, neither represents even the whole of the collier fleet of Whitby. Many known owners did not subscribe, so that the 121 vessels recorded in one list and 88 in another, while interesting as evidence of the existence of given vessels at certain dates, are useless for an overall picture of the fleet. However, on 2 March 1773, an unknown person commenced, in the small notebook referred to above, a comprehensive list of the vessels belonging to Whitby. There were later interpolations, without tonnage being given, and some vessels were later described as lost, taken, presumably in the War of American Independence, or sold. Even some changes of name were noted.

The 1773 list gives the most comprehensive picture of the state of Whitby's fleet at any one time, better even than the Port Register of 1786, for which 'registrations' came in so slowly that it is very difficult to obtain an exact 'snapshot' for that year. The muster rolls also suffered from late registration; some owners paid for up to ten years at a time, and even with modern data processing it is very difficult to know exactly what the state of the fleet was at any one time.

This transcript, however, is of a contemporary list of the state of the fleet on almost one day; given, perhaps, the possibility of the loss of the odd vessel as yet unrecorded.[5] That there should be such a loss was unlikely, since the average annual loss was probably only 4–5 per cent of the total, and would have amounted to around twelve vessels per annum. The 'snapshot' must have been as accurate as the writer's memory allowed. He listed 233 vessels, of 72,050 tons burthen, from 'one-sails' of 40 tons to very large ships and barques of up to 600 tons.

The unknown compiler gives the rule of thumb by which Whitby owners and masters converted tonnage burthen to measured tonnage. The so-called 'registered tonnage' is never mentioned and the term was probably never used in Whitby. The ratio seems to have been three measured tons to four tons burthen. Coal capacity was greater still, given that it was a high-bulk cargo carried loose in the hold. *Three Sisters* measured 240 tons, by which its purchase price

---

4   WLP/ Burnett Papers/PB5032; Percy Burnett was Clerk to Whitby Rural District Council for many years, and devoted his spare time to collecting and transcribing documents relevant to the history of Whitby. After his death he bequeathed his collections to Whitby Museum, but sadly some documents were apparently sold and some dispersed. Where it has been possible to check, however, his work was accurate.

5   Davis, p. 87.

was calculated; its deadweight or burthen tonnage was 320 tons, but its voyage books show that it routinely carried 400 tons of coal, the 20 keels recorded in Burnett's transcript.

Yet in that same year, BL Additional Ms 11,256 records a tonnage burthen for Whitby of 6,479, to which Dalley was presumably able to add the now-lost total of specialised tonnage, making, perhaps double the quantity, some 13,000 tons. However, that was only one-fifth of the total tonnage recorded in the port itself. Given that the figures collated and retained within the port were more likely to be accurate than any sent to authority, this begs the question as to the true size of the national fleet at this time. Corfield suggests that in 1751 the national fleet measured 420,000 tons; if the 'factor' shown by the Whitby evidence is accepted and true for every port, then the national fleet would have contained 2.1 *million* tons of shipping.[6] If the figures suggested by the Whitby list apply to Whitby alone, then Whitby should have ranked far higher than any other port outside London.

Were that the only instance in which the local figures differed from the national figures, then one might treat the local figures as an aberration. However, in 1782, the penultimate year of the War of American Independence, Francis Gibson wrote an impassioned plea for the augmentation of the defences of Whitby.[7] To it he attached formidable statistics and elegant maps.

Francis Gibson was Customer, then, initially, Lieutenant of Volunteers, later Commanding Officer of the Militia in Whitby, during the last two decades of the eighteenth century. He was also a cartographer, poet and playwright, kept the minutes of various organisations involved with shipping in Whitby, corresponded with the Russia Company and was a man central to Whitby's shipping affairs. In 1782, as Lieutenant of the Whitby Volunteers, he petitioned the Master General of the Ordnance to provide better defences for Whitby, during the War of American Independence.[8] His petition was accompanied by a plan and chart of the town and harbour and by a sheaf of papers containing statistical details about Whitby's trade. Among his statistics is the information that Whitby's fleet consisted of 320 ships of 78,000 tons 'King's measure-ment', a measure which probably, as does the measurement after 1786, equates with the measured tonnage quoted in the 1773 list. If this figure is multiplied up to the tonnage burthen suggested by that source, then the tonnage burthen of the Whitby fleet was 104,000. Yet Dalley calculated the non-specialised ton-nage for Whitby for the previous year, 1781, as 4,466 tons burthen, laughably short of Gibson's totals. All the energies of Whitby's busy ship-yards, capable of building up to twenty-five large vessels a year, could not have made such a difference in a single year.

Gibson included demographic statistics in his appeal, but these are seri-ously over-estimated, and as such were criticised by George Young, the first

6   Corfield, p. 37.
7   Francis Gibson was a polymath whose poetry and plays were widely read, and even produced at Drury Lane.
8   TNA/T1/430.

historian of Whitby, whose work was published in 1816.[9] However, Young was the Presbyterian minister in Whitby, and therefore much more aware of the size of households and the number of people in the town than was Francis Gibson, while Gibson, as Collector of Customs, was much more likely to be accurate about his shipping statistics. He was, of course, trying to make a serious point to a senior political figure, so exaggeration may have featured in his arguments. Gibson recorded *nine* times as great a tonnage as did the official figures. Certainly Dalley's comments about the low returns during the war applied, for a large number of Whitby's larger vessels were employed as transports and carried Letters of Marque so that they did not have to report.

After 1786, the figures were collated nationally from the registers and the figures, as seen in Table Appendix 1.1 above, reflect more accurately the state of the fleet. What the two local documents showing the differences between the national and the local estimates do is show that if other such local documents could be traced, then a far more accurate picture of the national fleet before 1786 could be obtained.

Dalley was apparently an enthusiastic statistician, but without all the evidence which he presumably amassed in a long career, it is impossible to estimate the true size of England's national fleet. Suffice to say that the two Whitby documents suggest that it was a great deal larger than has ever been realised. So too was the fixed and working capital of such a fleet. Perhaps it is time for the economic historians to take another look at Britain's seafaring wealth.

---

9   G. Young, *History of Whitby*, 2 vols, Whitby, 1817, p. 514.

# Appendix 2

## Pressgang Instructions

A copy of instructions to officers employed in the impress service; no date, but eighteenth century hand (source: WLP):

*By the Commissioners for Executing the Office of Lord High Admiral of Great Britain and Ireland, &c, &c, &c, -*

Instructions to Lieutenants of His Majesty's ships appointed to impress &c for the service of His Majesty's Fleet

**Ist** Whereas you will receive herewith a warrant empowering you to impress seamen for the service of His Majesty's Fleet, you are hereby strictly required and directed, carefully and diligently to attend the said service, and in the execution thereof to observe the following instructions, &c, &c.

You are to keep the said warrant in your own Custody & execute the same personally and never entrust it in the charge of any other.

**II** You are not to impress any Landmen, but only seamen and seafaring men, or such as are directed in the Impress warrants, and of these only such as are able and fit for his Majesty's Service, and not to take up boys or infirm persons, in order to magnify the number upon your accounts & bring on unnecessary charge upon his Majesty.

**III** You are not to impress any Boatswains, Carpenters, or First Mates, belonging to Merchant ships of Fifty Tons and upwards, or any Masters of small vessels.

**IIII** You are not to impress any whose names are entered in a Protection signed by us, though not exactly described provided they are actually in the ship or on the service for which they are protected, but if there are more seamen in the ship than the Protection is granted for, you are to impress those who are supernumerary, but not those who are duly protected in the said number.

**V** You are not to impress any men who are protected under the Hands of Three or more of the Commissioners of the Navy, or Victualling, or of the principal Officers of the Ordnance & the Seal of these respective offices, provided they are actually employed in the service of these offices.

**VI** You are to observe that protections are intended to protect only those Seamen, who are actually in the ship, or working near the ship, & and in the service of the ship, but if any men go on shore with the Protection it shall not, only be of use to Protect men ashore but these who are in the ship shall be liable to be impressed during the absence of the Protection.

**VII** You are not to impress any men being the age of 55 years or upwards, or any youth not the full age 18,: or any Foreigner, or any Landman whatsoever age he shall be, who shall use the sea, until he have served two full years to be completed from the time of his first going to sea; nor any person, who not having before used the sea, that shall bind himself apprentice to serve at sea, until he have served the full space of three years to be completed from the time of his binding himself apprentice; all such persons as are under the above description being exempted from being impressed by Act of Parliament. But if you shall find that Protections have been obtained from us by surprise for any person pretending to be under one of the above cases who are not really under the circumstances for which they are protected, you are to impress the person who shall appear to you to have imposed upon us, & send the Protection to our Secretary, but you are not to meddle with the other seamen who are protected.

**VIII** You are not to impress any Harpooneers, Boatsteerers, Line managers or Seamen who shall be in or belong to any ship or vessel in the Greenland Fishery trade from the said service, Harpooneers, Boatsteerers, Line managers or Seamen during the time of the year when they are not employed in the said Fishery Trade & have given security to the satisfaction of the Commissioners of the Customs that he or they shall proceed in the said ship or Vessel to Greenland or the Davis Straights on the whale fishery the next season, they may sail in the collier trade without being liable to be impressed.

**IX** And whereas the watermen belonging to each Insurance Office not exceeding 30 to each office are free by law from being impressed or compelled to go to sea, their names and place of abode being first registered in this office, you are to have a regard thereto.

**X** When you go on board any Merchant ship or vessel in order to get a seaman from her, you are first to call the crew upon deck & let them know that if any of them will declare willing to serve his Majesty & go with you, they shall receive two months' pay advance, before the ship they are to serve in proceed to sea, but otherwise if they refuse to go without your impressing them they will be excluded from that advantage, and when you take men from Merchant ships you are to take care they carry along with them their Clothes & Bedding.

**XI** When you take any seaman out of any ship or vessel homeward bound, as shall be proper, you are to put aboard of her an equal or sufficient number of good seamen in their room, under the care of a discreet officer, to whom you are to give directions to assist in navigating the ship safely to the place of her unloading, or any nearer port that the Master shall desire, and not to quit her sooner on any pretence whatsoever, and as you are strictly forbid yourself, so are you as strictly to charge the said officers and seamen not to demand any money or other gratification whatsoever upon that account, as you and they shall answer at your perils.

**XII** You are to give tickets of leave to men you send in Merchant ships for such time as you shall judge reasonable for their return to your ship, & if you send them into the River of Thames, you are to draw out a list of their names, and certificate at the foot thereof in the following form & you are to deliver the same sealed to the officer you send up, with directions, when he had seen the ship moored in safety, to repair with his men to the Clerk of the Cheques at Deptford, & to deliver the same sealed Certificate to him, who will thereupon give them Condition money back to their ship, & will indorse upon the ticket of leave, the time when and the sums paid them for that purpose.

# Appendix 3

## The Naming of Ships

One of the most intriguing aspects of maritime history is the considerable variety of names which were given to vessels by their owners. Vessels were, as explained earlier, identified by their names, followed by the surname of the master and the port 'belonging'. The last part, before the registration of shipping became universal, could seem an arbitrary concept, especially as it might well be wrongly recorded by the official at a port where a vessel had called. Variations in spelling had much to do with the way in which the names of ports might be recorded. Bridlington, in the East Riding of Yorkshire, often appears as 'Burlington', even in the records of neighbouring ports. Brightlingsea, in Essex, was easily confused with 'Brighthelmstone', or Brighton, in Sussex. The spelling of surnames was not finally stabilised until universal education arrived in 1870. Regional accents probably added to the confusion.

Even so, given a large enough sample from which to extrapolate, it is possible to discern the ways in which names were chosen. Given that they were probably carved into either the stem or the stern of even quite small vessels, they were probably less likely to be mis-spelt than the names of either masters or ports.

Many vessels were simply given personal names, possibly of the managing owner or a member of his family. These were often 'homely' names, diminutives or pet names of children. Some of course, were more dignified, indicative of the owner's status, at least in his own eyes. *Nancy*, a frequent choice over many decades, somehow seems more affectionate than *Harrison Chilton*, named after the early nineteenth-century owner. Brothers and sisters, sons and daughters, wives and parents were all commemorated. Sometimes the difficult business of choosing between siblings was solved by group names, like that of *Three Sisters*. Double names, adding *William* to *Jane*, as in the early eighteenth century, were common.

Places were also used, adding to confusion in documents. Whitby appears several times as a vessel's name in the eighteenth and early nineteenth centuries. So too do topographical names, such as *Esk*, from the river whose estuary was so important to the town. Indications of a classical education might spur new owners to call their vessels by names such as *Dryad*, *Nymph* or *Boreas*.

Many vessels were given names that reflected the allegiances, political, social or religious, of their principal shareholders. This was, of course, a way of networking, and finding customers. The Whitby fleet was a carrying fleet, seeking cargoes and transporting them wherever they were needed. The 'reactionary' *Earl of Eldon* must have left little doubt as to the Barry family's frame of political mind in the early nineteenth century. There was a *Freemason*, and several overtly Quaker names – *Brotherly Love, Friends' Adventure* and *Friendship*, as well as the now misunderstood *Freelove*, meaning 'grace'. Some names managed to look more ways than one; in 1752 was launched *Liberty and Property*, a Quaker phrase, favoured by William Penn. However, it was also the war-cry of the only English Jacobite regiment during the 1745/6 rebellion. It is of interest that during the *diaspora* which followed the '45, no fewer than twenty Highland surnames found their way into the Whitby parish registers. James Watt of Orkney, apprenticed to Jonas Brown of Whitby, was the son of 'William Watt the Jacobite' released from the Tower of London in 1747 to carry home the 'general pardon'.[10]

Abstract qualities which might appeal to a potential employer of shipping were also used. There were *Swift*, and *Speedy, Endeavour, Resolution* and *Fly*. One has to wonder about *Haddock*, but it may have been a surname, or perhaps an indication that the vessel could survive in the North Sea, where it usually plied its trade. There were other prosaic names: *Traveller's Habitation* carried coal and alum in the seventeenth century, as did vessels with more delicate names, like *Midsummer Blossom* and *Seaflower*. A century later, there was *Flora*, owned by Jonas Brown, who was willing to 'article' a Jacobite boy – was it called for Flora MacDonald?

Hero-worship had its place. The names of famous admirals were often given to vessels, as were those of generals. Perhaps the best known vessel so honoured now is *General Carleton*, named after General Guy Carleton, Governor of Quebec at the start of the War of American Independence.[11]

That the newspapers were intrigued by vessel names is perhaps best illustrated by the entry in the *Newcastle Chronicle* which dealt with the problems caused by the Baltic embargo of 1800–01. The following is extracted from the *Newcastle Chronicle* of 17 January 1801:

> The embargo laid by Russia on the English shipping is a much more serious evil than we at first imagined. From a list of vessels it appears the Emperor has by it provided himself with *Admiral Nelson, Lord Rodney, Earl Howe*, and several others of our best Admirals. Thus supported, no wonder that he has taken from us our *Commerce*, our *Prosperity*, our *Performance, Industry* and *Resolution*, leaving us without our *Fortune, Friendship, Union, Concord, Peace, Amity* and *Hope*. He has parcelled out all *Albion*, and possessed himself of *Manchester, Bedford*, etc., and deprived us of the *Prince of Wales, Lord Carrington*, and a long train of fashionable *Nymphs, Betseys, Annes, Fannys* and *Marys*. Even the winds of heaven are not suffered to visit us, as he has seized upon *Zephyr, Boreas* etc. In this situation, we are left without *Expedition, Enterprise* and *Chance*.

---

10 OA/D2 and D3, Papers of Balfour and of Watt of Breckness. The letters of James Watt and his wife, spanning 40 years, and sent to family in Orkney, are a useful source for the social side of Whitby's shipping in the second half of the eighteenth century.

11 S. Baines, 'The History of *General Carleton*, and some of those connected with her', in W. Ossowski (ed.), *The* General Carleton *Shipwreck*, Gdansk, 2008, pp. 66-9.

Most whimsical, or perhaps ironic, were two vessels laid down during the white heat of the Napoleonic Wars, but launched in the peace – and slump in shipping – that followed. One, a ship of 356 tons, launched during the '100 days' of supposed peace in 1814, was named *Regret*, and the other, a 131-ton barquentine, laid down after the war had restarted, was named *Crisis* in 1816.

# Appendix 4

## The Burnett Papers

A major source of information about Whitby is kept in Whitby Museum and known collectively as The Burnett Papers. The late Percy Burnett (1903–1972) was Deputy Treasurer to Whitby Urban District Council. He assembled a very large collection of manuscripts, both loose-leaf and books, and transcribed these, translating from Latin where necessary. This collection was bequeathed to Whitby Literary and Philosophical Society on his death, and was largely deposited in North Yorkshire County Record Office. Where both the original document and the transcript can be compared, it is clear that Burnett's work was meticulous.

Burnett also made transcripts of other documents which remained in private hands. From time to time the originals of such transcripts re-surface and can be photocopied if not acquired. When this happens and comparison is made with the transcript, it is again clear that the work was accurate. It is safe, therefore, to assume that where documents exist only in Burnett's transcripts, and the original can no longer be traced, such transcripts are almost certainly equally accurate.

# Glossary and Definitions

A vessel was generally defined in official documents by its name, and usually by its master's name, with its home port, and less often, particularly in the early modern period, by its tonnage or rig. Thus the vessel might be recorded as, '*Judith*, Rogers, of Whitby'. This is one of the areas in which Rediker's work makes comparison difficult, since, he, with other historians, fails to use this means of identifying vessels, despite its almost universal use in the archives. Whether tonnage, the means by which the cost of the hull was calculated, or the tonnage burthen, a vessel's theoretical capacity, is measured is not always clear in the documents. The importance attached to the master's name reveals much of the way in which the two were perceived as a unit. The master was often part-owner, acted as agent, ship's husband or factor, and was often retained for many years, even in vessels whose crew changed with much greater frequency.

Since this book deals with a highly technical subject, it is important to make some of the terminology quite clear. The industry with which this book deals is correctly referred to as 'shipping'. The same collective noun may be used for groups of vessels in given circumstances. However, 'shipping' was not necessarily made up of 'ships'. In the period of the study, shipping was made up of many sailing vessels, some of which, but only some, were ships.

## Terminology

**Buoyage**: the fee paid for passing a fixed buoy indicating either a channel or a natural hazard or a wreck.

**Brig**: a vessel with two square-rigged masts, anything from 60 to 150 tons.

**Charter**: the practice of hiring a vessel to undertake a specific voyage either to deliver a cargo or to pick one up and return it to the charterer. The legal document which bound both the charterer and the master was called a 'charter-party'.

**Corrodians**: medieval religious houses often accepted 'corrodians' as permanent guests in return for endowments or large gifts of money or property. Sometimes the Crown presented such guests as a reward for services rendered.

**Displacement**: modern shipping, with its carefully marked 'Plimsoll' lines, measures accurately the difference in displacement between fresh and saline water, and indeed between seas which are of variable salinity.[1] *Judith* (1677–82) undertook voyages to London, which was tidal and saline, and Rouen, which was a river port on the Seine in France, and though certainly tidal, with a notorious bore like that of the Severn, certainly much less saline. The conditions must have produced some differential in freeboard which were visible to the experienced eye. Unfortunately Rogers made no comment in his voyage accounts, yet in fact he appears to have carried the same amount of cargo both in river and in off-shore trade. It may be that the Seine varies less in this respect, since Rogers's voyages to Rouen were very successful. It would be of interest to consider river trade on the Humber or the Severn to see whether or not adjustments had to be made. Inland water transport was cheaper than road transport, but for a salt-water vessel to have taken to fresh-water work must in theory have affected the sale price of the goods relative to the reduced cargo, and must also have varied the amount of ballast carried. Fresh water and tidal rivers also meant more stops to allow for the rise and fall of tides, and these are clearly shown as 'postidge' in the voyage accounts of Rogers's *Judith*.

**Factoring**: the practice of buying cargo at the port of outset, and selling it at the destination. Some vessels engaged in long-distance voyages carried a 'supercargo' whose responsibility this was, but in practice in the North Sea fleet it was the master who factored the cargo, unless he had been chartered.

**Fleet**: the term is normally used as a collective noun for a group of vessels, often thought by laymen to be naval in application. In this study, it has several definitions, each of which will be clear whenever the term is used. The assumption will be, unless otherwise stated, that the term is used in its mercantile context. The term may be used to describe the total stock of merchant shipping belonging to a single nation, such as the English, the Dutch or the Scots. It may also indicate a large number of vessels sailing at any one time to a single destination, such as the Baltic, or else on a particular trade, such as fishing, or carrying convicts to the colonies. Some such fleets have become immortalised, particularly the 'First Fleet', which reached Port Jackson with the first convicts and settlers in New South Wales in 1788, and included two Whitby-built vessels. The shipping stock of a particular port, such as Whitby or Bristol, may be described as a fleet, and so may the group of vessels managed by a single owner or company.

**Knees**: naturally-grown curved timber used to construct the brackets supporting deck beams where they join the ribs of the hull.

**Lightage**: a fee prepaid or collected en route for passing a specific navigation light, such as a leading-light guiding shipping into a particular port or channel,

---

1  E. A. Stokoe, *Reed's Ship Construction for Marine Engineers*, Reed, 1964, pp. 113-15, quoting the Load Line Rules of 1932 which were formed by an international convention: The freeboard marking for moving from salt to fresh water is based on the calculation:

Fresh Water Allowance $\dfrac{\Delta}{40T}$ inches

where $\Delta$ is the displacement and T the tons per inch immersion.

or a warning lighthouse or other fixed light associated with a natural hazard, such as rocks or a sandbank.

**Money**: sums have been converted into decimal currency, except where that would seriously diminish the sense, in order to maintain consistency with the spreadsheets of accounts which have formed a major part of the data management of this study. However, for that purpose, a simple formula used in a spreadsheet such as MS Excel can be used to convert £ s d accounts to modern decimal sums.[2]

**Pontage**: the right to collect a levy on passing shipping for the upkeep of an opening bridge within a harbour.

**Quayage**: a similar right to collect a levy for the upkeep of a quay protecting a harbour.

**Ship**: a vessel with three masts, square-rigged on each mast, whose tonnage, certainly in Whitby, might vary, particularly at the end of the eighteenth century, between 230 measured tons and 600 measured tons. If the term 'ship' is used of a vessel, then that must be taken to imply the correct rig.

**Tonnage**: there are two methods of measuring a fleet, by the number of its vessels and by its tonnage, both important in different ways. Most of the published benchmark tables comparing the fleets of the more important port towns are calculated in tonnage, tonnage burthen until 1786, and measured tonnage thereafter. Even given this confusing method of ranking ports by the tonnage belonging, there is no instance before 1702 of Whitby's fleet being ranked in any national list. At this early period the only way of estimating the size of Whitby's fleet is by enumerating vessels from a wide range of references.

Since any consideration of the size of a fleet must therefore take account of tonnage, it is important to try to define 'tonnage'. There were several concepts of tonnage; *registered tonnage, measured tonnage* and *tonnage burthen*. Problems of analysis arise when an attempt is made to convert from one to the other, or when particular listings offer no indication as to the kind of tonnage implied.[3] The broad range of documents extant in Whitby, for the seventeenth and eighteenth centuries, carries no reference at all to *registered tonnage* as a concept, while m*easured tonnage* was a system designed for the calculation of the purchase price of a vessel, and is found among the accounts for

2  The method requires four columns (£, s, d and ¼d) which are then converted in a fifth column, using the formula: =SUM(B2+(C2/20)+(D2/240)+(E2/960)). Column A is used to indicate the nature of the payment.

3  C. J. French, 'Notes: The eighteenth-century shipping tonnage measurements', *Journal of Economic History*, vol. 33, 1973, pp. 435, refers to work by McCusker and Walton on *registered tonnage* prior to 1773, but there are no Whitby vessels' 'registers' extant from before 1800, so it is not possible to relate Whitby's concepts of tonnage to registered tonnage.

building in some Whitby voyage books.[4] *Tonnage burthen* is a term found in relation to Whitby vessels in lists of dues, such as Pierage, or in Port Books, mainly derived from outside the town.[5] In 1782, Francis Gibson, Collector of Customs, calculated the size of Whitby's fleet by 'King's Measurement', by which he presumably meant *measured tonnage*.[6]

Until 1786, when the first systematic scheme for shipping registration was established, using *measured tonnage* for the purposes of the registration, it is often difficult to determine from the given figures in most sources which kind of *tonnage* is being intended. Some early lists of Whitby colliers give the size of Whitby vessels by their capacity in keels (20–21 tons), and it seems that capacity for coal was the most used factor for those involved in Whitby shipping. Even that measure, however, was not the only means of calculation.

A twentieth-century transcript of a Whitby notebook, dated 1773, appears to set out a rule-of-thumb to calculate one kind of tonnage from another, and then relate both to the capacity in keels *at that time*.[7] This document, 'A List of all SHIPS and Vessels belonging to the Port of Whitby with their Burthen and Tonnage', may have been compiled in response to, or in anticipation of the 1773 Act. It suggested a ratio of 4:3 for *dead tonnage* to *measured tonnage*. *Dead tonnage* is calculated to be twenty times the capacity in keels, and this *dead tonnage* is the nearest that Whitby's extensive archive comes to attempting a definition of *tonnage burthen*.[8] There is a further dimension to this problem of definition, in that the voyage books of several vessels indicate that vessels routinely carried 25 per cent more coal than either their capacity in keels or their *dead tonnage* suggests, even in the seventeenth century, when

---

4 Ibid. pp. 434–5, charts the differences between the rules in 1695, when the measured tonnage was calculated by this formula:

$$\text{tonnage} = \frac{\text{length} \times \text{breadth} \times \frac{1}{2}\text{ breadth}}{94}$$

and 1773, by which date the formula had become more complex:

$$\text{tonnage} = \frac{(\text{length - } 3/5\text{ breadth}) \times \text{breadth} \times \frac{1}{2}\text{ breadth}}{94}$$

M. Marshall, *Ocean Traders from the Portuguese Discoverers to the Present Day*, Batsford, 1989, pp. 97–8, goes back to 1582, when the divisor was even more bizarre, 97½! The formula was used to calculate the cost of the hull, which was always itemised separately in the building accounts, at £n per ton, even where, as in the case of *Judith*, built 1677, the actual *dimensions* of the vessel are not given. Later voyage books, especially after 1786, tended to give much more information about the dimensions of vessels.

5 TNA/E190, and NYCRO/SBC/Pierage Accounts.

6 TNA/T1/430, Maps and notes sent to the Board of Ordnance by Francis Gibson, concerning the defence of Whitby, 1782; he probably used this term under the Act 13 Geo III, c. 74, 1773.

7 WLP/PB5032, transcript of a notebook, now lost, dated 2 March 1773; it also gives the capacity for coal in keels (which at that time held 20–21 tons), although there is evidence from voyage books that in fact the colliers were capable of carrying a much greater tonnage of coal than this notebook suggests. *Three Sisters* (1761–87), was of 240 measured tons, and 320 tons burthen, and regularly carried up to 400 tons of coal. At the same time it often came home with only 90 tons of ballast, indicating a well-balanced and sea-worthy vessel.

8 Davis, p. 35, gives a note on the ratio accepted for Scarborough at this time.

Davis suggests that measured tonnage was much greater than tonnage burthen.[9] *Judith* (1677–82), 74¾ measured tons when built, carried up to 90 tons of alum.[10] This may indicate a deliberate understatement of capacity in order to reduce beaconage and buoyage dues, often by as much as 50 per cent.[11] It is thought, however, that the heavier scantlings, or construction timbers, of much seventeenth-century shipping meant that their tonnage burthen was more than their actual capacity.[12]

**Trade**: another term that requires some comment; it is used, particularly in the context of Whitby's fleet, and by the participants in the shipping industry, in three ways. It may simply denote commerce itself; it is also used in association with a particular commodity, especially coal, and the expression 'coal trade' is commonly found. At other times it is used with equal frequency to mean trade with a particular region, such as for the notorious 'triangular trade', to Africa with trading goods, thence to the New World with slaves, and back to Britain with sugar or tobacco. It might refer to trade with the countries bordering the Baltic, or, as the Levant trade, to the countries of the Near East. It is not feasible to reduce the use of the term to any common denominator, such as place or commodity, simply because trade in a particular commodity, such as coal, involved a variety both of outset ports and of destinations, including overseas, and trade with a particular region involved a range of commodities. The term 'trade' will be used as it is found in the source material.

9   Davis, p. 7, n. 1.
10  WLP/Voyage Accounts of *Judith*, 1677–82
11  NYCRO/DC/SBC/Scarborough Borough Records, Pierage Accounts, show that the crucial tonnage was 50 tons, with a due of 4 pence for vessels below that, and 8 pence above. All Whitby vessels paid 4 pence.
12  Appendix 1 gives a more detailed analysis of the problems of estimation of tonnages for ports and for the national fleet.

# Selected Bibliography and further reading

## PRIMARY SOURCES:

### *MANUSCRIPTS:*

#### UNITED KINGDOM
**The National Archives (TNA/)**
**Audit Office:**
AO1/2486/349–50 and AO1/2487/351–4, Accounts of Alum Monopoly, 1614–27; AO3/1243/3A, Account Book, for the Yorkshire Alum Works, of Richard Wyllys, 1612/13

**Colonial Office:**
CO388/18, Ship clearances from Whitby for overseas, 1710–18

**Customs and Excise:**
CUST90/74, Committee of Shipowners of Whitby for the regulation of the coal trade; CUST90/76, Licence book relevant to 47 Geo. 3, c.66

**Exchequer:**
E179/261/32, Hearth Tax Returns, Wapentake of Whitby Strand

**Foreign Office:**
FO181, Various Letter Books

**High Court of Admiralty:**
HCA1–30: various Mss relevant to Whitby

**Miscellaneous:**
T1/430, Maps and notes sent by Francis Gibson, concerning the defence of Whitby, 1782, 1794

**Port Books, Whitby:**
E190/185–207, 1600–1698

**Port Books, Other:**
E190/45–958, 1600–1699

**Prerogative Court of Canterbury:**
TNA/PROB 11/447, Will of Thomas Rogers, senior, of Northshields

**Privy Council:**
APC/1623–5, Petition of Andrew Dickson

**State Letters and Papers:**
SP16/ and SP29/ Trinity House certificates and Baltic passes

**British Library (BL/)**
Additional Ms 32656
Musgrave Papers, Additional Mss 11255–6, 69087 and 61579

**National Archives of Scotland (NAS/)**
E72/1 and E15/4, Port books, 1681
GD217 Watt papers

**COMMONWEALTH**

**Province of Manitoba, Canada**
Winnipeg, Hudson's Bay Company Archives (HBCA/)

**UK PROVINCIAL REPOSITORIES**

**Borthwick Institute, University of York (Borthwick)**
Archdeaconry of Cleveland, will of John Haggas, 1637; will and inventory of Jonas
    Haggas, 1689
Consistory Court of York, will and inventory of Jonathan Porritt, 1764
Records of the Vice-Admiralty Court

**Essex Record Office (ERO/)**
D/P 170 and 174, Harwich and Dovercourt Parish Registers

**Ipswich and Suffolk Record Office (SRO/)**
C9/27 *et seq.*, Ipswich Borough Council, Coalmeters' Accounts

**Norfolk Record Office (NRO/)**
NRO/HMN7/186, 771X7; Winterton Lights Accounts, 1687/8
Y/C16/12–15, Admiralty Court Books for Great Yarmouth

**North Yorkshire Record Office (NYCRO/)**
Port Register, Port of Whitby, 1786 *et seq.*, ZWvi 11/10/1–9, Correspondence of
    Whitby Shipowners' Society; DC/SBC/Scarborough Borough Records; Whitby
    Parish Church Registers of Baptisms, Burials and Marriages from 1600; Records
    of Quarter Sessions

**Orkney Archives (OA/)**
D2 and D3, Papers of Balfour; Papers of Watt of Breckness

**Tyne and Wear Record Office (TWRO/)**
Certified copy of John Brand's *History and Antiquities of the Town and County of
    Newcastle upon Tyne*, vol. 2, 1789, p. 677

**Whitby Literary and Philosophical Society (WLP/)**
**Selected Voyage Books:**
*Judith*, 1677–82; *Hannah*, 1714–18; *Blessing*, 1715–26; *William and Jane*, 1718–27;
    *William and Anne*, 1755; *Swallow*, 1757–63; *Four Brothers*, 1758–75; *Three Sisters*,
    1761–88

**Ships' Logs:**
*Flora* 1764–71; *Swallow*, 1757–63

**Insurance Ledgers:**
Policies at Lloyds, Barry ships

**Other:**
Burnett Papers
Crispin Bean's Apprentices Notebook, 1789–99

**Whitby Seamen's Hospital:**
Seamen's Sixpence Muster rolls

Seamen's Sixpence Ledgers
Minute Books
Disbursements
Appeals
Letters
**Private Hands:**
St Ninian Papers
Will of Nathaniel Langborne
Journal of Thomas Etty
Will and Inventory of Jonathan Porritt

## *PRINTED PRIMARY SOURCES:*

*A Seaman's Pocket Book, June 1943*, Conway, 2006

Ashcroft, M. Y. (ed.), *Scarborough Records 1600–1640*, North Yorkshire County Record Office Publication No. 47, (Draft) 1991

Atkinson, J. C. (ed.), *Quarter Sessions Records*, North Riding Records, vols 7 and 8, 1890

Binns, J., *Sir Hugh Cholmley's Memoirs*, Yorkshire Archaeological Society, vol. 153, 2000

Brown, W. (ed.), *The Lay Subsidy of 1301*, Yorkshire Archaeological Society, vol. 21, 1896

*Calendars of Close Rolls, Patent Rolls and State Papers*

Childs, W. (ed.), *The Customs Accounts of Hull, 1453–90*, Yorkshire Archaeological Society Record Series, vol. 144

Christy, M. (ed.), *The Voyages of Captain Luke Foxe and Captain Thomas James in Search of a North-West Passage*, Hakluyt Society Nos. 88 and 89, 1894

D. (*sic*), 'Records of the Council for New England', *Proceedings of the American Antiquarian Society*, 1867, vol. 2, No. 6

Dendy, F. W. (ed.), *Records of the Newcastle upon Tyne Merchant Venturers*, Surtees Society 93 and 101, 1895 and 1899

Dendy, F. W. (ed.), *Records of the Newcastle upon Tyne Hostmen's Company*, Surtees Society 105, 1901

English, T., *Whitby Prints*, Horne, Whitby, 1931

Foxe, L., *North-West Foxe, or Foxe from the North-West Passage*, London, 1635, reprinted by Johnson Reprint Corporation, Canada, 1965

Hainsworth, D. R. (ed.), *The Correspondence of Sir John Lowther of Whitehaven, 1693–1698*, British Academy Records of Social and Economic History, New Series, vol. 7, 1983

Harris, G. G. (ed.), *Trinity House of Deptford, Transactions 1609–35*, London Record Society, vol. 19, 1983

Perrin, W. G. (ed.), *The Autobiography of Phineas Pett*, Navy Records Society, 1918

Powell, J. R. and Timings, E. K., *Documents Relating to the Civil War 1642–1648*, Navy Records Society, vol. 105, 1963

Purvis, J. S., *Records of the Admiralty Court in York*, St Anthony's Hall Publication No. 22, 1962

Roseveare, H., *Markets and Merchants of the Late Seventeenth Century; The Marescoe-David Letters 1668–1680*, British Academy Records of Social and Economic

History, New Series vol. 12, 1991

Rowe, D. J. (ed.), *Records of the Newcastle upon Tyne Company of Shipwrights*, Surtees Society, vol. 181, 1971

Scott, P. H., *1707: The Union of Scotland and England*, The Saltire Society and Chambers, 1979

Troup, J. A., *The Ice-bound Whalers: the Story of the* Dee *and the* Grenville Bay *1836–7,* Orkney Press, 1987

Twiss, T. (ed.), *The Black Book of the Admiralty*, vols 1–5, 1871–76, Rolls Series, vol. 55

Vickers, N. (ed.), *A Yorkshire Town of the Eighteenth Century: The Probate Inventories of Whitby, North Yorkshire, 1700–1800,* Brewin, 1986

Woodward, D. (ed.), *Descriptions of East Yorkshire: Leland to Defoe*, East Yorkshire Local History Series, No. 39, 1985

*NEWSPAPERS:*

*Lloyds List* and *Lloyds Register of Shipping*
*Newcastle Chronicle*


## SECONDARY SOURCES:

*UNPUBLISHED WORKS:*

Barker, R. R., 'A Demographic History of the Tendring Hundred, Essex, 1538–1835', unpubd SSRC Report HR5014/2, 1980

Barrow, A., 'The North-east Coast Whale Fishery', unpubd PhD thesis (CNAA), Newcastle Polytechnic, 1989

Binns, J., 'Sir Hugh Cholmley of Whitby, 1600–1657: His Life and Works', unpubd PhD thesis, Leeds University, 1990

Evans, F. M., 'Seaborne Trade of Ipswich and its Members 1558–1640', unpubd PhD thesis, University of East Anglia, 1987

Lewis-Simpson, S., 'Sources of Whitby History Pre–1700', collated for the Friends of Whitby Abbey, 2005

Jones, S. K., 'A Maritime History of the Port of Whitby 1700–1914', unpubd PhD thesis, University College, London, 1982

Starkey, D. J., 'British Privateering 1702–1783, with Particular Reference to London', unpubd PhD thesis, Exeter University, 1985

Storey, G., 'The Registers of the Presbyterian Chapel, Flowergate, Whitby, 1695–1824', unpubd transcript and comment

*BOOKS:*

Abel, W., *The Shipwright's Trade*, first pubd 1948, Conway Maritime, 1981

Allen, D. E., and Hatfield G., *Medicinal Plants in Folk Tradition: An Ethnobotany of Britain and Ireland*, Timber, 2004

Anderson, R. C., *The Rigging of Ships in the Days of the Spritsail Topmast 1600–1726,* Conway Maritime, 1982

Bang, N. E., and Korst, K., *Tabeller over Skibsfart og Varetransport gennem Oresund, 1497–1783*, 7 vols, Copenhagen and Leipzig, 1906–1953

Barker, R. R., *Prisoners of the Tsar: East Coast Sailors Held in Russia, 1800–1801*, Highgate Publications, 1992

Barker, R. R., *Plague in Essex*, Essex Record Office, 1982

Barrett, C. R. B., *The Trinity House of Deptford Strond*, London, 1893

Barrow, T., *The Whaling Trade of North-East England, 1750–1850*, University of Sunderland Press, 2001

Barry, J. (ed.), *The Tudor and Stuart Town: A Reader in English Urban History*, Longman, 1990

Binns, J., *Yorkshire in the Civil Wars*, Blackthorn, 2004

Boxer, C. R., *The Dutch Seaborne Empire 1600–1800*, Penguin, 1990

Brown, R., *Economic Revolutions in Britain 1750–1850*, Cambridge University Press, 1992

Burwash, D., *English Merchant Shipping, 1460–1540*, University of Toronto, 1947, David and Charles Reprint, 1969

Capp, B., *Cromwell's Navy*, Oxford University Press, 1989

Charlton, L., *The History of Whitby*, York, 1779

Clark, A., *Working Life of Women in the Seventeenth Century*, 1st edn, 1919, 3rd edn, A. L. Erickson (ed.), Routledge, 1992

Clark, C. and Hosking, J. (eds) *Population Estimates of English Small Towns, 1550–1851*, revised edition, University of Leicester Press, 1993

Clark, P. and Slack, P., *English Towns in Transition 1500–1700*, Oxford University Press, 1976

Clark, P. (ed.), *Country Towns in Pre-Industrial England*, Leicester University Press, 1981

Coleman, D. C., *Industry in Tudor and Stuart England*, Studies in Economic History, Economic History Society, 1975

Coleman, D. C., *The Economy of England 1450–1750*, Oxford University Press, 1977

Corfield, P. J., *The Impact of English Towns 1700–1800*, Oxford University Press, 1982

Cottrell, P. L., and Allcroft, D. H., *Shipping Trade and Commerce: Essays in Memory of Ralph Davis*, Leicester University Press, 1981

Credland, A., *The Hull Whaling Trade*, Hutton Press, 1995

Crowhurst, P., *The Defence of British Trade 1689–1815*, Dawson, 1977

Davis, R., *The Rise of the English Shipping Industry in the Seventeenth and Eighteenth Centuries*, Macmillan, 1962

Donaldson, G., and Morpeth, R. S., *A Dictionary of Scottish History*, John Donald, 1977

Earle, P., *The Last Fight of the* Revenge, Collins and Brown, 1992

Falconer, W., *Universal Dictionary of the Marine*, London, 1769

Finberg, H. P. R., *The Local Historian and his Theme*, Leicester University Press, 1952

Flinn, M. W. (with Stoker, D.) *The History of the British Coal Industry*, vol. 2, *1700–1830: The Industrial Revolution*, Clarendon Press, 1984

Floud, R., and McCloskey, D. (eds), *The Economic History of Britain since 1700, 1: 1700–1860*, Oxford University Press, 1987

Food Standards Agency, *Manual of Nutrition*, 10th edn, HMSO, 1995

Frank, P., *Yorkshire Fisherfolk*, Phillimore, 2002

Gaskin, R. T., *The Old Seaport of Whitby*, first published Forth, Whitby, 1909, Caedmon reprints, 1986

Gillett, E. and MacMahon, K. A., *A History of Hull*, Hull University Press, 1989

Goel, K. (ed.), *Captain John Smith's* A Sea Grammar, Joseph, 1970

Hartley, W. C. E., *Banking in Yorkshire*, Dalesman Books, 1975

Hatcher, J., *The History of the British Coal Industry*, vol. 1, *Before 1700: Towards the Age of Coal*, Clarendon Press, 1993

Hoppit, J., *A Land of Liberty? England 1689–1727*, Oxford University Press, 2002

Jackson, G., *Hull in the Eighteenth Century: A Study in Economic and Social History*, Oxford University Press for the University of Hull, 1972

Kay, J., *The Honourable Company*, Harper Collins, 1991

Lamb, H. H. and Frydendahl, K. *Historic Storms of the North Sea, the British Isles and North-west Europe*, Cambridge University Press, 1991

Langford, P., *A Polite and Commercial People; England 1727–1783*, Oxford University Press, 1989

Laurence, A., *Women in England, 1500–1760*; Weidenfeld and Nicolson, 1994

Lewis, D. B. (ed.), *The Yorkshire Coast*, Normandy Press, 1991

Marcombe, D., *English Small Town Life: Retford 1520–1642*, Department of Adult Education, University of Nottingham, 1993

Marshall, M., *Ocean Traders from the Portuguese Discoverers to the Present Day*, Batsford, 1989

McKay, J., *The Armed Transport Bounty*, Conway Maritime Press, 1989

Mitchison, R., *A History of Scotland*, 2nd edn, Routledge and Kegan Paul, 1990

Morgan, G. and Rushton, P., *Rogues, Thieves, and the Rule of Law*, UCL Press, 1998

Naish, J., *Seamarks: Their History and Development*, Stanford Maritime, 1985

Nef, J. U., *The Rise of the British Coal Industry*, 2 vols, London, 1932

Osborne, R., *The Floating Egg; Episodes in the Making of Geology*, Jonathan Cape, 1998

Ossowski, W. (ed.), *The* General Carleton *Shipwreck*, Gdansk, 2008

Palmer, S., *Politics, Shipping and the Repeal of the Navigation Laws*, Manchester University Press, 1990

Phythian-Adams, C., *Rethinking English Local History*, Leicester University Press, 1987

Platt, C., *The English Medieval Town*, Paladin, 1979

Rediker, M., *Between the Devil and the Deep Blue Sea*, Cambridge University Press, 1987

Rodger, N., *The Wooden World: An Anatomy of the Georgian Navy*, Fontana, 1988

Rodger, N., *The Safeguard of the Sea: A Naval History of Britain, 660–1649*, Harper Collins, 1997

Rodger, N., *The Command of the Ocean: A Naval History of Britain, 1649–1815*, Allen Lane, 2004

Roseveare, H., *The Financial Revolution 1660–1760*, Longman, 1991

Schurer, K. and Arkell, T., *Surveying the People: The Interpretation and Use of Document Sources for the Study of Population in the later Seventeenth Century*, Local Population Studies Supplement, 1992

Scoresby, W., *Essay on the Improvement of the Town and Harbour of Whitby*, 1818

Slack, P., *The Impact of Plague in Tudor and Stuart England*, Routledge and Kegan Paul, 1985

Smith, R., *Sea-coal for London: The History of the Coal Factors in the London Market*, Longman, 1961

Smyth, W. H., and Belcher, *The Sailor's Word-Book: An Alphabetical Digest of Nautical Terms*, Blackie, 1867, reprinted Conway Maritime Press, 1991

Stokoe, E. A., *Reed's Ship Construction for Marine Engineers*, Reed, 1964

Tawney, R. H. and Power, E. (eds), *Tudor Economic Documents*, vols 1–3, Longmans, 1951

Thomson, W. P. L., *Kelp-making in Orkney*, Orkney Press, 1983

Unger, R. W., *Dutch Shipbuilding before 1800*, van Gorchum, 1978

Victoria History of the North Riding of Yorkshire

Victoria History of Yorkshire

Ville, S. P., *English Shipowning during the Industrial Revolution: Michael Henley and Son, London Shipowners 1770–1830*, Manchester University Press, 1987

Waters, D. W., *The Art of Navigation in England in Elizabethan and Early Stuart Times*, Hollis and Carter, 1958

Weatherill, R., *The Ancient Port of Whitby and its Shipping*, Horne, Whitby, 1908

Weaver, L. T., *The Harwich Story*, 2nd edn (privately published) Harwich, 1976

White, A., *The Buildings of Georgian Whitby*, Keele University Press, 1995

Whiteman, A., *The Compton Census of 1676*, Records of Social and Economic History, New Series vol. 10, British Academy, 1986

Willan, T., *The English Coasting Trade, 1600–1750*, Manchester University Press, 1938

Williams, G. (ed.), *Captain Cook: Explorations and Reassessments*, Boydell, 2004

Williams, N. J., *The Maritime Trade of the East Anglian Ports, 1550–1590*, Clarendon Press, 1988

Woodward, D., *Men at Work: Labourers and Building Craftsmen in the Towns of Northern England, 1450–1750*, Cambridge University Press, 1995

Wrigley, E. A. and Schofield, R. S., *The Population History of England*, Cambridge University Press (paperback), 1989

Wrigley, E. A., Davies, R. S., Oeppen, J. E., and Schofield, R. S., *English Population History from Family Reconstitution, 1580–1837*, Cambridge University Press, 1997

Young, G., *History of Whitby*, 2 vols, Whitby, 1817

Zupko, R., *A Dictionary of English Weights and Measures*, University of Wisconsin, 1968

### *ARTICLES:*

Barker, R. R., 'An Account of Unnatural Death in the Harwich Peninsula, 1550–1838', *East Anglian History Workshop Journal*, vol. 1, no. 2, September, 1980, pp. 3–10

Barker, R. R., 'Comparing Demographic Experience: Harwich and Whitby', *Local Population Studies*, vol. 46, 1991, pp. 32–38

Barker, R. R., 'Ipswich Coalmeters' Accounts', *Suffolk Review*, New Series, vol. 19, 1992

Barker, R. R. 'The Stock in Her: A Maritime Enigma', *Business Archives: Sources and History*, No. 86, 2003, pp. 18–26

Barker, R. R., 'Whitby, North Yorkshire: Changes in Shipping Practice and their Effect on the Town', *Vernacular Building*, No. 29, 2005, pp. 6–14

Barker, R. R., 'Thomas Rogers and the Judith of Whitby: The Voyage Accounts of a Seventeenth-Century Merchant Ketch', *The Northern Mariner/Le Marin du Nord*, vol. XVII, No. 3, 2007, pp. 19–39

Binns, J., 'Captain Browne Bushell: North Sea Adventurer and Pirate', *Northern*

*History*, vol. 27, 1991, pp. 90–105

Binns, J., 'Scarborough and the Civil Wars, 1642–1651', *Northern History*, vol. 22, pp. 95–122

Binns, J., 'Sir Hugh Cholmley: Whitby's Benefactor or Beneficiary?' *Northern History*, vol. 30, pp. 87–104

Fisher, F. J., 'The Development of the London Food Market, 1540–1640', *Economic History Review*, 1st series, vol. 5, 1935, pp. 46–64

Gould, J., 'The Newcastle Port Books and the Coastal Trade: The Results of a Computer-based Investigation into Vessel Utilisation and Shipping Losses in the Eighteenth Century', paper given at the New Researchers in Maritime History Conference, March, 2000

Holderness, B. A., 'Credit in English Rural Society before the Nineteenth Century, with Special Reference to the Period 1650–1720', *Agricultural History Review*, vol. 24, part 2, 1976, pp. 97–109

Jarvis, R. C., 'Ship Registry to 1707', *Maritime History*, vol. 1, 1971, pp. 29–45

Jarvis, R. C., 'Ship Registry 1707 to 1786', *Maritime History*, vol. 2, 1971, pp. 151–167

Phythian-Adams, C., 'Local History and Societal History', *Local Population Studies*, vol. 51, 1993, pp. 30–45

Pybus, D. P. and Rushton, J., 'Alum and the Yorkshire Coast', in D. B. Lewis (ed.), *The Yorkshire Coast*, Normandy Press, 1991

Waites, B., 'The Mediaeval Ports and Trade of North-east Yorkshire', *Mariners' Mirror*, vol. 63, 1977, pp. 137–149

Woodward, D., 'The Port Books of England and Wales', *Maritime History*, vol. 2, 1972, pp. 147–164

# Index

Acts of Parliament
  Navigation Ordinances and Acts, (1651–72), 14, 109
  Poor Relief or Settlement Act, (1662), 94, 128
  Bill of Rights, (1689), 98
  Whitby Harbour Acts, (1702, 1734), 4 n.14, 103–4
  East India Act, (1813), 154
  Passing Tolls Act, (1861), 104
Admiralty, 3
Admiralty courts 9, 11, 79 n.54, 83, 85, 152–53
alum 5, 24–7, 45, 72, 80, 81–3, 109–10, 156, 169
apprentices *see* servants
Atlantic 3, 5

Bagdale Hall 40, 70
ballast 92, 130–31
Barkers
  Peter 112
  William 136–7
Barrys 154
bartering 82
Baxtergate 74, 111 n.29,
Bean, Crispin 10
Beecroft, John 8, 12
Bell Island 56
Benson, Dorothy 112
Blome, Richard 75
Bocking and Braintree 72
Botany Bay 153
bridge 20, 115, 118 plate 6.2
Browne, Jonas 135–6, 169
burgess court 7, 21, 109
Bushell, Browne, 38, 46–9, 50, 77, 86, 94, 96
butter 54 n.14, 46, 109

Calvert, John 135–6
cargoes 20, 26, 45, 53–5
Carnaby, Anne 112
chaldrons 119–20
Chambers, George 8
chandlery 13, 105, 125–6

Chapman family 8, 12, 126
Charlton, Lionel 65, 126 map 0.2
Cholmleys 21, 27, 34 n.1, 41 n.24, 43–4, 49, 52, 64, 105
  Hugh I 4, 25 n.33, 34 n.1, 38 n.18, 40 n.20 and n.23, 47, 50–2, 56–7 n.23, 94
  Hugh II 51, 56, 68
  Henry 27, 40 n.23
  Richard 4, 40 n.23
  Lady 50
coal-meters 11, 69
Coates, Jarvis 110 n.25
Commonwealth 16
Compton Census 74
Constable, Sir William 50
Cook, James 8, 137–8, 156, 157
cooperage 55
Court of Chancery 11
Coverdale, Norrison 154
crew lists 131
Cromwell's Navy 53
Customs and Excise 3, 20, 159

demurrage 91
Dickson, Andrew 21
dry-docks 126
Dudgeon light 59–61

East Anglia 27
East Indies 154
education 14, 64–5 n.12, 95
entrepôt 55, 81, 108
Exchequer 20–1

factoring 47, 91
Fairfax, Lord 50, 61
Farne Islands 130–1
fertility 81
First Fleet (1788) 153
fleet 108, 123
Fishburn, Thomas 16
Fishburns 126
Foxe, Luke 8, 35–9, 41, 83
freight 53

Galilee
   George 11, 119–20, 124, 125, 136–7, 140–1
   John 125
Gibson
   Edmund 105
   Francis 163–4
Gill, Bartholomew 152–3
Great Barrier Reef 157
Greenwich Hospital 9, 128
Guernsey 86

Haggas
   John 49
   Jonas 49, 55
   Nicholas 51
Hanseatic League 78
harbour 8 n.9, 103, 126, 154–5
harbour of refuge 103
Harraton colliery 34
Hawsker, 40
Hearth Tax 8 n.17, 65, 66 n.22–74, 84, 94–7
Helmsley 51
Holts 126
Hotham
   Sir John 34 n.1, 38, 46–7, 94 n.29
   Captain John 46–7
Hostmen 56–7 n.24, 104
Hudson's Bay 8
Huguenots 92
Hull 19

impost 78
impress service 79, 128–9 n.3, 160, Appendix 2

Jacobites 135, 169
Jersey 92
Johnsons, Timothy and Martha 83
Jones, William 51–2

keels 130–1
Knaggs, Francis 111–12 n.27–9,

lagan 79
Langborne, George and Nathaniel 16
Laws of Oléron 12 n.24, 13, 152–3
lay subsidy, 1301 19
Legendre, Thomas 77–8 n.47
letters of marque 124, 159 n.2
Lloyds Register 8, 125
London 7
Lowthers 75

manor court 7, 110
Marescoe-David company 65 n.18

masters 129–135, 150
mates 131–4
monarchies
   Charles I 15
   Charles II 92
   Edward I 10, 20 n.7
   Edward II 20 n.7
   Edward VI 21
   Henry VIII 21
   James VI and I 15
   John 18
   Louis XIV (France) 92, 101
   Robert I (Scots) 19
   William and Mary 15, 101
Mulgrave, Earl of 76 n.45, 92–3
Musgrave Papers 159

Navy 101, 143
Netherlands 23, 78
New England Company 21
Newcastle, Earl of 50
Newton, Isaac 34 n.1, 38 n.18, 41 n.23–4, 48
   n.41
North York Moors 24
Norway 103
Norwich 32

occupations 61–5
Ogilby, John 76
Orkney 9, 10, 102 n.6, 139
parish registers 102

Percy, William de, 18
pierage 9
piers 7, 20, 104–5, 106–7, plates iv and 6.1
Piper, Nicholas 124
pitch 91
plague 28–9 n.49, 40–1, 70, 85
port books 3
port registers 3, 162
ports
   Aldeburgh 21, 109
   Amsterdam 46
   Antwerp 152
   Blyth Nook 54
   Bridlington 72, 168
   Brightlingsea 60, 168
   Brighton 168
   Bristol 32, 109
   Chester 21, 150, 155
   Coatham 24
   Colchester 68
   Cowes 91
   Cullercoats 54

Deal 91
Dieppe 108
Dover 91
Dunkirk 46, 108
Elsinore 22
Exeter 32, 109
Gloucester 6
Great Yarmouth 8, 34, 58, 79, 109, 148
Harwich 29–31, 71 n.29, 109, 155
Havre 108
Hull 21, 32, 33, 36–7 n.15, 69 n.26, 94,
    98, 109
Ipswich 8, 34, 109, 150, 155
King's Lynn 32, 34, 60, 148
Leigh 21
Liverpool 8, 109, 155
London 7, 108, 122, 148
Newcastle upon Tyne 21, 35, 81, 104, 109,
    138, 155, 162, 169
Nottingham 6
Plymouth 119
Robin Hood's Bay 21, 129
Rotterdam 54
Rouen, 77, 86
Runswick 21
Sandsend 129
Scarborough 7, 21, 32 n.57, 90, 103, 105,
    118–19, 121, 124, 159
Seaton Sluice 54
South Shields 72
Southampton 32, 109
St Malo 96, 108,
Staithes 21, 129
Stockton on Tees 21
Sunderland 21, 86–7, 91, 109, 121,130–1
Whitehaven 75, 109
York 94
primage accounts 54
pressgang see impress service
profit 113–24
probate 74 n.36–7, 111
protest 130–1

Quakers 5, 66, 102, 129, 130, 138–9, 140–1
quarantine 85

railway 155
risk 84 n.8,
Rivers
    Esk 8, 68, 110
    Humber 8, 72
    Orwell 68
    Ouse 72
    Stour (Essex) 29

Tees 8
Thames 27, 103 125
Tyne 9, 69, 77, 81, 103, 122, 125, 129–30,
    141
Wear 103, 130
Rogers
    Thomas, senior, 79 n.48, 86 n.13
    Thomas, junior, 77, 86–94, 153
Rogers, John 92–3
roperies plate vii, 127
Ruswarp 18, 94

sail-cloth weaving 63 n.9, 127
Saltwick 56
Scoresby
    William, senior, 8, 10
    William, junior, 8, 10
Scots 9, 109
Scurvy plate ix a,b,c, 79 n.53
Seamen's Sixpence 9, 110, 128, 160
select vestry 7, 19 n.4–5, 110
servants and apprentices 126, 131, 135–9, 148
share-owning 7, 11, 84, 88, 110–11 n.25,
    113–51, 116–17
Sheffield 72
ship-building 5, 7, 23, 33–4, 35–6, 83, 104,
    111 n.29
ships
    Alert plate 0.1, 16
    Allome An 25, 83
    Amity 25
    Anna 142, 153
    Archer 142–7
    Benjamin 25
    Blessing, 119, 121–4
    Brotherly Love 169
    Bonhomme Richard (American) 140
    Camden 154
    Charity 74
    Charles 26, 36
    Coverdale 154
    Crisis plate v, 170
    Durtie Megge (Burntisland) 23 n.3
    Earl of Eldon 154, 168
    Endeavour 169
    Esk 168
    Fishburn 153
    Flora 132 n.1, 156
    Fly 169
    Fortune 25
    Four Brothers 125
    Fox 25
    Freelove 169
    Freemason 168

*Friends' Adventure* 169
*General Carleton* xi, 169
*George* 24, 129 n.3, 135
*Golden Grove* 153
*Great Neptune* 23, 36, 47, 83
*Haddock* 169
*Hannah* 111–14, 119, 121–3, 134
*Harrison Chilton* 168
*Heaven* 25
*Henry* 25
*Hopeful Katherine* 54, 57
*Isabel* 23
*Isabella* 83 n.2
*Jacob* 23
*John* 25, 38, 47–49
*Judith* 54 n.9, 66 n.2, 77–9, 81, 83, 86–94,
     121, 131, 133–4, 139–40, 141, 153
*Liberality*
*Liberty and Property* 16,17
*Marie* 33
*Mary* 23
*Mary and Rebecca* 130–1
*Midsummer Blossom* 169
*Nancy* 168
*Pelican* (of Newcastle) 35
*Prince of Wales* 141
*Prosperous Adventure* 141
*Regret* 170
*Resolution* 169
*Robert* 25
*Rose* 25
*Seaflower* 169
*Speedy* 169
*Swallow* 124–5, 133 fn
*Swift* 169
*Thomasin* 66
*Three Sisters* 11, 119–20, 124, 125,
     136–37, 140–1, 162
*Traveller's Habitation* 169
*True Briton* 150
*Welcome* 49, 74
*William and Jane* 115, 116–17, 119, 121–4,
     135, 141
*William and Anne* 124–5
shipowners 10, 50, 155
shipwrights 131
Shipton, Thomas 76
Sibbald, Alexander 135–7
Sledway 56 n.21, 57
social control 148
Society of Friends *see* Quakers
Sound tolls 22
South Sea Bubble 121, 123

Stainbridge 126
stock 47 n.38, 123–4

Tangier 56 n.22
tea 133
timber plates vi, vii, viii, 111
tonnage owned 108, 159, 162–4
trade
    alum 82
    American 109
    Baltic 16, 22 n.20, 103
    coal 16, 3 n.2
    East Indies 154
    naval transport 5, 139, 142–8, 160
    retail 13
    timber plate viii, 103
    whaling 155
Trinity House, London 9, 39
trust 152–53
Tynemouth Castle 130

urban development 127, plates i–iii
Usherwoods 126

victualling 48, 83–4 n.7, 125
Virginia 83
voyage books 11
voyage times 87

wages 89–90, 92, 126, 139
Walker, John 138
Walker Yeomans 126
wars
    Civil, (1642–51), 4, 50
    Dutch, 1–4, (1652–84) 54, 76
    Spanish War (1655–60) 55 n.16
    King William's War (1681–97) 101
    First Jacobite Rebellion (1715) 121
    Second Jacobite Rebellion (1745–6) 169
    Seven Years' War (1757–63) 124, 139–41,
       149–150, 161
    Spanish Succession (1701–14) 55, 101
    War of American Independence (1776–83)
       124, 139–40, 161–2
    Napoleonic (1803–1815) 170
    Second world war (1939–45) 12
Watt family 10
Wentworth, Thomas 40
Weatherill, Richard 14
whaling 36, 131–32, 142, 154, 156
whins 48, 91
White Sea 103, 142
Winterton Lights 4 n.14, 58–9
winter-work 90, 118–19

Whitby Literary and Philosophical Society 5
Whitby Seamen's Hospital 9, 110, 128,
    148–51
Whitby Shipowners' Society 10

York 10, 19
York, James, Duke of, 93
Young, Revd George 163–4

## Volumes Already Published

Volume I: *The Durham Liber Vitae and its Context*, edited by David Rollason, A. J. Piper, Margaret Harvey and Lynda Rollason, 2004

Volume II: *Captain Cook: Explorations and Reassessments*, edited by Glyndwr Williams, 2004

Volume III: *North-East England in the Later Middle Ages*, edited by Christian D. Liddy and Richard H. Britnell, 2005

Volume IV: *North-East England, 1850–1914: The Dynamics of a Maritime-Industrial Region*, Graeme J. Milne, 2006

Volume V: *North-East England, 1569–1625: Governance, Culture and Identity*, Diana Newton, 2006

Volume VI: *Lay Religious Life in Late Medieval Durham*, Margaret Harvey, 2006

Volume VII: *Peasants and Production in the Medieval North-East: The Evidence from Tithes, 1270–1536*, Ben Dodds, 2007

Volume VIII: *The Church of England and the Durham Coalfield, 1810–1926: Clergymen, Capitalists and Colliers*, Robert Lee, 2007

Volume IX: *Regional Identities in North-East England, 1300–2000*, edited by Adrian Green and A. J. Pollard, 2007

Volume X: *Liberties and Identities in the Medieval British Isles*, edited by Michael Prestwich, 2008

Volume XI: *The Bishopric of Durham in the Late Middle Ages: Lordship, Community and the Cult of St Cuthbert*, Christian D. Liddy, 2008

Volume XII: *Northern Landscapes: Representations and Realities of North-East England*, edited by Thomas Faulkner, Helen Berry and Jeremy Gregory, 2010

Volume XIII: *The Keelmen of Tyneside: Labour Organisation and Conflict in the North-East Coal Industry, 1600–1830*, Joseph M. Fewster, 2011

Printed and bound by CPI Group (UK) Ltd, Croydon, CR0 4YY

24/04/2025

14661365-0001